PRAISE FOR

The Smartest Kids in the World

"[Ripley] gets well beneath the glossy surfaces of these foreign cultures and manages to make our own culture look newly strange. . . . [A] masterly book."

—*The New York Times Book Review*

"Compelling. . . . What is Poland doing right? And what is America doing wrong? Amanda Ripley, an American journalist, seeks to answer such questions in *The Smartest Kids in the World*, her fine new book about the schools that are working around the globe. . . . Ms. Ripley packs a startling amount of insight in this slim book."

—*The Economist*

"Intriguing. . . . Ripley is a talented writer. . . . [*The Smartest Kids in the World*] has the most illuminating reporting I have ever seen on the differences between schools in America and abroad."

—Jay Mathews, education columnist, *The Washington Post*

"[*The Smartest Kids in the World* is] a riveting new book. . . . Ripley's policy recommendations are sensible and strong. . . . The American school reform debate has been desperately in need of such nononsense advice, which firmly puts matters of intellect back at the center of education where they belong."

—*The Daily Beast*

"*The Smartest Kids in the World* should be on the back-to-school reading list of every parent, educator and policymaker interested in understanding why students in other countries outperform U.S. students on international tests."

—*U.S. News & World Report*

"Gripping. . . . Ripley's characters are fascinating, her writing style is accessible, and her observations are fresh. . . . If you're interested in how to improve public schools, read Ripley's book today."

—*The Huffington Post*

"Ripley's reporting leads her, and us, to valuable insights into today's standards debate. . . . Ripley helps us see clearly that shifting philosophical gears—making drive rather than talent the cornerstone of our educational system—is a key to achieving our academic aspirations."

—*Washington Monthly*

"Ripley's reporting is top-notch, fluidly presented, and well-documented, and her coverage of the teenagers' personal journeys and experiences, both social and academic, make this a must-read for anyone interested in getting American schools back on track."

—*School Library Journal*

"In riveting prose . . . this timely and inspiring book offers many insights into how to improve America's mediocre school system."

—*Publishers Weekly*, starred review

"Fascinating. . . . Ripley's voice is engaging, and *Smartest Kids* is impeccably researched and packed with interesting interviews and anecdotes. . . . The book ends on a positive note. . . . [While] the issues are complex, we certainly get the message that we can improve our educational system for our kids."

—*Washington Independent Review of Books*

"Ripley's evaluation of education in a changing world is revealing and thought-provoking."

—*Rocky Mountain Telegram*

"Engaging . . . well-researched."

—*Scholastic Administrator*

"Amanda Ripley observes with rare objectivity and depth. She finds a real and complex world 'over there'—schools with flaws of their own but also real and tangible lessons about how to do better by our kids. *The Smartest Kids in the World* gave me more insights, as a parent and as an educator, than just about anything else I've read in a while."

—Doug Lemov, author of *Teach Like a Champion*

"Such an important book! Amanda Ripley lights the path to engaging our next generation to meet a different bar. She makes an enormous contribution to the national and global discussion about what must be done to give all our children the education they need to invent the future."

—Wendy Kopp, founder and chair, Teach For America, and CEO, Teach For All

"*The Smartest Kids in the World* is a must-read for anyone concerned about the state of American public education. By drawing on experiences, successes, and failures in education systems in the highest-performing countries across the globe, Amanda Ripley lays out a course for what we must do to dramatically improve our nation's schools."

—Michelle Rhee, founder and CEO, StudentsFirst

also by amanda ripley

The Unthinkable: Who Survives When Disaster Strikes—and Why

the
smartest
kids in
the world

and how they got that way

amanda ripley

simon & schuster paperbacks

new york london toronto sydney new delhi

Simon & Schuster Paperbacks
A Division of Simon & Schuster, Inc.
1230 Avenue of the Americas
New York, NY 10020

First Simon & Schuster trade paperback edition July 2014

SIMON & SCHUSTER PAPERBACKS and colophon are registered trademarks of Simon & Schuster, Inc.

For information about special discounts for bulk purchases, please contact Simon & Schuster Special Sales at 1-866-506-1949 or business@simonandschuster.com.

Designed by Nancy Singer
Illustrations by John Del Gaizo

Manufactured in the United States of America

10 9 8 7 6 5 4

The Library of Congress has cataloged the Simon & Schuster hardcover edition as follows:
Ripley, Amanda.
    The smartest kids in the world : and how they got that way / Amanda Ripley.
      pages cm
    Includes bibliographical references and index.
    1. Comparative education. 2. Education—Finland. 3. Education—Korea (South)
4. Education—Poland.
    I. Title.
    LB43.R625 2013
    370.9—dc23

                                                                                    2013002021

ISBN 978-1-4516-5442-4
ISBN 978-1-4516-5443-1 (pbk)
ISBN 978-1-4516-5444-8 (ebook)

PHOTO CREDITS

Page 1: IvanBautista.com
Page 3: Hanushek and Woessmann, *The Knowledge Capital of Nations*
Page 13: OECD/Michael Dean
Page 21: OECD (2009), Take the Test: Sample Questions from OECD's PISA Assessments, PISA, OECD Publishing; http://dx.doi.org/10.1787/9789264050815-en
Page 26: Courtesy of Kim's family
Pages 46, 67, 81, 104, 151: Amanda Ripley
Page 124: Adam Lach/Napo Images
Page 169: Jean Chung
Page 180: NewWaySolutions.com

contents

for louise s. ripley

principal characters

germany

Thomas Neville Postlethwaite. British scientist. Pioneered the study of what children know around the world. Mentor to Andreas Schleicher.

Andreas Schleicher. German scientist at the OECD who helped create the PISA test, designed to measure twenty-first century skills in fifteen-year-olds around the world.

united states

Scott Bethel. Football coach and teacher of Kim's Algebra I class in Sallisaw, Oklahoma.

Mark Blanchard. Principal of Tom's high school in Gettysburg, Pennsylvania.

Charlotte. Kim's mother and an elementary school teacher in Sallisaw, Oklahoma.

Scott Farmer. Superintendent of Kim's school district in Sallisaw, Oklahoma.

Deborah Gist. Education Commissioner in Rhode Island.

Elina. Finnish exchange student who left Helsinki at sixteen to spend a year in Colon, Michigan.

Ernie Martens. Principal of Kim's high school in Sallisaw, Oklahoma.

William Taylor. Public-school math teacher in Washington, D.C.

south korea

Cha Byoung-chul. Head of a study-curfew enforcement squad at Gangnam district office of education in Seoul, South Korea.

Lee Chae-yun. Owner of a chain of five tutoring academies in Seoul, South Korea.

Eric. American exchange student who left Minnetonka, Minnesota, at age 18 to spend the 2010-11 school year in Busan, South Korea.

Jenny. Korean student who had lived in the United States and became friends with Eric in Busan, Korea.

Lee Ju-ho. South Korea's Minister of Education, Science and Technology. An economist with a PhD from Cornell University.

Andrew Kim. English teacher who made his fortune at Megastudy, one of Korea's biggest private tutoring academies.

poland

Mirosław Handke. A chemist who served as Poland's Minister of Education from 1997 to 2000, during a period of intense reform.

Urszula Spałka. Principal of Tom's high school in Wrocław, Poland.

Tom. American exchange student who left Gettysburg, Pennsylvania, at age seventeen to spend the 2010-11 school year in Wrocław, Poland.

Paula Marshall. CEO of the Bama Companies in Oklahoma, China, and Poland.

finland

Kim. American exchange student who left Sallisaw, Oklahoma, at age fifteen to spend the 2010–11 school year in Pietarsaari, Finland.

Tiina Stara. Teacher of Kim's Finnish class in Pietarsaari, Finland.

Susanne. Kim's host mother for the first six months of her stay in Pietarsaari, Finland.

Heikki Vuorinen. Teacher at the Tiistilä School, where a third of the students are immigrants. Located in Espoo, Finland, just outside Helsinki.

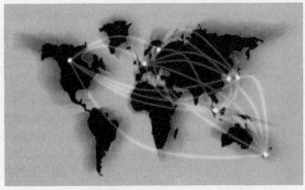

Heat Map: In a handful of countries scattered across the world, virtually all kids are learning to think critically in math, reading, and science.

prologue

the mystery

For most of my career at *Time* and other magazines, I worked hard to avoid education stories. If my editors asked me to write about schools or tests, I countered with an idea about terrorism, plane crashes, or a pandemic flu. That usually worked.

I didn't say so out loud, but education stories seemed, well, kind of soft. The articles tended to be headlined in chalkboard font and festooned with pencil doodles. They were brimming with good intentions but not much evidence. The people quoted were mostly adults; the kids just turned up in the photos, smiling and silent.

Then, an editor asked me to write about a controversial new leader of Washington, D.C.'s public schools. I didn't know much about Michelle Rhee, except that she wore stiletto heels and tended to say "crap" a lot in interviews. So, I figured it would be a good story, even if it meant slipping into the fog of education.

But something unexpected happened in the fog. I spent months talking to kids, parents, and teachers, as well as people who have been creatively researching education in new ways. Pretty soon I realized that Rhee was interesting, but she was not the biggest mystery in the room.

The real mystery was this: Why were some kids learning so much—and others so very little?

Education was suddenly awash in data; we knew more than ever about what was happening—or failing to happen—from one neighborhood or classroom to the next. And it didn't add up. Everywhere I went I saw nonsensical ups and downs in what kids knew: in rich neighborhoods and poor, white neighborhoods and black, public schools and private. The national data revealed the same peaks and valleys, like a sprawling, nauseating roller coaster. The dips and turns could be explained in part by the usual narratives of money, race, or ethnicity. But not entirely. Something else was going on, too.

Over the next few years, as I wrote more stories about education, I kept stumbling over this mystery. At Kimball Elementary School in Washington, D.C., I saw fifth graders literally begging their teacher to let them solve a long division problem on the chalkboard. If they got the answer right, they would pump their fists and whisper-shout, "Yes!" This was a neighborhood where someone got murdered just about every week, a place with 18 percent unemployment.

In other places, I saw kids bored out of their young minds, kids who looked up when a stranger like me walked into the room, watching to see if I would, please God, create some sort of distraction to save them from another hour of nothingness.

For a while, I told myself that this was the variation you'd expect from one neighborhood to the next, from one principal or teacher to another. Some kids got lucky, I supposed, but most of the differences that mattered had to do with money and privilege.

Then one day I saw this chart, and it blew my mind.

The United States might have remained basically flat over time, but that was the exception, it turned out. Look at Finland! It had rocketed from the bottom of the world to the top, without pausing for breath. And what was going on in Norway, right next door, which

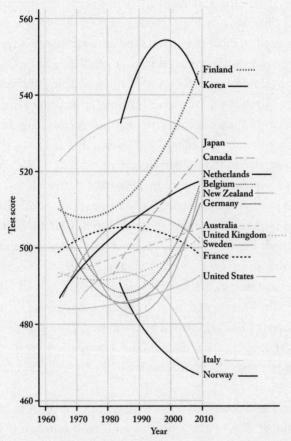

Dance of the Nations: Over a half century, different countries gave eighteen different tests to their children. Economists Ludger Woessmann and Eric Hanushek projected kids' performance onto a common measuring stick. The results suggest that education levels can—and do—change dramatically over time, for better and worse.

seemed to be slip sliding into the abyss, despite having virtually no child poverty? And there was Canada, careening up from mediocrity to the heights of Japan. If education was a function of culture, could culture change that dramatically—that fast?

Worldwide, children's skills rose and fell in mysterious and hopeful ways, sometimes over short periods of time. The mystery I'd noticed in Washington, D.C., got far more interesting when viewed from outer space. The vast majority of countries did *not* manage to educate all their kids to high levels, not even all of their better-off kids. Compared to most countries, the United States was typical, not much better nor much worse. But, in a small number of countries, really just a handful of eclectic nations, something incredible was happening. Virtually *all* kids were learning critical thinking skills in math, science, and reading. They weren't just memorizing facts; they were learning to solve problems and adapt. That is to say, they were training to survive in the modern economy.

How to explain it? American kids were better off, on average, than the typical child in Japan, New Zealand, or South Korea, yet they knew far less math than those children. Our most privileged teenagers had highly educated parents and attended the richest schools in the world, yet they scored below privileged kids in twenty-seven other nations in math, well below affluent kids in New Zealand, Belgium, France, and Korea, among other places. The typical child in Beverly Hills performed below average, compared to all kids in Canada (not some other distant land, Canada!). A great education by the standards of suburban America looked, from afar, exceedingly average.

At first, I told myself to resist the hype. Did it really matter if we ranked number one in the world in education outcomes? Or even number ten? Our elementary students did fine on international tests, thank you very much, especially in reading. The problems arose in math and science, and they became most obvious when our kids grew into teenagers. That's when American students scored twenty-sixth on a test of critical thinking in math, below average for the developed world. But, so what? Our teenagers had performed at or below average on international tests for as long as anyone had been counting. It had not mattered much to our economy so far; why should it matter in the future?

The United States was a big, diverse country. We had other advantages that overwhelmed our K-12 mediocrity, right? We still had world-class research universities, and we continued to invest more in research and development than any other nation. It was easier to start a business here than in most places on earth. The values of hard work and self-sufficiency coursed like electricity through the United States, just as they always had.

But everywhere I went as a reporter, I saw reminders that the world had changed. The 2,300 days that our kids spent in school before high-school graduation mattered more than ever before. In Oklahoma, the CEO of the company that makes McDonald's apple pies told me she had trouble finding enough Americans to handle modern factory jobs—during a recession. The days of rolling out dough and packing pies in boxes were over. She needed people who could read, solve problems, and communicate what had happened on their shift, and there weren't enough of them coming out of Oklahoma's high schools and community colleges.

The head of Manpower, a staffing and recruiting firm with offices in eighty-two countries, said one of the hardest jobs to fill anywhere was the sales job. Once upon a time, a salesperson had to have thick skin and a good golf game. Over the years, however, products and financial markets had become wildly more complex, and information had become available to everyone, including the customer. Relationships were no longer everything. To succeed, salespeople had to understand the increasingly sophisticated and customizable products they were selling almost as well as the engineers who worked on them.

Rather suddenly, academic mediocrity had become a heavier legacy to bear. Without a high-school diploma, you couldn't work as a garbage collector in New York City; you couldn't join the Air Force. Yet a quarter of our kids still walked out of high school and never came back.

Not long ago, zero countries had a better high-school graduation rate than the United States; by 2011, about twenty countries did. In an era in which knowledge mattered more than ever, why did our kids know less than they should? How much of our problems could be blamed on diversity, poverty, or the vastness of the country? Were our weaknesses mostly failures of policy or of culture, of politicians or of parents?

We told ourselves that we were at least raising more creative children, the kind who might not excel in electrical engineering but who had the audacity to speak up, to invent, and to redefine what was possible. But was there a way to know if we were right?

the mythical nordic robots

Education pundits had worked mightily to explain different countries' wildly different results. They had visited faraway schools on choreographed junkets. They'd debriefed politicians and principals and generated PowerPoints for the folks back home. However, their conclusions were maddeningly abstract.

Take Finland, for example, which ranked at the top of the world. American educators described Finland as a silky paradise, a place where all the teachers were admired and all the children beloved. They insisted that Finland had attained this bliss partly because it had very low rates of child poverty, while the United States had high rates. According to this line of reasoning, we could never fix our schools until we fixed poverty.

The poverty narrative made intuitive sense. The child poverty rate in the United States was about 20 percent, a national disgrace. Poor kids lived with the kind of grinding stress that children should not have had to manage. They learned less at home, on average, and needed more help at school.

The mystery was not so simply solved, however. If poverty was the main problem, then what to make of Norway? A Nordic welfare state with high taxes, universal health care, and abundant natural resources, Norway enjoyed, like Finland, less than 6 percent child poverty, one of the lowest rates in the world. Norway spent about as much as we did on education, which is to say, a fortune, relative to the rest of the world. And, yet, Norwegian kids performed just as unimpressively as our own kids on an international test of scientific literacy in 2009. Something was amiss in Norway, and it wasn't poverty.

Meanwhile, the Finns themselves offered vague explanations for their success. Education, I was told, had always been valued in Finland, going back hundreds of years. That explained it. But, then, why did only 10 percent of children finish high school in Finland in the 1950s? Why were there huge gaps between what rural and urban kids knew and could do in Finland in the 1960s? Back then, Finland's passion for education had seemed rather uneven. What had happened?

At the same time, President Barack Obama and his education secretary said that they envied the South Korean education system, lauding its highly respected teachers and its demanding parents. On the surface at least, Korea appeared to have nothing in common with Finland. The Korean system was driven by testing, and Korean teenagers spent more time studying than our kids spent awake.

Listening to this cacophony, I kept wondering what it would be like to actually be a kid in these mystical lands of high scores, zero dropouts, and college graduates. Were Finnish kids really the Nordic robots that I kept reading about? Did Korean kids think they were getting such a sweet deal? What about their parents? No one talked about them. Didn't parents matter even more than teachers?

I decided to spend a year traveling around the world on a field trip to the smart-kid countries. I wanted to go see these little bots for myself. What were they doing at ten on a Tuesday morning? What did their parents say to them when they got home? Were they happy?

field agents

To meet the Nordic robots, I needed sources on the inside: kids who could see and do things that I could never do on my own. So, I recruited a team of young experts to help.

During the 2010–11 school year, I followed three remarkable American teenagers as they experienced smarter countries in real life. These kids volunteered to be part of this project as they headed off for year-long foreign-exchange adventures, far from their families. I visited them in their foreign posts, and we kept in close touch.

Their names were Kim, Eric, and Tom, and they served as my escorts through borrowed homes and adopted cafeterias, volunteer fixers in a foreign land. Kim traveled from Oklahoma to Finland, Eric from Minnesota to South Korea, and Tom from Pennsylvania to Poland. They came from different parts of America, and they left for different reasons. I met Kim, Eric, and Tom with the help of AFS, Youth for Understanding, and the Rotary Clubs, outfits that run exchange programs around the world.

I chose these Americans as advisers, but they turned out to be straight-up protagonists. They did not stand for all American kids, and their experiences could not reflect the millions of realities in their host countries. But, in their stories, I found the life that was missing from the policy briefings.

Kim, Eric, and Tom kept me honest. They didn't want to talk about tenure policies or Tiger Moms; unburdened by the hang-ups of adults, they talked a lot about other kids, the most powerful influences in teenagers' lives. All day long, they contemplated the full arc of their new lives, from their host families' kitchens to their high-school bathrooms. They had much to say.

In each country, my American field agents introduced me to other kids, parents, and teachers, who became co-conspirators in this quest. In Korea, for example, Eric sent me to his friend Jenny, a teenager who had spent half her childhood in America and the other half in Korea. Jenny, an accidental expert on education, patiently answered questions that Eric could not. (Video interviews with my student sources can be found on the website for this book at www.Amanda Ripley.com.)

To put the conclusions of these informants in context, I surveyed hundreds of other exchange students about their experiences in the United States and abroad. Unlike almost everyone else who proffers an opinion about education in other countries, these young people had first-hand experience. I asked them about their parents, schools, and lives in both places. Their answers changed the way I thought about our problems and our strengths. They knew what distinguished an American education, for better and for worse, and they did not mind telling.

When I finally came back to the United States, I felt more optimistic, not less. It was obvious that we'd been wasting a lot of time and money on things that didn't matter; our schools and families seemed confused, more than anything else, lacking the clarity of purpose I saw in Finland, Korea, and Poland. Yet I also didn't see anything anywhere that I didn't think our parents, kids, and teachers could do just as well or better one day.

What I did see were whole generations of kids getting the kind of education all children deserve. They didn't always get it gracefully, but they got it. Despite politics, bureaucracy, antiquated union contracts and parental blind spots—the surprisingly universal plagues of all education systems everywhere—it could be done. And other countries could help show us the way.

part I

fall

chapter 1

The Map Maker: Andreas Schleicher in Paris.

the treasure map

Andreas Schleicher sat down quietly toward the back of the room, trying not to attract attention. He did this sometimes; wandering into classes he had no intention of taking. It was the mid-1980s and, officially speaking, he was studying physics at the University of Hamburg, one of Germany's most elite universities. In his free time, however, he drifted into lectures the way other people watched television.

This class was taught by Thomas Neville Postlethwaite, who called himself an "educational scientist." Schleicher found the title curious. His father was an education professor at the university and had always talked about education as a kind of mystical art, like yoga. "You cannot measure what counts in education—the human qualities," his father liked to say. From what Schleicher could tell, there was nothing scientific about education, which was why he preferred physics.

But this British fellow whose last name Schleicher could not pronounce seemed to think otherwise. Postlethwaite was part of a new, obscure group of researchers who were trying to analyze a soft subject in a hard way, much like a physicist might study education if he could.

Schleicher listened carefully to the debate about statistics and sampling, his pale blue eyes focused and intense. He knew that his father would not approve. But, in his mind, he started imagining what might happen if one really could compare what kids knew around the world, while controlling for the effect of things like race or poverty. He found himself raising his hand and joining the discussion.

In his experience, German schools had not been as exceptional as German educators seemed to think. As a boy, he'd felt bored much of the time and earned mediocre grades. But, as a teenager, several teachers had encouraged his fascination with science and numbers, and his grades had improved. In high school, he'd won a national science prize, which meant he was more or less guaranteed a well-paying job in the private sector after college. And, until he stepped into Postlethwaite's lecture, that was exactly what he'd planned to do.

At the end of class, the professor asked Schleicher to stay behind. He could tell that there was something different about this rail-thin young man who spoke in in a voice just above a whisper.

"Would you like to help me with this research?"

Schleicher stared back at him, startled. "I know nothing about education."

"Oh, that doesn't matter," Postlethwaite said, smiling.

After that, the two men began to collaborate, eventually creating the first international reading test. It was a primitive test, which was largely ignored by members of the education establishment, including Schleicher's father. But the young physicist believed in the data, and he would follow it wherever it took him.

the geography of smart

In the spring of 2000, a third of a million teenagers in forty-three countries sat down for two hours and took a test unlike any they had ever seen. This strange new test was called PISA, which stood for the Program for International Student Assessment. Instead of a typical test question, which might ask which combination of coins you needed to buy something, PISA asked you to design your own coins, right there in the test booklet.

PISA was developed by a kind of think tank for the developed world, called the Organisation for Economic Co-operation and Development, and the scientist at the center of the experiment was Andreas Schleicher. It had been over a decade since Schleicher had wandered into Postlethwaite's class. He'd worked on many more tests since then, usually in obscurity. The experience had convinced him that the world needed an even smarter test, one that could measure the kind of advanced thinking and communication skills that people needed to thrive in the modern world.

Other international tests had come before PISA, each with its own forgettable acronym, but they tended to assess what kids had memorized, or what their teachers had drilled into their heads in the classroom. Those tests usually quantified students' preparedness for more schooling, not their preparedness for life. None measured teenagers' ability to think critically and solve new problems in math, reading, and science. The promise of PISA was that it would reveal which countries were teaching kids to think for themselves.

By December 4, 2001, the results were ready. The OECD called a press conference at the Château de la Muette, the grand Rothschild mansion that served as its headquarters in Paris. Standing before a small group of reporters, Schleicher and his team tried to explain the nuances of PISA.

"We were not looking for answers to equations or to multiple choice questions," he said. "We were looking for the ability to think creatively."

The reporters stirred, restless for a ranking. Eventually he gave them what they wanted. The number-one country in the world was . . . Finland. There was a pause. Schleicher was himself a bit puzzled by this outcome, but he didn't let it show. "In Finland, everyone does well," he said, "and social background has little impact."

Finland? Perhaps there had been some kind of mistake, whispered education experts, including the ones who lived in Finland.

Participating countries held their own press conferences to detail the results, and the Finnish announcement took place fifteen hundred miles away, in Helsinki. The education minister strode into the room, expecting to issue a generic statement to the same clutch of Finnish journalists she always encountered, and was astonished to find the room packed with photographers and reporters from all over the world. She stammered her way through the statement and retreated to her office.

Afterward, outside the Ministry of Education, foreign TV crews interviewed bewildered education officials in below-freezing December temperatures, their jackets flapping in the sea breezes off the Gulf of Finland. They had spent their careers looking to others—the Americans or the Germans—for advice on education. No one had ever looked back at them.

The Germans, meanwhile, were devastated. The chair of the education committee in the Bundestag called the results "a tragedy for German education." The Germans had believed their system among the best in the world, but their kids had performed below average for the developed world in reading, math, *and* science—even worse than the Americans (the *Americans!*)

"Are German Students Stupid?" wondered *Der Spiegel* on its cover. "Dummkopf!" declared the *Economist*. Educators from every country, including Germany, had helped Schleicher and his colleagues write the test questions, so they couldn't dismiss the results outright. Instead, some commentators blamed the teachers; others blamed video games. PISA entered the German vernacular, even inspiring a prime-time TV quiz program, *The PISA Show*. Education experts began making regular pilgrimages to Finland in search of redemption. Even

Schleicher's father came around, reading through the results and debating them with his son.

Across the ocean, the United States rang in somewhere above Greece and below Canada, a middling performance that would be repeated in every subsequent round. U.S. teenagers did better in reading, but that was only mildly comforting, since math skills tended to better predict future earnings.

Even in reading, a gulf of more than ninety points separated America's most-advantaged kids from their least-advantaged peers. By comparison, only thirty-three points separated Korea's most-privileged and least-privileged students, and almost all of them scored higher than their American counterparts.

U.S. Education Secretary Rod Paige lamented the results. "Average is not good enough for American kids," he said. He vowed (wrongly, as it would turn out) that No Child Left Behind, President George W. Bush's new accountability-based reform law, would improve America's standing.

Other Americans defended their system, blaming the diversity of their students for lackluster results. In his meticulous way, Schleicher responded with data: Immigrants could not be blamed for America's poor showing. The country would have had the same ranking if their scores were ignored. In fact, worldwide, the share of immigrant children explained only 3 percent of the variance between countries.

A student's race and family income mattered, but *how much* such things mattered varied wildly from country to country. Rich parents did not always presage high scores, and poor parents did not always presage low scores. American kids at private school tended to perform better, but not any better than similarly privileged kids who went to public school. Private school did not, statistically speaking, add much value.

In most countries, attending some kind of early childhood program (i.e., preschool or prekindergarten) led to real and lasting benefits. On average, kids who did so for more than a year scored much higher in math by age fifteen (more than a year ahead of other students). But in the United States, kids' economic backgrounds overwhelmed this advantage. The quality of the early childhood program seemed to matter more than the quantity.

In essence, PISA revealed what should have been obvious but was not: that spending on education did not make kids smarter. Everything—*everything*—depended on what teachers, parents, and students *did* with those investments. As in all other large organizations, from GE to the Marines, excellence depended on execution, the hardest thing to get right.

Kids around the world took the PISA again in 2003, 2006, 2009, and 2012. More countries had signed on, so, by 2012, the test booklet came in more than forty different languages. Each time, the results chipped away at the stereotypes: Not all the smart kids lived in Asia, for one thing. For another, U.S. kids did not have a monopoly on creativity. PISA required creativity, and many other countries delivered.

Money did not lead to more learning, either. Taxpayers in the smartest countries in the world spent dramatically less per pupil on education than taxpayers did in the United States. Parental involvement was complex, too. In the education superpowers, parents were not necessarily *more* involved in their children's education, just differently involved. And, most encouragingly, the smart kids had not always been so smart.

Historical test results showed that Finnish kids were not born smart; they had gotten that way fairly recently. Change, it turned out, could come within a single generation.

As new rounds of data spooled out of the OECD, Schleicher became a celebrity wonk. He testified before Congress and advised prime ministers. "Nobody understands the global issues better than he does," said U.S. Education Secretary Arne Duncan. "And he tells me the truth—what I need to hear, not what I want to hear." U.K. Education Secretary Michael Gove called him "the most important man in English education," never mind that Schleicher was German and lived in France.

On every continent, PISA attracted critics. Some said that the test was culturally biased, or that too much was lost in translation. Others said the U.S. sample size of 5,233 students in 165 schools was too small or skewed in one direction or another. Many said that Schleicher and his colleagues should just collect test scores and stop speculating about what might be leading to high or low scores.

For the most part, Schleicher deflected his critics. PISA was not perfect, he conceded, but it was better than any other option, and it got better each year. Like a Bible salesman, he carried his Power-Point slides from country to country, mesmerizing audiences with animated scatter plots of PISA scores over time and across oceans. His last slide read, in a continuously scrolling ticker, "Without data, you are just another person with an opinion . . . Without data, you are just another person with an opinion . . ."

test pilot

I met Schleicher for the first time in April 2010 in Washington, D.C., just after the cherry trees had blossomed on the National Mall. We spoke in the lobby of an office building next to the U.S. Capitol, during his only break in a whirlwind day of meetings. By then, Schleicher had white hair and a brown Alex Trebek mustache. He was pleasant but focused, and we got right down to business.

I told him I was impressed by PISA, but skeptical. By the time of my quest, the United States had wasted more time and treasure on testing than any other country. We had huge data sets from which we had learned precious little. Was PISA really different from the bubble tests our kids had to zombie walk through each spring?

Without bothering to sit down, he took each of my questions in turn, quietly rattling off statistics and caveats, like C-3PO with a slight German accent.

"PISA is not a traditional school test," he said. "It's actually challenging, because you have to think."

No test can measure everything, I countered.

Schleicher nodded. "PISA is not measuring every success that counts for your life. I think that's true."

I felt vindicated. Even Schleicher had admitted that data had its limitations. But he went on, and I realized I'd misunderstood.

"I do think PISA needs to evolve and capture a broader range of metrics. There is a lot of work going on to assess collaborative problem-solving skills, for example. We are working on that."

I got the sense that there was almost nothing, in his mind, that PISA could not measure. If not now, then, one day. Already, he insisted, PISA was radically different from any other test I'd ever taken.

We shook hands, and he headed back inside for his next meeting. As I left, I thought about what he had said. Schleicher, of all people, was a man to be taken literally. If PISA was really different from any test I'd ever taken, there was only one way to know if he was right.

my PISA score

I got there early, probably the only person in history excited to take a standardized test. The researchers who administered PISA in the United States had an office on K Street in downtown D.C., near the White House, wedged between the law firms and lobbyists.

In the elevator, it occurred to me that I hadn't actually taken a test in fifteen years. This could be embarrassing. I gave myself a quick pop quiz. What was the quadratic formula? What was the value of pi? Nothing came to mind. The elevator doors opened.

A nice young woman who had been ordered to babysit me showed me to an office. She laid out a pencil, a calculator, and a test booklet on a table. She read the official directions aloud, explaining that the PISA was designed to find out "what you've been learning and what school is like for you."

For the next two hours, I answered sixty-one questions about math, reading, and science. Since certain questions could reappear in later versions of the test, the PISA people made me promise not to reveal the exact questions. I can, however, share similar examples from past PISA tests and other sample questions that PISA has agreed to make public. Like this math question:

A TV reporter showed this graph and said: "The graph shows that there is a huge increase in the number of robberies from 1998 to 1999."

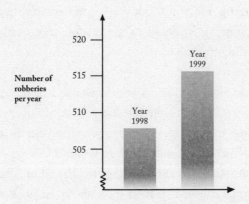

Do you consider the reporter's statement to be a reasonable interpretation of the graph? Give an explanation to support your answer.

Several questions like this one asked for my opinion, followed by rows of blank lines for writing my answer; that was odd. Since when did a standardized test care about anyone's opinion?

Other questions reminded me of problems I'd encountered as an adult—having to decipher the fine print of a health-care policy before choosing it, or comparing the fees of checking accounts offered by competing banks. It seemed more like a test of life skills than school skills.

All the math formulas were provided, thank God, including the value of pi. But I noticed that I had to really *think* about my answers. When I tried to speed through a math section, I had to go back and erase several answers.

One sample reading question featured a company flu-shot notice—the kind of bland announcement you might find hanging on the bulletin board at your job. The flyer, designed by an employee named Fiona, was not remarkable in any way. Just like a real HR flyer! The test asked for an analysis of Fiona's work:

> Fiona wanted the style of this information sheet to be friendly and encouraging. Do you think she succeeded? Explain your answer by referring in detail to the layout, style of writing, pictures or other graphics.

For me, the science section was the trickiest. I resorted to guessing more than once. Many of the questions were about everyday science you might use in real life. What happened to your muscles when you exercised? Which foods were high in vitamin C?

I finished with about twenty minutes to spare. Unlike a real student, I got to grade my own test. It took about an hour, since each answer could receive zero, full, or partial credit, depending on how close it came to the many options listed in the answer key. Smart tests usually had to be graded by humans, at least in part, which is what made them expensive and rare.

For the question about robberies, full credit was given for any version of ten different possible answers, as long as the answer was basically *no*—and included a critique of the distorted graph, which didn't start at 0, or pointed out that the increase in robberies was actually fairly small on a percentage basis. (Only about one-third of participants in Finland, Korea, and the United States got this question right, by the way.)

For the question about the flu-shot flyer, there was no one right answer. Yes or no, the only way to get full credit was to defend your opinion by citing at least one specific feature of the flyer and evaluating it in detail. It wasn't enough to merely repeat that the style was "friendly" and "encouraging;" those words were already included in the question. "Interesting," "easy to read," and "clear" were considered too vague. The assessment had to be original, and expectations were high. Worldwide, only four out of ten teenagers got that question right.

The questions varied slightly from country to country. Students from Mexico, for example, would not have been asked to measure the diameter of Lake Erie. Details like that didn't matter very much, because PISA was not just a test of facts. It was a test of the ability to do something useful with facts.

Finally, I announced my score to my chaperone, since there was no one else to tell. I had gotten just one wrong (a science question). "Good job!" she said generously. We both knew I had twenty-two more years of life experience than normal PISA takers, including four years of college.

After I left the building, my sense of relief faded. My score, I realized, did not bode well for teenagers in my own country. This test was not easy, but it wasn't that hard, either. On one question that I'd gotten right, only 18 percent of American fifteen-year-olds were with me. There were other questions like that, which many or most of the Finns and the Koreans were getting right, just as I was, but most young Americans were getting wrong.

PISA demanded fluency in problem solving and the ability to communicate; in other words, the basic skills I needed to do my job and take care of my family in a world choked with information and subject to sudden economic change. What did it mean for a country if most of its teenagers did not do well on this test? Not all of our kids had to be engineers or lawyers, but didn't all of them need to know how to *think*?

I still didn't believe PISA measured everything, but I was now convinced that it measured critical thinking. The American Association of University Professors had called critical thinking "the hallmark of American education—an education designed to create thinking citizens for a free society." If critical thinking was the hallmark, why didn't it show itself by age fifteen?

It was hard to escape the conclusion that American kids and taxpayers had been squandering a lot of time and money. In 2009, U.S. teenagers ranked twenty-sixth on the PISA math test, seventeenth in science, and twelfth in reading. We ranked second in the world in just one thing, spending per pupil. (The only country that spent more was Luxembourg, a place with fewer people than Nashville, Tennessee.)

The implications of that waste were painful to think about. Economists had found an almost one-to-one match between PISA scores and a nation's long-term economic growth. Many other things influenced economic growth, of course, but the ability of a workforce to learn, think, and adapt was the ultimate stimulus package. If the United States had Finland's PISA scores, GDP would be increasing at the rate of one to two trillion dollars per year.

For students, PISA scores were a better predictor of who would go to college than report cards. Kids who scored poorly on the PISA reading test were far more likely to drop out of high school. PISA wasn't measuring memorization; it was measuring aspiration.

I left the test with an unsettled feeling. The exam and the one thousand pages of analysis that came with the PISA results sketched out a kind of treasure map of the world. This map could help me sort out which countries were teaching all of their children to think, and which were not.

Most successful or improving countries seemed to fit into three basic categories: 1) the utopia model of Finland, a system built on trust in which kids achieved higher-order thinking without excessive competition or parental meddling; 2) the pressure-cooker model of South Korea, where kids studied so compulsively that the government had to institute a study curfew; and 3) the metamorphosis model of

Poland, a country on the ascent, with nearly as much child poverty as the United States, but recent and dramatic gains in what kids knew.

Still, PISA could not tell me how those countries got so smart, or what life was like for kids in those countries, day in and day out, compared to life in America. Children's life chances depended on something beyond what any test could measure. Were Korean girls and boys driven to *learn*, or just succeed? There was a difference. Did Finnish teenagers have as much character as they had math skills? I had the data, and I needed the life.

I set out to visit Finland, Korea, and Poland to see what the rest of the world could learn from the kids who lived there. I studied other places, too, places with sky-high scores like Shanghai, China, and Singapore. But I decided to focus most of all on developed democracies, countries where changes could not be made by fiat. I wanted to go where parents, kids, and teachers had to tolerate the vagaries of politics and the dull plod of compromise, and succeeded anyway. That was a magical thing that had to be seen to be believed.

The Quest: To raise money to go to Finland, Kim held a bake sale outside a supermarket in her hometown of Sallisaw, Oklahoma.

chapter 2

leaving

If the town of Sallisaw, Oklahoma, was famous for anything, it was for something the locals did not often discuss. In the 1939 book, *The Grapes of Wrath*, a fictional family called the Joads fled the Dust Bowl during the Great Depression. When they drove off in search of better life, it was Sallisaw they were running from.

"The ancient overloaded Hudson creaked and grunted to the highway at Sallisaw and turned west," John Steinbeck wrote, "and the sun was blinding."

In early 2008, when Kim was twelve, Sallisaw was on the brink of the second worst depression in U.S. history. It wasn't obvious, not right away anyway. Highway I-40 ran alongside the town, connecting Oklahoma to Arkansas. A chain of economy motels had opened up to cater to the truckers who came and went. In an empty field less than a mile from Kim's house, Walmart had built a Superstore.

Just down the road, a big Indian-owned casino drew a decent crowd at lunch hour. Older men in cowboy hats worked slot machines in the cool darkness. Retirees came for the three-dollar-and-fifty-cent lunch special. On the bathroom wall, a red plastic sharps container installed for diabetic gamblers held dozens of used insulin needles.

Despite this modest commerce, Sallisaw was still a rural town, home to just under nine thousand people. The bank that Pretty Boy Floyd had robbed during the Depression was now a vacant lot. The train station, where his body had arrived in a pine box after he was shot dead, housed a small public library.

Like Kim, most everyone in Sallisaw looked white, but people's identity shifted depending on which form they were filling out. Half the kids had their Indian cards, identifying them as certified blood descendants of Native Americans. Even if you were only 1/512 Indian, you could get the card, and it came with certain benefits, like free school supplies or access to a Cherokee food pantry. About a quarter of the kids in the Sallisaw school district were officially classified as poor, so the Indian benefits were as much about sustenance as heritage.

The schools in Sallisaw were considered just fine—not the best, nor the worst. A lot depended on where you were standing when you were doing the considering, however. On the state test, Kim and most of her classmates did all right, but that test was notoriously easy. On a more serious test used nationwide, just one in four Oklahoma eighth graders performed competently in math. (Sallisaw kids likely fared about the same, though not enough kids took the test at a local level to know for sure.)

The farther away you got, the worse things looked. If states were countries, Oklahoma would have ranked about eighty-first in the world in math, or around the same level as Croatia and Turkey.

Kim had lived in Sallisaw all her life. Each winter, she and her grandfather participated in the Christmas rodeo, steering antique tractors through the old downtown. She liked the slow rumble of the Model H tractor, the jangle of the marching bands behind her, and the way children shrieked when she threw candy into their out-stretched hands.

Still, like many twelve-year-olds, Kim felt like maybe she be-longed somewhere else. She'd tried to succeed in Sallisaw in all the ways that mattered. Since she wasn't very good at traditional sports, she'd started doing cheerleading in kindergarten. She'd posed straight-backed and smiling for pictures in her daffodil-yellow uniform. But, by third grade, she still could not do a cartwheel, so she quit.

After that, she'd started dreaming about playing in the school marching band. That felt right: a path into the football stadium, the center of the town's culture, without the forced smiles and front handsprings. She'd taken up the flute and practiced each day until her jaw ached. After two years, though, the notes still came out breathy and thin, and the band leader had assigned her to the fourth chair.

What came more naturally to Kim was a curiosity about the world. She took her schoolwork seriously and felt connected to injustice in faraway places. In second grade, she'd watched a TV news segment about scientists using rats to detect bombs. It was the year after 9/11, and the country had just gotten its first Secretary of Homeland Secu-rity. The reporter explained that scientists were inserting electrodes in rats' heads to make them go left or right or wherever humans dared not go, turning them into remote-controlled bomb detectors.

Kim felt a prick of conscience. She had no particular affection for rats and understood that a rat's life was less valuable than that of a human. But it seemed wrong to infiltrate the brain of any creature. It was creepy, possibly even immoral. She thought about her pet turtles and imagined if the government took over their brains, too. Where would it stop? Surely there was a better way to make animals go left or right. Maybe offer them a treat?

Then Kim did something unusual for a child, or for an adult, for that matter. She took action to rectify a faraway problem that had little to do with her. That afternoon, she sat by the vending machine at her elementary school and wrote a letter to President George W.

Bush detailing her concerns about the rat experiments. She'd made sure to be polite and respectful, looping her letters in careful penmanship in her spiral notebook.

When two of her friends walked by, Kim told them the story of the rats. She asked if they wanted to sign the letter. Maybe they could start a petition, get the whole school to sign.

After staring at her for a beat, the girls squealed.

"Ewwwww! Gross, Kim! Who cares about *rats?!*"

Their laughter echoed down the fluorescent-lit hallway. Then they made up a little song about Kim and her crusade. It was more of a jingle really; not very lyrically inspired. "Save the rats! Save the rats!" But it caught on anyway.

Kim felt a space open up between her and her friends. She wouldn't have minded if they'd thought the robo-rats were a good idea; what had upset her was that they didn't seem to care at all. Why didn't they care? At times like this, it felt like her friends were speaking another language, one she could imitate but never really understand.

She stopped talking about the rats, and she pretended she didn't hear the save-the-rats jingle when she walked down the hallway. Still, she sent the letter to the White House.

an invitation

One day, in seventh grade, Kim's English teacher asked to speak with her in the hallway.

"You've been invited to go to Oklahoma City and take the SAT," her teacher told her. "It's an honor."

Kim was confused; she was only twelve. She stared back at the teacher, her dark brown eyes awaiting more information. The teacher explained that Kim's standardized test scores had qualified her and other students for something called the Duke University 7th Grade Talent Search. The scores wouldn't count, but it might be an interesting experience.

In the car on the way home from school, Kim handed her mom the pamphlet. "I want to go to Oklahoma City and take the SAT," she announced. Looking over the top of her small wire-frame glasses, her mom stared at the information and then at her daughter. Oklahoma City was a three-hour drive from Sallisaw. But Kim hadn't sounded this emphatic about anything in a while.

Kim's mom, Charlotte, was a teacher at the local elementary school. She was a petite woman with short, curly hair, an unabashed Oklahoma drawl, and a quick laugh. She doted on Kim, driving her to and from school each day so she didn't have to take the bus. At their small ranch house, she lined the walls with pictures of Kim visiting the Oklahoma State Senate and Kim in her cheerleader uniform.

Lately, she'd become worried about her daughter's attitude. When she wasn't alone, reading in her room, Kim spent a lot of time complaining about school and Sallisaw. Charlotte had several theories about this behavior. For one thing, she and her husband had been fighting too much. It was an old, worn fissure in the family, but as Kim had gotten older, she'd started to take sides, defending her mom against her dad and pleading with her to get divorced.

Another theory was middle school. In sixth grade, Kim had come home with her first C. She'd said she was afraid to ask for help because her teacher got angry when kids didn't understand. Charlotte eventually complained to the principal, but nothing happened. She made Kim ask for the teacher's help anyway, and Kim went into school early for a series of strained tutoring sessions. By the end of the year, she'd decided that she was terrible at math and vowed to avoid it whenever possible.

As a mother, Charlotte figured Kim was going through a phase. She was nearly a teenager after all; she was entitled to slam doors and play Avril Lavigne at excessive volume. But, as a teacher, she also knew that middle school was a kind of limbo for children, the years when American kids began to slip behind—and when it became obvious that some of them would eventually drop out altogether.

This Kim, the one who wanted to drive three hours to take the SAT, reminded her of the old Kim, the one with plans. As she drove home, Charlotte silently added up the cost of going to Oklahoma City. They would probably need to spend the night in a hotel to get to the test on time, not to mention gas and food. As they pulled into the driveway, she made up her mind: "Okay, let's go see how you do."

A few weeks later, at a mostly empty Oklahoma City high school, Kim sat down with a small group of kids to take the SAT. She answered the essay question as best she could, twisting her long brown hair round and round her index finger. She'd always liked to write, and people had told her she was good at it.

When she got to the math section, though, the problems had letters in them where there should have been numbers. Maybe it was a misprint? She looked around; no one else seemed confused, so she focused on the word problems and guessed on the rest. By the end, she'd twirled her hair into a nest of knots. She had a grinding headache, like her brain had been slowly cooked over a low flame. She took four aspirin and slept the whole ride home.

One month later, Kim's teacher handed her an envelope with her SAT scores. When her mom picked her up from school, the two of them sat in the car and stared at the paper, trying to decipher what the numbers meant.

"Oh, look here: It says you've done better than 40 percent of college-bound Oklahoma high-school seniors in critical reading!" her mom said.

"What?" said Kim, grabbing the paper. "That can't be right."

Kim read and reread the words. How could she have done better than *any* college-bound high school seniors, let alone 40 percent? What had those kids been doing for the past five years?

"Wow, I am very disappointed in my state right now."

"Oh, Kim," her mom said, rolling her eyes and putting the car into drive.

But as they drove home, Kim had a second reaction. This was the first time she had ever won anything. It wasn't a cheerleading trophy, but still. She looked down at the scores again. Then she turned to look out the window so her mom wouldn't see her smile.

Later that spring, Kim and her parents drove to Tulsa for a recognition dinner for the top-scoring SAT takers. Kim wore the yellow flowered sundress she'd gotten for the band recital. The *Sequoyah County Times* ran a short article, along with a picture of Kim and her silver medal. Usually, the newspaper ran stories about Sallisaw basketball and football players, the local celebrities; it felt strange to see her name in the same font.

Back at home, Kim put the medal in her desk drawer. It made her nervous to have it out in the open. What if it was the last thing she won? Better to forget about the whole episode until she took the SAT for real in high school.

But a few weeks later, a brochure arrived from Duke's summer camp for the gifted and talented. Her SAT scores had gotten their attention; the story was not over after all. She was invited to learn Shakespeare and study psychology in Durham, North Carolina.

Reading the pamphlet, Kim felt disoriented, as if she'd stumbled upon a new planet. The program was billed as "intense and demanding," equivalent to one year of high school in just three weeks. How was that possible? The camp looked like an unusual place: the kind of place where it was acceptable to care about things like Shakespeare and psychology.

She ran to tell her mom; her mind buzzed with the idea of meeting people her own age who wanted to have serious conversations. "This is my chance to be normal. We can discuss things—real things!"

Kim had never been good at small talk; it felt awkward and fake. Maybe this camp was a place where she could be herself, where she could go left or right at will, and let her questions come tumbling out into the open.

But the program cost money and, besides, Charlotte was in no hurry to let her youngest child leave home for the summer. She said no.

"at least they are trying."

Oklahoma, like the rest of America, had been trying to fix its schools for a long time. Between 1969 and 2007, the state had more than doubled the amount of money it spent per student in constant dollars. Over the years, Oklahoma had hired thousands of new teachers' aides, granted badly needed raises to teachers, and lowered the student-to-teacher ratio. By 2011, over half the state budget went to education, but most of Oklahoma's kids still could not demonstrate competency in math.

To motivate kids and schools to do better, state lawmakers decided to create an incentive. In the late 1980s, they passed a law requiring students to take a test to graduate from high school. This kind of end-of-school test was standard in the countries that performed at the top of the world on the PISA test. It gave kids and teachers a clear mission, and it made a diploma mean something.

A few years later, however, Oklahoma's lawmakers delayed the test. It was a matter of compassion, or so they said. The lawmakers were worried too many students would fail. How would that look? Those kids would have attended four years of high school without getting a diploma. That didn't feel right. The parents wouldn't like it, either. So, the test was set aside, and the kids were left to fail a little later, in the real world, if they didn't know enough math to take college classes for credit, or couldn't get a job that paid above minimum wage.

After that, the governor of Oklahoma tried a kinder, gentler strategy. He signed an executive order requiring kids to pass a series of literacy tests, starting in eighth grade. That meant they had four years to retake the tests if they failed. However, just before the new mandate could take effect, Oklahoma's legislature scrapped this requirement, too. Lawmakers said they were worried about lawsuits from angry parents.

The state's history read like a slow-motion tug of war between hopes and fears, as if no one could agree what Oklahoma's children were capable of doing—a lack of faith that surely trickled down to the students. "Kids have a really good detector about what adults take seriously and what counts," as a 1997 teachers' union report noted, "If they see that it doesn't count, then they're not going to do the hard work."

In 2005, Oklahoma tried yet again, passing a law to require students to show a mastery of English, algebra, geometry, biology, and U.S. history in order to receive a diploma. The state had seven years to phase in the requirement, gently and humanely. Kids who failed could retake the test up to three times in one year, or they could take alternate tests, like the SAT. They could even opt to do special projects demonstrating their competence in any subject that they'd failed.

In 2011, as the graduation test was finally about to take effect, local newspapers warned that thousands of kids might not graduate. An Oklahoma School Boards Association official predicted that the results would be "devastating." One superintendent told the *Tulsa World* that the graduating class of seniors might be known as the "lost generation." A Republican legislator introduced a bill to delay the test for two more years.

When I first visited Kim's hometown, the young new superintendent of Sallisaw gave me a tour of the brick, one-story high school, past the orange and yellow lockers lining the cinderblock hallways. The last high school had been built by WPA workers during the Depression. This one, opened in 1987, looked like many American high schools: institutional but tidy, with blocks of color and light. The basketball court was the school's jewel. The school's black-diamond mascot, gleaming on the hardwood floor, dated back to the 1920s, when coal mining was a major local industry.

Scott Farmer had just been appointed the town's first new superintendent in twenty years. He had short brown hair and a boyish face. The state of Oklahoma had 530 superintendents like him, each with their own fiefdom. There were about as many superintendents in

Oklahoma as there were members of Congress for the entire country. This tradition of hyperlocal control, hard-wired for inefficiency, hinted at one reason that the United States spent so much more than other countries on education.

Farmer made about $100,000 per year, which made him one of the top earners in Sallisaw. He had an assistant superintendent, too, along with eight director-level managers and a school board. It was quite an operation for a district that included just four schools. But it was hardly unusual. Compared to the rest of the state, in fact, Sallisaw was one of the more efficient school districts in Oklahoma.

When I asked Farmer to describe Sallisaw High School's biggest challenge, he talked mostly about parental involvement, lamenting the low turnout for parent-teacher conferences. "I'm just not convinced that parents quit caring," Farmer said, shaking his head, "but that's something we need to work on—reminding them of the importance of lifelong learning."

I'd heard this argument often in U.S. schools, not just in Oklahoma. It seemed to be common knowledge that parents were AWOL in our schools. Even other parents thought so. In a survey about the best ways to improve education, most American adults cited more involved parents.

Reality was more complicated, however. Whatever U.S. parents were doing wrong, they were in fact showing up at their children's schools more often than they had in twenty years. In 2007, nine out of ten parents said they'd attended at least one parent-teacher conference or school meeting that school year. Some were coming to school for disciplinary meetings—uncomfortable encounters with assistant principals and stone-faced kids. But whether they came for positive reasons or negative, American parents were not as hands-off as most of us seemed to think.

So, what explained the disconnect? It might have depended on how you defined *involved*. When I talked to Ernie Martens, Sallisaw High School's principal for the past decade, he had no complaints about parental involvement. Sure, parent-teacher conferences weren't as well attended as they were in the younger grades, but that was okay, he said. High-school students didn't need that kind of handholding. Instead, about three-quarters of the Sallisaw parents got involved in some other way, usually with the football booster club, the basketball booster club, or the Future Farmers of America chapter. Only about one in four of his parents were what he would consider uninvolved.

In fact, Principal Martens said his biggest problem was not parental involvement at all. His biggest problem was expectations; they were, he said, too high.

Politicians and so-called reformers expected too much from his students. "We have a lot of our kids who come from dysfunctional homes," he said. "We're the only normal thing they have in their life." It was all well and good to talk about high expectations in political speeches, but he lived in the real world, in a part of the country where some parents read to their children, and some never did. In his world, some mothers thought breakfast was a bag of potato chips, and some fathers hid methamphetamines in the backyard barbecue.

In Sallisaw, nearly one in four students failed to graduate high school within four years. Martens and Farmer had different narratives about why that was, but they were both looking in the same direction. Neither saw education itself as the primary problem or the main solution. Both pointed to external forces: negligent parents, social ills, or out-of-touch government expectations. That, too, was a common refrain among educators all over the United States. Whatever the problem, it was, it seemed, largely outside their control.

And they were right, of course. A long list of grim factors lay beyond their reach, from how much kids slept to how much television they watched. The stress that kids endured in many families taxed their bodies and minds, doing damage that no school could undo.

The only problem with this narrative was that it was habit forming. Once you start locating the source of your problems outside your own jurisdiction, it is hard to stop, even when the narrative is wrong.

For example: Sallisaw had plenty of good students, too. Other than the destitute and the dropouts, Sallisaw High School had its success stories, like every town. About half the kids who graduated from Sallisaw enrolled in public colleges and universities in Oklahoma. Others went to out-of-state colleges or looked for jobs.

What happened to these success stories after they left? Their colleges tested their basic skills and found them wanting. More than *half* these students were promptly placed into remedial classes at Oklahoma public colleges. That meant that some of Sallisaw's best students were paying good money for college, often in the form of student loans, but they weren't getting college credit.

These young men and women had been told their whole lives to get a high-school diploma and go to college; that was the dream. But when they got there, they were stalled in limbo, redoing algebra or English as if they'd never left high school. It wasn't hard to understand why, as their debt mounted, many quit college altogether. One out of two Oklahoma university students failed to graduate within six years.

I asked Principal Martens about all the Sallisaw alumni who were retaking math or English. "That really doesn't bother me," he said, "because at least they are trying." The main goal was to go to college. Whether his graduates succeeded there was out of his control, or so it seemed.

The fact that those kids had spent four years in his school preparing to get to college—and that he'd given them a diploma that was supposed to mean they were ready—did not seem relevant.

"rich people do that. we don't do that."

It was July Fourth weekend, the year after she took the SATs, and Kim and her mom were visiting Kim's older half-sisters in Texas. It was too hot to do anything ambitious, so they stayed close to the air conditioning, playing Scrabble and petting the dogs. When her mom went outside to smoke a cigarette, Kim told her sister Kate she wanted to leave Sallisaw.

"I'd like to live somewhere where people are curious."

Kate listened and nodded. She was a woman of action. She worked a retail job, but on her days off, she liked to jump out of planes and explore caves. In her opinion, if Kim wanted to go away, she should think big.

"Why don't you become an exchange student?"

"You mean like go to another country?" In her head, Kim imagined a kid with floppy hair and leather flip-flops, backpacking around Europe.

"Why not?"

Kim laughed. "Rich people do that. We don't do that."

It wasn't until Kim went home to Sallisaw that she thought about the idea again. If Kate thought she could go to another country, maybe it wasn't a totally absurd idea. She Googled "exchange programs" and spent an hour clicking on random countries, imagining herself in each one.

She learned that one or two thousand American high school students went abroad each year. She found AFS, one of the largest exchange programs, by reading the blog of an American girl posted in Sweden. Kim liked the story of AFS. It had started out as the American Field Service, an ambulance convoy set up by American volunteers to help ferry wounded soldiers to safety during the World Wars. After liberating concentration camps at the end of World War II, the ambulance drivers were tired of carnage. They decided to reinvent the group, dedicating it to building trust between countries through cultural exchanges.

The more Kim read, the less ridiculous the whole idea sounded. She decided to bring the idea up to her mother. But, this time, she tried a new strategy.

"I am applying to go on an exchange program," she said one evening, keeping her voice level and free from doubt. "I want to live in Egypt for a year."

Charlotte looked up from her tea. "Wow, how exciting," she said, trying to act like this was not a completely insane notion. Kim had never left the country, and neither had she.

The obvious response was no, just like it was when Kim had asked to go to Shakespeare summer camp at Duke. But, this time, she tried a new approach.

Charlotte and Kim's dad had gotten divorced not long before. It was a long time coming, and Kim said she was relieved by the split. Still, Charlotte was trying to handle her daughter with care. So, if Kim wanted to rebel by vowing to go far away, she would not stop her; she would just wear her out.

"Egypt sounds a little unsafe," Charlotte said in her most reasonable voice. "Why don't you pick another country and write me up a little report on why you want to go there?"

"Okay, fine," Kim answered, with a tight smile. Then she got up and walked toward the extra bedroom, the one with the computer in it.

Charlotte felt a sliver of anxiety. What had she just done? "And, Kim," she called out after her, "nowhere with sand!"

At the computer, Kim contemplated her remaining options. She didn't want to go to France or Italy. She wanted to be original, so she started reading about places she knew nothing about, obscure countries with languages she'd never heard and food she'd never eaten.

One day, she read about Finland—a snow-castle country with white nights and strong coffee. She read that the Finns liked heavy metal music and had a dry sense of humor. Every year, the country hosted something called the Air Guitar World Championship. That sounded promising—a place that didn't take itself too seriously.

Then she read that Finland had the smartest kids in the world. Could that be right? Teenagers in Finland did less homework than Americans, but scored at the top of the world on international tests, which was weird, since Finland had been until fairly recently a largely illiterate farming and logging nation.

Nothing about it made much sense. Sure, Finland was a small country full of white people, but not even the smallest, whitest states in America could compete with Finland's education results. Not even tiny New Hampshire, which was 96 percent white and had the highest median income in the nation and one of the lowest child poverty rates. Why hadn't New Hampshire done what Finland had done? Apparently, every kid in Finland got a decent education, regardless of how much money their parents made. It sounded like upside-down world in every way.

Kim had found her destination. If Finland was the smartest country in the world, that's where she wanted to go. She wrote up a report for her mom, as agreed. She emphasized the education angle; her mom was a teacher after all, so she would find this argument hard to refute. She added blurbs about the population (a little over 5 million), the religion (mostly Lutheran), and the food (fish, dark rye bread, and lots of berries with mystical names like arctic brambles and lingonberries).

One fall morning, she handed the Finland report to her mom. Charlotte took it and promised to read it. Then they left for Sallisaw High School, where Kim was now a freshman. Her mom dropped her off by the flagpole and watched as Kim walked slowly into the orange brick building.

Like many places in the United States, Oklahoma's curriculum was not rigorous by international standards. The state's science standards ranked among the least challenging in the nation, especially at the high school level. The word *evolution* did not appear anywhere in the thirty-one-page document, for example. Kim was taking biology that year. She spent the class period that day copying terms and definitions into her notebook. She wasn't sure why; maybe copying information from one piece of paper to another would help her memorize the information, maybe not. Whatever the case, the time passed slowly.

Kim's favorite class was English, which Oklahoma and most states took more seriously. She was reading *Tuesdays with Morrie*, and she loved it. The best days were the days her teacher pushed the desks into a circle and everyone talked about the book.

Her most dreaded subject, by far, was math. After the misery of sixth grade, she had decided that math was not for her; she just wanted to get through the requirements that she needed to graduate.

When Kim walked into Algebra I that day, her teacher was talking to the football players in her class. They had a lot to talk about since he was also a football coach and a former star football player at the same school. He was a nice guy, but, like most everyone in Sallisaw, he seemed to care more about football than Kim did.

She stared out the window at the American flag waving in the breeze. She wondered if her Finnish teachers would be different. She had read that being a teacher in Finland was prestigious, like being a doctor here. That was hard to imagine. She wished her mom was treated like a doctor at the elementary school where she taught.

She knew Finland didn't have American football; would they be obsessed with ice hockey instead? Would they spend so much class time on ESPN.com?

That afternoon, when her mom picked her up, Kim slid into the Hyundai Sonata's passenger seat and tried to refrain from asking if she had read the Finland report yet.

"How was your day?" Charlotte asked.

"I feel bored out of my skull," Kim answered, looking straight ahead.

Charlotte let that go. She had read the report, and she had an ultimatum for Kim.

"If you get all the papers filled out, and you raise all the money, then you can go to Finland."

Kim turned toward her mom. "It costs ten thousand dollars."

"I know."

beef jerky dreams

Kim posted the pictures of her flute on eBay and set the price at eighty-five dollars. It was after midnight in early October 2009, and her mom had long since gone to sleep. Kim had done this once before with her old dresses from middle school; she'd gotten no bids at all. A humiliating defeat. This time, she tried not to get her hopes up. She stared at the screen for a while, unblinking, then made herself go to sleep.

Two days later, Kim logged into eBay. Her eyes widened. Offers had come in from around the world, including a top bid from the United Arab Emirates for $100. Her flute was wanted. She yelped and jumped up out of her chair, breaking into a little dance on the carpet. Her flute would travel farther than she ever had. She started looking for a box. Honestly, she couldn't wait to get rid of it.

That fall, Kim spent all of her free time raising money for Finland. The rational part of her brain thought she would never get to $10,000, but the rest of her was desperate enough to try. She bought a case of beef jerky online and sold it door to door. Total profit: $400. Not bad.

She baked Rice Krispies Treats all night long and sold them at a table outside of Marvin's grocery store. Profit: $100. At that rate, she'd have to hold a bake sale every three days to get to Finland.

She tried the Internet, which everyone knew was the best place to find easy money in twenty-first century America. She created a blog, asking strangers to sponsor her quest: "I understand our economy's down right now, but I'll gladly accept even the smallest amount of money," she wrote. "I hope you'll part with just a few dollars for some girl with a crazy dream." To show people where Sallisaw was, she included a map of the I-40 corridor.

To her surprise, small donations started trickling in. They were all from relatives, who probably just felt sorry for her, but she took the money.

Still, she didn't dare tell her grandfather about Finland; she was sure he'd think this was another one of her hippie-dippie plans, like the time she'd become a secret vegetarian for three months. How could she tell him she wanted to move to Europe for a year? *Europe.* As it was, he kept referring to President Obama as "Kim's president."

Kim was very close to her grandfather, a retired drilling super-intendent for an oil company. They spent hours together, neither of them talking very much. He was an old-fashioned man with no de-sire to leave the countryside of Oklahoma. She feared he would never understand why anyone would want to move to Finland.

Meanwhile, all around Kim, the Oklahoma economy was coming apart. The Therma-Tru door and window factory, citing the down-turn in the housing market, announced plans to shut down its nearby manufacturing plant, taking 220 jobs with it. A horse-racing track called Blue Ribbon Downs, one of Sallisaw's larger attractions, also closed its doors. The unemployment rate hit 10 percent. For a brief period, the county jail ran out of money.

Even the good news came laced with anxiety: The Bama Com-panies, the Oklahoma-based supplier of McDonald's apple pies, was expanding. The company already had four facilities in the state. That year, it opened another new factory—in Guangzhou, China.

To Kim, these headlines were like smoke signals, warning her to get out while she could. She sent in her AFS application and got tested for tuberculosis. She started teaching herself Finnish, watch-ing videos of Finnish bands on YouTube, impressed that any lan-guage could deploy six syllables just to convey the word *pink*. She bought a hermit crab and named it Tarja, after the first female Finn-ish president.

Money wasn't her only problem. AFS couldn't find anyone in her area to do an in-home interview; apparently, she lived too far from civilization. Her mom was willing to drive her to Tulsa, but AFS insisted that the interviewer had to come to her home, to see Kim in her native living room. She waited and worried.

To distract herself, she wrote blog posts and tried to explain her-self to the world. Sometimes she succeeded, hitting just the right note between self-aware and sincere. "Basically I'm just a walking contra-diction. For example, on the outside I appear sarcastic and cold, but in actuality I'm a bleeding heart," she wrote. "I get a little sad whenever a spider is killed . . . [But] I think squirrels are pure evil (chased twice, bitten twice—three separate occasions by the way).”

In November, she mustered her courage and sat down with her grandparents to tell them about her plan; her grandmother interrupted her: “You mean your trip to Finland?” Kim was shocked. They had known for weeks, as it turned out. Kim’s grandmother was on Facebook and checked it daily. *Daily!* To Kim’s relief, they had no objections. Kim’s grandfather asked her if she knew the capital of Finland. *Helsinki.* He didn’t say much more about it, and Kim didn’t ask. She remembered then that he had traveled to oil wells in seven different countries as a younger man. He must have known that the world was a big place and worth seeing.

Just after Thanksgiving, Kim got a three-thousand-dollar scholarship. She wasn’t sure where the rest of the money would come from, but she noticed that her grandparents started talking about “when” Kim went to Finland, not “if.”

That December, she and her mom went to Walmart to get her passport photos taken. She didn’t want to jinx anything, but she was impatient for her life to start. Then she got lucky again, winning a two-thousand-dollar scholarship intended for someone from Arkansas. AFS officials decided Sallisaw was close enough.

Finally, AFS found someone to interview her. It took three months, and the woman had to drive for hours to get to Sallisaw. Kim and her mom tidied up the bathroom, set out some scented candles, and waited, nervously. When her interviewer arrived, Kim felt herself rambling. She heard herself criticizing her town, and she knew she’d made a mistake. The woman looked worried.

“You sound like you are trying to escape.”

Kim tried to reassure her; okay, yes, maybe she wanted to escape a little, but she also wanted to explore, to see what life was like somewhere else—what *she* was like somewhere else.

The letter arrived soon afterward. Despite the tortured interview, Kim had made it. She was officially an exchange-student-to-be.

Finally, just a couple of months before she was supposed to leave, Kim got one last donation—from her grandparents. She tried to refuse, but her grandmother wrote her the check and walked away.

With that, Kim had $10,000.

One thing led to another, and soon everything became tangible and specific. That summer, Kim was sitting on her grandfather's recliner when the phone rang. She recognized the country code and jumped out of the chair. She pulled out her retainer and ran outside to get a better signal.

"Hello?"

"Hello, this is Susanne from Finland!" Her host mother's voice sounded far away. She spoke excellent English, with only a slight, hard-edged Nordic clip. "We can't wait to meet you!"

Kim walked in circles, barefoot on the hot rock pathway. Susanne told her she was a journalist and a single mother of twin five-year-old girls. They lived in an apartment in Pietarsaari, a small town on Finland's west coast. Kim would be going from one country town to another; from one single mother to another. Susanne told her to bring her warmest clothes.

From Minnesota to South Korea: Eric in Busan.

chapter 3

the pressure cooker

Nothing seemed real until he saw the sign. It was dark pink with blue letters, and he spotted it through the sliding glass doors in front of him, as he rolled his luggage cart toward the arrivals lounge at Gimhae International Airport in Busan. "Welcome to Korea, Eric!" it said in bubbly script, the kind waitresses use to write *Thank You!* on the bottom of their checks. That boy holding the sign must be his host brother, standing next to his host mother and host father. His new *omma* and *appa*, he thought. Or maybe it was *appa* and *omma*.

He slowed down, his small frame finally absorbing the implications of this decision. He'd spent all eighteen years of his life in Minnetonka, Minnesota, a white, affluent suburb of Minneapolis. That was over now. For the next year, he had chosen to live in Busan, South Korea, with total strangers. He ran his fingers through the thick pelt of brown hair on his forehead, which was growing frizzier by the second. The humidity had wrapped around him like a wool blanket from the moment he'd gotten off the plane. The glass doors opened and closed and opened again. Then, he took a breath and rolled his cart through.

Before he'd even left the United States Eric was, in some ways, living in a different country than Kim in Oklahoma. Minnesota was one of the very few states that ranked among the top twenty nations in the world in education outcomes. Minnesota did not make it into the top tier with Finland or Korea, but in math, the state's teenagers performed about as well as teenagers in Australia and Germany.

Even by those standards, Eric had attended a particularly high-powered high school. *Newsweek* regularly ranked Minnetonka High School among the top high schools in America. The place had four gymnasiums and a hockey rink and looked more like a small college than a high school.

Eric had opted to join the International Baccalaureate Diploma Programme, an intense track within the school that was benchmarked to international standards. He had several teachers who were legendary in Minnetonka. Ms. Duncan, his history teacher, held an annual trial for Napoleon; her students picked sides, researched their arguments, and then presented their case in full costume to a jury of alumni. On paper, anyway, Eric was going from one of the smartest states in the United States to one of the smartest countries in the world.

Eric had already practiced what to do when he met his host family. Following Korean protocol, he bowed deeply from the waist as a sign of gratitude and respect. He also smiled widely, like a proper Midwestern boy. His Korean family all bowed in response—not as deeply, but it was clear that they were pleased with his effort.

Then Eric froze. He had not planned out what to do after the bow. Should he hug them? Too much. Should he shake their hands? Too businesslike. Instead, he tried to introduce himself in Korean. This was a mistake; his lips would not cooperate. The sounds squeaked out of his mouth like the chirps of a spastic parakeet. *Rosetta Stone* had not gotten him far.

"Don't worry," his Korean mother said in English, interrupting him with a smile. "We'll teach you how to do that."

Then, his Korean brother gave him a hug and started chattering away, excited to deploy his choppy English on a real American as they all walked together to the parking garage. Eric stuffed his heavy suitcases into the trunk of the Daewoo hatchback, and they headed off to his new home.

At first, the car sped through a long tunnel that went on and on, revealing nothing of Eric's new city. But then, suddenly, the Daewoo surged into the open air. He looked back through the rear window and saw a steep, lush mountain behind them. They had driven through the middle of the rock and now emerged into the heart of Busan, a pulsing city with nearly ten times the population of Minneapolis.

To Eric, Busan (pronounced PU-san) looked like a city stacked on top of a city, a kaleidoscope of commerce and color. He strained his neck, looking up through the window, and he recognized what looked like a pharmacy, built on top of a police station, perched on top of a Dunkin' Donuts, their glowing green, yellow, and pink signs cantilevered out over the street. Cranes sliced up the skyline like windmills, each marking a high-rise in progress.

"This is amazing!" Eric exclaimed in English, as the car merged onto the Diamond Bridge, a suspension bridge that sheared across the sea, running the length of eighty football fields. From the front seat, his host mother smiled.

On one side of the bridge, Eric could see the Pacific Ocean stretching out to the horizon, calm and polished. It was nighttime by then, and the bridge's white spotlights spilled out onto the expanse of water below. On the other side of the bridge, he saw a city in full. It was like watching split-screen television. Neon-lit skyscrapers were lined up like dominoes along the edge of the water, as if the gods had dropped a booming metropolis right onto a beach.

The host family lived in an apartment on the seventh floor of a luxury skyscraper complex called Lotte Castle. Eric got his own bathroom, a rare amenity in Korea's crowded cities.

One morning shortly after his arrival, he and his host mother walked outside to catch the number eighty bus. By then, Eric had emerged from the fog of jet lag and was eager to visit Namsan, the Korean high school he would be attending for the next year. He had read that Korean students performed at the top of the world on international tests, just like the Finns. He also knew that Korea had one of the highest high-school graduation rates in the world, far higher than the United States, despite having dramatically less wealth.

Getting on the bus, he felt nervous in a detached way, like an anthropologist on a field visit. Eric had already graduated from high school in Minnesota, so he was not worried about passing exams or getting credit. He was in Korea for a break, or so he thought.

A lot had happened in the last few years of his life. He'd worked extremely hard to keep up with his International Baccalaureate classes, pushing himself to stay up later and study harder. He'd also come out to his family at age sixteen. His parents had been supportive, and he was now comfortable talking about his sexuality openly. He didn't plan to talk about being gay often in Korea, a very conservative country, but he didn't plan to lie to anyone either. He hoped that, as an outsider, he would be exempt from the worst cultural strictures. He was here for the experience, determined to keep his mind open to whatever he found. Next year, he would go to college, and it was hard to say when he'd have this kind of adventure again.

The bus stopped at the top of a long hill, outside a flimsy metal archway. Eric and his host mother got off and walked across a dirt field, where a group of students were playing pick-up soccer, kicking up a cloud of dust in the humid morning air. Looming behind the field, up on an incline, was Namsan high school. It was a massive four-story, red-brick compound that stretched on and on, bending at an angle at one point as if to fit between all the neighboring high-rises.

Inside, a single hallway ran the full length of each floor. It felt very cramped and very vertical compared to Eric's school back home. Nothing looked dirty exactly, but the school had clearly seen a lot of use. The walls were dinged and the white boards were scuffed. The curtains were tied back haphazardly to let in fresh air—not to look nice. In this school, function clearly came before form.

Eric and his host mother met up with an exchange student from Canada who had also just arrived. The hallway was quiet, and, through the open doors, Eric could see students sitting behind rows of desks.

The shrieking began without warning. First one girl and then another and soon dozens of girls were screaming in unison. Eric froze. What had happened? Had he done something wrong, triggered some invisible alarm?

The shrieking was the kind of screeching he'd heard on old news footage of the Beatles appearing on *The Ed Sullivan Show*. It was high pitched and sustained, and it started a chain reaction. Students from other classrooms spilled into the hallway to investigate.

Groups of girls approached in gaggles, still shrieking, which was when Eric realized that this hysteria was for them. "Hello!" one of the boys shouted in thickly accented English. "How are you?" Eric smiled, eyebrows raised, uncertain whether to be flattered or frightened. A boy reached out to high-five him, and he cautiously complied. "We're rock stars," he whispered to the Canadian girl.

The adults ushered them away for a brief meeting with the principal. They didn't stay long; for the exchange students, classes would begin the next week. Soon afterward, he and the Canadian left to catch the bus home.

Walking down the front steps and across the dirt field, they heard yelling behind them. Eric looked back and saw kids hanging out of five or six classroom windows to wave goodbye. They were smiling, high up in the air. He smiled and waved back. Strange as the experience had been, it felt good to be so warmly welcomed.

Before turning the corner to catch the bus a few minutes later, Eric glanced back one last time. The kids were still there, lined up at the institutional windows with their arms dangling out—as if they wanted to get as far from the building as they could, without actually falling.

Watching them, the feeling of gratitude faded slightly. In its place, he felt something more foreboding.

"have you ever shot anyone?"

He hoped that the uniform would help him blend in. It was early in the morning on his first full day of school, and Eric was putting on the dark-blue pants and the white collared shirt required for all Namsan students. His exchange counselor from the Rotary Club had gotten it for him. She'd also explained that he would be assigned to a class with kids two years younger than he was. The older kids, she'd said, were too busy to talk to him. They had to study for the college entrance test. This exam was so important, so all consuming, that going to school with them would be like going to school in solitary confinement. Eric had nodded as though he understood; the SAT was a big deal in Minnetonka, too.

As Eric made his way to sociology, his first class, he tried to make himself as small as possible, to minimize the screaming. In the back of his classroom, he put his outdoor shoes in a nook and traded them for indoor flip-flops, just like the other students. He noticed that many of the kids wore colorful socks with sayings he couldn't understand—or cartoon images of Batman. The school banned makeup, earrings, long hair, and hair dye, so socks seemed to be the main outlet for free expression.

Eric found an empty seat near the front and waited for class to begin. Looking around, he noticed that the classroom looked a lot like a Minnesota classroom might have looked thirty years earlier. There were wooden and metal desks lined up in rows and a faded chalkboard at the front.

At his high school in Minnetonka, every classroom had an inter-active, electronic white board that usually cost a couple of thousand dollars, and teachers had wireless clickers to hand out to students for instant polling. However, Korea's cultural obsession with digital toys did not seem to extend to this classroom, which was utilitarian and spare.

As the other students filed into the classroom, they crowded around Eric's desk. The class was large by Eric's standards, bursting with over thirty students, but typical for Korean classes.

"Have you ever ridden a horse?"

"Have you met Brad Pitt?"

"Do you own a farm?"

"Have you ever shot anyone?"

Eric remembered hearing that the Koreans were known as the Italians of Asia, more emotive and chatty than the Japanese or Chinese. Now that the shrieking had diminished, he found the kids' curiosity charming. And he had always liked to talk.

"Yes, I have ridden a horse," he said. "I have not met many celebrities. I don't own a farm, and I have never shot anyone."

The teacher walked into the room and stood at the front of the class. She was tall compared to most Korean women, and wore glasses. She carried a delicate microphone in one hand and a stick with a stuffed frog on the end of it in the other hand. It looked like a backscratcher, something you might find in a gift shop at the mall. Eric stopped talking and sat up straight at his desk, wondering what to make of the frog.

Strangely, no one else seemed to react. The kids kept chatting with one another while the teacher stood there, waiting. It was painful to watch. Finally, the teacher tapped her frog stick on a desk to get everyone's attention, and the students slowly took their seats. As she lectured, a few of the kids talked over her in the back. Eric was surprised. He had seen worse behavior back in the States, but for some reason, he had expected Korean kids to be more deferential.

A few minutes later, he glanced backwards at the rows of students behind him. Then he looked again, eyes wide. A third of the class was asleep. Not nodding off, but flat-out, no-apology sleeping, with their heads down on the desks. One girl actually had her head on a special pillow that slipped over her forearm. This was pre-meditated napping.

How could this be? Eric had read all about the hard-working Koreans who trounced the Americans in math, reading, and science. He hadn't read anything about shamelessly sleeping through class. As if to compensate for his classmates, he sat up even straighter and waited to see what happened next.

The teacher lectured on, unfazed.

At the end of class, the kids woke up. They had a ten-minute break and made every second count. Girls sat on top of their desks or on overturned trash cans, chatting with each other and texting on their phones. A few of the boys started drumming on their desks with their pencils. They were strangely comfortable in the classroom, as if they were in their own living rooms at home.

Next was science class. Once again, at least a third of the class went to sleep. It was almost farcical. How did Korean kids get those record-setting test scores if they spent so much of their time asleep in class?

Soon he discovered the purpose of the teacher's backscratcher. It was the Korean version of wake-up call. Certain teachers would lightly tap kids on the head when they fell asleep or talked in class. The kids called it a "love stick."

At lunch, Eric followed the other students to the cafeteria and copied everything they did, filling up his tray with *kimchi*, a kind of spicy, fermented cabbage that appeared at every meal in Korea, along with transparent noodles and what looked like vegetable and beef stew. He was relieved to see the Canadian and sat down with her to eat. It was a treat to have a real, freshly cooked meal, not the warmed-up, pre-fab entrees he got at Minnetonka.

For a moment, sitting there in the warm cafeteria twirling noodles with chop sticks, Eric felt as though he'd made the right decision in coming to Korea. The kids he'd graduated with were all starting college now. They'd bought their extralong twin sheets at Bed Bath

& Beyond and met their roommates; they were going to freshman writing seminars and fraternity parties. Eric had deliberately chosen to step off the treadmill. He'd spent thirteen years in school and been politely bored much of the time. Like a lot of kids all over the world, he'd spent a lot of time staring at clocks, doodling in margins, and wondering whether this was all there was.

For the last two years of high school, the International Baccalaureate program had challenged him in a way nothing else had. And it had reminded him how it felt to really learn—to think and discover things for the sake of discovery, not because it was what he was supposed to do.

So, after he'd gotten accepted into DePaul University in Chicago, he'd checked the box to defer. He'd wanted to live in Asia—to discover a totally different world in which he understood nothing at all whatsoever—and marinate in the strangeness for a while. Then, he could come back and decorate a dorm room and let his life after high school begin.

The Korean kids bolted down their food and then raced outside to claim the small amount of free time they had left. Some of the boys played soccer in the dirt, and a few of the girls sat on the steps and, hunched over their smart phones, logged on to CyWorld, which was like Facebook with more privacy controls. Eric was one of the last students to finish his food and leave the cafeteria.

Between classes, Eric asked one of the other students about this test he kept hearing about—the one Korean high school seniors took before they graduated. "It's like your SAT in America," the boy told Eric. Except that your score determined the rest of your life.

"In Korea, your education can be reduced to a number," the boy explained. "If your number is good, you have a good future."

The highest score guaranteed acceptance into one of Korea's three most prestigious universities and, with that, you were destined for a good job, a nice house, and a lifetime of ease. Everyone would respect you. You were chosen by God, as another student put it, only half joking.

But there was a problem: only 2 percent of seniors got into these top three schools. So, the exam was a chokepoint for the ambitions of millions of kids and their parents. Eric's classmates talked about this test with dread. They would spend the next two years of their lives studying, planning, and praying to do well on this test. Not one of them looked forward to it.

Minnesota had a graduation test of its own. Eric had taken the math portion his junior year, but it was so easy that he couldn't imagine failing it. Kids who scored below the cutoff were automatically enrolled in a special class and allowed to retake the test again and again until they passed. The Korean test, by contrast, was offered one day each year, and it was designed to be very difficult. Students who did poorly could take it again, but they had to wait a year.

In Eric's next class, the teacher wrote each student's test score on the chalkboard, using ID numbers, not names. But all the kids knew each other's numbers. It was the first of many times that Eric would see his classmates publicly ranked. One girl put her head in her hands, and another just shook her head.

Most of the tests at the school were graded on a curve, so only 4 percent of kids could get the top score, regardless of how hard they worked. On and on went the hierarchy, all the way to the ninth and worst possible score, which the bottom 4 percent of the class earned, every time.

Everyone in Eric's class knew everyone else's ranking, not just on this test but on everything. The top twenty-eight kids in the grade were the class heroes, and also the martyrs. Because they had the most to lose, they worked hardest of all.

At ten past two, Eric left school early. Since he was an exchange student, he was exempt from having to experience the full force of the Korean school day. He asked one of his classmates what would happen after he left.

"We keep going to school."

Eric looked at him blankly.

"Until when?"

"Classes end at ten after four," he said.

Then he went on: After classes, the kids cleaned the school, mopping the floors, wiping the chalkboards, and emptying the garbage. The kids who had received demerits—for misbehaving or letting their hair grow too long—had to wear red pinnies and clean the bathrooms. Work, including the unpleasant kind, was at the center of Korean school culture, and no one was exempt.

At four thirty, everyone settled back in their seats for test-prep classes, in anticipation of the college entrance exam. Then they ate dinner in the school cafeteria.

After dinner came *yaja*, a two hour period of study loosely supervised by teachers. Most kids reviewed their notes from the day or watched online test-prep lectures, as the teachers roamed the hallways and confiscated the occasional illicit iPod.

Around nine in the evening, Eric's classmates finally left Namsan.

But the school day still wasn't over. At that point, most kids went to private tutoring academies known as *hagwons*. That's where they did most of their real learning, the boy said. They took more classes there until eleven, the city's hagwon curfew. Then—finally—they went home to sleep for a few hours before reporting back to school at eight the next morning.

Eric listened to this epic regimen with a mounting feeling of dread. How could teenagers do nothing—literally nothing—but study? Suddenly, he understood what he had seen in class that day. The kids had acted like they lived in the classroom because they essentially *did*. They spent more than twelve hours there every weekday—and they already went to school almost two months longer than kids back in Minnesota. His classmates slept in their classes for one primal reason: because they were exhausted.

Suddenly, Eric wanted very badly to leave early.

By quarter past two, he and the Canadian girl were walking across the dirt field, headed away from Namsan—*seven hours* before their classmates could leave. While the Korean kids worked, the exchange students went into a convenience store. Eric noticed an ice cream bar made with red-bean paste, molded into the shape of a fish. He bought it, hoping it wouldn't taste like fish. It didn't! It tasted like vanilla. Around two-thirty, he caught the bus back home. The Korean kids kept working.

Lying on his bed back at his host family's apartment, Eric thought more about what the boy had told him. Korean kids essentially went to school *twice*—every weekday. He had found one possible explanation for Korea's PISA scores, and it was depressing. Kids learned a lot, but they spent a ridiculous amount of time doing so. They had math classes at school—and math classes in hagwons. He was astounded by the inefficiency of it all. In Korea, *school never stopped*.

Staring out the window at the city, he recalibrated. Before he'd left the United States, he had thought that American schools did too much standardized testing and put too much pressure on kids and teachers. Everyone always seemed to be complaining about tests and over-programmed kids. Now, thinking back on the rhetoric about high-stakes testing and stressed-out kids, Eric almost laughed.

American tests were not high stakes for students. In fact, the stakes couldn't have been much lower, especially for standardized tests. The consequences, if there were any, extended mostly to the adults who worked at the school; their school might, for example, be labeled in need of improvement by the federal government and, in a few places, a small fraction of teachers with extremely low scores might eventually lose their jobs. But for most kids, standardized tests were frequent, unsophisticated, and utterly irrelevant to their lives.

Even regular classroom tests did not mean as much in the United States as they did in Korea. If kids did poorly in the United States, there was always a caveat: *The test was unfair.* Or, *That's okay! Not everyone can be good at math.* In Korea, the lesson was cleaner: *You didn't work hard enough, and you had to work harder next time.*

He started to realize that pressure was a relative term, and so was testing. From what Eric had seen so far, Namsan seemed designed to convey, through austere classrooms and brutal hierarchies, one message: that kids' futures depended not on their batting averages, their self-esteem, or their Facebook status, but on how hard they worked to master rigorous academic material.

Was this what it took, he wondered, to score at the top of the world on international tests? If so, Eric wasn't sure he'd want to be number one.

iron child competition

I met Korea's education minister, Lee Ju-Ho, at his office in Seoul. He had a boyish cowlick and a default expression of mild amusement, both of which artfully masked the ambition that had powered his career up to this point.

Lee was a product of the Korean pressure cooker. He had attended an elite high school and Seoul National University, one of the country's top three universities. Then he'd earned his PhD in economics at Cornell. He'd risen swiftly up the Korean hierarchy, becoming a professor, then a politician. But when he became the Minister of Education, he did so with the goal of dismantling the pressure cooker, piece by piece.

We drank tea around a large table with his entourage of advisers, none of whom spoke. When I asked if he agreed with President Obama's glowing rhetoric about the Korean education system, he smiled a tired smile. It's a question he got asked often, usually by Korean reporters who could not understand what the U.S. president—or anyone—would find to like about Korea's system.

"You Americans see a bright side of the Korean education system," he said. "But Koreans are not happy with it."

In some ways, Korea was an extreme manifestation of a very old Asian tradition. Chinese families had been hiring test-prep tutors since the seventh century. Civil-service exams dated back before the printing press. In tenth-century Korea, ambitious young men had to pass an exam to get a government job. The high-stakes test was, in practice, accessible only to the sons of the elite, who could afford the ancient version of test prep.

Despite the American stereotype that Asians excelled in math and science, regular Koreans were not historically so smart. Confucius may have instilled Koreans with an appreciation for the value of long, careful study, but the country had no history of excelling in math. In fact, the vast majority of its citizens were illiterate as recently as the 1950s. When the country began rebuilding its schools after the Korean War, the Korean language did not even have words for modern concepts in math and science. New words had to be coined before textbooks could be published. In 1960, Korea had a student-teacher ratio of fifty-nine to one. Only a third of Korean kids even went to middle school. Poverty predicted academic failure. If PISA had existed back then, the United States would have trounced Korea in every subject.

Over the next fifty years, Korea became what Lee called a "talent power." The country had no natural resources, so it cultivated its people instead, turning education into currency. This period of frenetic economic growth created a kind of lottery for Korean parents: If their children got into the best middle schools, which put them on track for the best high schools, which gave them a chance at getting into the top universities, then they would get prestigious, well-paying jobs, which would elevate the entire family.

This competition followed very explicit rules: Score above a certain number on the college exam, and you were automatically admitted to a top university. Forever after, you would be paid more than others, even for doing the same work. The system was as predictable as it was brutal. It sent a very clear message to children about what mattered: University admissions were based on students' skills as measured by the test. Full stop. Nobody got accepted because he was good at sports or because his parents had gone there. It was, in a way, more meritocratic than many U.S. colleges had ever been.

Without this education obsession, South Korea could not have become the economic powerhouse that it was in 2011. (Since 1962, the nation's GDP had risen about 40,000 percent, making it the world's thirteenth largest economy.) Education acted like an anti-poverty vaccine in Korea, rendering family background less and less relevant to kids' life chances over time.

But there weren't enough of those university slots or coveted jobs, so the lottery morphed into a kind of Iron Child competition that parents and kids resented, even as they perpetuated it. It was an extreme meritocracy for children that hardened into a caste system for adults. Even when more universities opened, the public continued to fixate on the top three. There was a warning for the rest of the world. Competition had become an end unto itself, not the learning it was supposed to motivate.

The country had created a monster, Lee told me. The system had become overly competitive, leading to an unhealthy preoccupation with test scores and a dependence on private tutoring academies. Even over summer break, libraries got so crowded that kids had to get tickets to get a space. Many paid $4 to rent a small air-conditioned carrel in the city's plentiful supply of for-profit self-study libraries.

Korea's sky-high PISA scores were mostly a function of students' tireless efforts, Lee believed, not the country's schools. Kids and their families drove the results. Motivation explained Korea's PISA scores more than curriculum, in other words.

Per student, Korean taxpayers spent half as much money as American taxpayers on schools, but Korean families made up much of the difference out of their own pockets. In addition to hagwon fees, they had to pay for public school, since the government subsidy didn't cover all the expenses. Eric's school was not the most elite public school in Busan, but it still cost about fifteen hundred dollars per year.

On paper, Eric's high schools in Minnesota and Korea had some things in common. Both Minnetonka and Namsan boasted dropout rates of less than 1 percent, and both schools paid their teachers similarly high salaries. However, while Minnetonka kids performed in musicals, Namsan kids studied and studied some more. The problem was not that Korean kids weren't learning enough or working hard enough; it was that they weren't working smart.

The Iron Child culture was contagious; it was hard for kids and parents to resist the pressure to study more and more. But all the while, they complained that the fixation on rankings and test scores was crushing their spirit, depriving them not just of sleep but of sanity.

collateral damage

One Sunday morning during that school year, a teenager named Ji stabbed his mother in the neck in their home in Seoul. He did it to stop her from going to a parent-teacher conference. He was terrified that she'd find out that he'd lied about his latest test scores.

Afterwards, Ji kept his secret for eight months. Each day, he came and went to school and back again as if nothing had changed. He told neighbors his mother had left town. To contain the odor of her decomposing body, he sealed the door to her room with glue and tape. He invited friends over for ramen. Finally, his estranged father discovered the corpse, and Ji was arrested for murder.

This ghastly story captivated the country, as might be expected, but for specific and revealing reasons. Ji's crime was not, in the minds of many Koreans, an isolated tragedy; it was a reflection of a study-crazed culture that was driving children mad.

According to his test scores, Ji ranked in the top 1 percent of all high school students in the country, but, in absolute terms, he still placed four thousandth nationwide. His mother had insisted he must be number one at all costs, Ji said. When his scores had disappointed her in the past, he said, she'd beaten him and withheld food.

In response to the story, many Koreans sympathized more with the living son than the dead mother. Commentators projected their own sour memories of high school onto Ji's crime. Some went so far as to accuse the mother of inviting her own murder. A *Korea Times* editorial described the victim as "one of the pushy 'tiger' mothers who are never satisfied with their children's school records no matter how high their scores."

As for Ji, he confessed to police immediately, weeping as he described how his mother had haunted his dreams after he'd killed her. At the trial, the prosecutor asked for a fifteen-year prison sentence. The judge, citing mitigating circumstances, sentenced the boy to three and a half years.

Meanwhile, Korean politicians vowed anew to treat the country's education fever, as it was called. Under Lee's tenure, the ministry had hired and trained 500 admissions officers to help the country's universities select applicants the way U.S. universities did, which is to say, based on something other than just test scores.

Almost overnight, however, new hagwons cropped up to help students navigate the new alternative admissions scheme. Hundreds of students were accused of lying about their hometowns to get preferential spots reserved for underprivileged rural families. One parent fabricated a divorce to take advantage of a preference for single-parent children. The fever raged on.

The country's leaders worried that unless the rigid hierarchy started to nurture more innovation, economic growth would stall and fertility rates would continue to decline as families felt the pressure of paying for all that tutoring.

To retroactively improve public schools, so that parents would feel less need for hagwons, Lee tried to improve teaching. Korea already had highly educated elementary school teachers, relative to the United States and most countries. Korean elementary teachers came from just a dozen universities that admitted the top 5 percent of applicants, and they were well trained. Middle school teachers-in-training in Korea performed at the top of the world on a mathematics test administered in six countries, trouncing future teachers in the United States.

Korea's high-school teachers were not as impressive, however. During a shortage of teachers decades earlier, the government had made a fateful mistake, allowing too many colleges to train secondary teachers. Those 350 colleges had lower standards than the elementary training programs. Like the more than 1,000 teacher-training colleges in the United States, the Korean programs churned out far more teachers-to-be than the country needed. Teacher preparation was a lucrative industry for colleges, but the lower standards made the profession less prestigious and less effective. Because, as one Korean policymaker famously said, "The quality of an education system cannot exceed the quality of its teachers."

To elevate the profession, Lee rolled out a new teacher evaluation scheme to give teachers useful feedback and hold them accountable for results. Under the new system, teachers were evaluated in part by their own students and their parents, who filled out online surveys, as well as other teachers, an approach meant to approximate the 360-degree review used in many businesses. (Unlike the model used by many U.S. districts, Korea's teacher evaluation scheme did not include student test-score growth; officials I talked to seemed to want to use this data, but they didn't know how to assign accountability, since so many students had multiple teachers, including outside tutors, instructing them in the same subjects.)

Under Korea's new rules, low-scoring teachers were supposed to be retrained. But, as in U.S. districts where reformers have tried imposing similar strategies, teachers and their unions fought back, calling the evaluations degrading and unfair. Pretty policies on paper turned toxic in practice. As a form of protest, some Korean teachers gave all their peers the highest possible reviews. In 2011, less than 1 percent of Korea's teachers were actually sent for retraining, and some simply refused to go.

After his first year in office, one of Lee's biggest accomplishments was that spending on hagwons had declined. The figures went down just 3.5 percent, but he considered it a major victory nonetheless.

Listening to Lee, I realized that the rest of the world could learn as much from what worked in Korea as from what didn't work. First, countries could change. That was hopeful. Korea had raised its expectations for what kids could do despite epidemic poverty and illiteracy. Korea did not wait to fix poverty before radically improving its education system, including its teacher colleges. This faith in education and people had catapulted Korea into the developed world.

Second, rigor mattered. Koreans understood that mastering difficult academic content was important. They didn't take shortcuts, especially in math. They assumed that performance was mostly a product of hard work—not God-given talent. This attitude meant that all kids tried harder, and it was more valuable to a country than gold or oil.

As Eric had noticed on his first day, Korean schools existed for one and only one purpose: so that children could master complex academic material. It was an obvious difference. U.S. schools, by contrast, were about many things, only one of which was learning. This lack of focus made it easy to lose sight of what mattered most.

For example, U.S. schools spend a relatively large sum of money on sports and technology, instead of, say, teachers' salaries. When I surveyed 202 exchange students from fifteen countries, they overwhelmingly agreed that they saw more technology in U.S. schools. Even students from high-performing countries said they saw more technology in their U.S. classrooms than back home. Seven out of ten American teenagers who had been abroad agreed. Americans had tricked-out classrooms with interactive white boards, high-tech projectors, and towers of iPads. However, there was little evidence that these purchases had paid off for anyone other than the technology vendors themselves.

Third, and this was Lee's most immediate problem: In places with extreme levels of student drive, winning the competition could become the goal in and of itself. Families and kids could lose sight of the purpose of learning and fixate obsessively on rankings and scores. In some high-income American neighborhoods, kids experienced a version of this compulsion, working day and night to get into an Ivy League college and prove themselves perfect on paper, perhaps only later wondering why. This obsession remained relatively mild in the United States, as shown by the persistently low math performance of even the wealthiest U.S. kids and the fact that only 15 percent of teenagers took afterschool lessons in the United States (a rate below average for the developed world). However, a small number of kids (many of them Asian-American) lived their own Westernized version of the Iron Child competition.

Finally, it was clear that the real innovation in Korea was not happening in the government or the public schools. It was happening in Korea's shadow education system—the multimillion-dollar afterschool tutoring complex that Lee was trying to undermine. I realized that, if I wanted to see what a truly free-market education system looked like, I would have to stay up late.

Personally, Lee thought Finland was a far better model than his own country. After all, Finland spent less per pupil on education, and just one in ten kids took afterschool lessons. In Korea, seven in ten took extracurricular lessons. Both countries scored at the top of the world on PISA, but, however you looked at it, Finnish children got a far better deal. There was more than one way to become a superpower, Lee warned; take care to choose the high road.

claustrophobic in korea

After visiting the minister in Seoul, I took a high-speed train to Busan, the booming beachfront city on the southern coast of Korea. Eric offered to give me a tour. He showed up at the lobby of my hotel in his white-rimmed sunglasses and a messenger bag, eager to please.

"Do you feel like Korean food or are you already sick of it? Have you had Korean pizza? It's crazy! Or we could do sushi."

Eric loved Korea. As we walked through the clamor of the shopping stalls, he pointed out socks with Barack Obama's face on them and made me try his favorite yogurt drink. We made a special stop at a gift store so he could show me the infamous napping pillows—demonstrating how they slipped over the wrist for effortless comfort.

"I adapt really well to places," he told me. He had diligently worked on his Korean and could now navigate gracefully through restaurants and casual conversations. He ordered sweet-potato pizza for both of us. By this time, he'd spent a night at a Buddhist temple high in the mountains; he'd learned Taekwondo; on one harrowing evening at a fish market, he'd even forced himself to eat a live baby octopus, wrapped around his chopstick.

Eric appreciated the weirdness of Korea and the warmth of Koreans. Really, the only problem was school. He had tried to keep his mind open, but he dreaded those days at Namsan, sitting for six hours with students too stressed—or exhausted—to talk for more than five minutes between classes, then taking the bus home alone.

It wasn't that Eric couldn't be alone. In fact, he had a lot of experience with isolation. He'd spent years as a closeted gay teenager in America. He knew about loneliness.

But he had discovered that the pressure to conform extended well beyond sexuality in Korea. Teenagers were in all kinds of closets, sometimes literally, locked into small, airless spaces, studying for the test. "The students I've talked to despise the system," he said, shaking his head. "They absolutely loathe it."

Eric admired one part of the Korean system—the high expectations that everyone had for what kids could do. He was curious about the hagwons, where his classmates said they learned so much. However, he was learning that the top of the world could be a lonely place, and the important question was not just which kids lived there, but what they had gone through to get there.

From Pennsylvania to Poland: Tom outside his high school in Wrocław.

chapter 4

a math problem

Five thousand miles away, Tom's teacher asked him a question.

It was his first day of school in Poland. He'd sat quietly in the back, trying to make himself small and unremarkable. But now she stared back at him, waiting. So he repeated the one sentence he knew by heart:

Nie mówię po polsku. I don't speak Polish.

Then he smiled, the clueless exchange student. This tactic had worked well for him so far.

Tom would turn eighteen in two weeks. He had a perpetual five o'clock shadow and dark eyes, the face of a young man hovering precariously atop a boy's body. When he smiled, flashing the dimples he'd inherited from his mother, he looked at least three years younger. American teachers had accepted Tom's excuses, generally speaking.

Yet this teacher spoke back to him, repeating the question in English.

"Could you please solve the problem?" She held out a piece of chalk and motioned for Tom to come to the front of the room. It was math class, and she'd written a polynomial problem on the board.

Tom got up, heart surging, and walked slowly to the board. The other twenty-two Polish students watched the American, wondering what would happen.

The story of Poland, a symphony of suffering and redemption, will come later in this book. But, for now, suffice to say that Tom found himself in a brooding country with a complicated past, which was precisely why he'd wanted to live there.

In America, Tom had lived in Gettysburg, Pennsylvania, the site of the bloodiest battle in the American Civil War. Some fifty-one thousand men were wounded or killed on the hills of Tom's home-town. Thousands of tourists stalked the empty, silent battlefields each year, looking for relics or ghosts or a lingering sensation of some kind.

However, since the 1800s, Gettysburg had become much less in-teresting, in Tom's opinion. It was a rural village two hours and a world away from Washington, D.C. As a little boy, Tom had no interest in Union or Confederate toy soldiers, the kind sold by the sackful in the town souvenir shops. He played with World War II soldiers instead.

As a teenager, Tom played the cello, listened to Sonic Youth, and watched Woody Allen movies. He occupied himself in the margins of the high school culture, which revolved around sports and the Fu-ture Farmers of America. In August, the Gettysburg Warriors foot-ball team held an all-you-can-eat pig roast to kick off the season. The local coffee house closed before the sun had set.

Early on, Tom had learned that the world outside of his home could be a complicated place. His father was a family law attorney, facilitating divorces and waging custody battles. His mother was the town's chief public defender. She worked out of a windowless base-ment office, representing Gettysburg's least popular residents, in-cluding a young man facing the death penalty for killing a wildlife conservation officer.

To escape the strain of their jobs, Tom's parents read. They read the way other families fished or watched television, together but apart. On Friday nights, they took Tom and his two brothers to Barnes & Noble, where they would wander off in their separate directions to choose their own adventures; on rainy Saturdays, they might all be found reading, sometimes in different rooms. The only noise was the sound of the rain.

Tom's two older brothers read leisurely, but Tom read hungrily, as if in search of a metaphor that he could never quite find. In the summer, his mom would see him in the backyard reading for hours on end. One winter, he read nothing but Anton Chekhov. He read *The Pianist*—twice.

For his senior year of high school, Tom had decided to exchange Gettysburg for one of his old-world novels. He'd wanted to go to Eastern Europe because he'd thought it would be romantic to live somewhere where people knew the names Dostoyevsky and Nabokov. He hadn't traveled much, but he believed in the promise of a faraway place, one that could sustain the kind of romance he'd read about and conjured in his head. He'd imagined himself learning to play Chopin in the homeland of Chopin.

And there he was, in Poland at last. Everything was more or less going according to his plan. The thing is: When Tom walked to the front of that classroom in Poland that day, he was carrying an American burden no one could see. Despite his Yo La Tengo T-shirt and his winter of Chekhov, Tom was in at least one way a prototypical American teenager.

Tom was not good at math.

He'd started to lose his way in middle school, as so many American kids did. It had happened gradually; first he hadn't understood one lesson, and then another and another. He was too embarrassed to ask for help. He hadn't wanted to admit that he wasn't as smart as other kids. Then he'd gotten a zero on a pre-algebra quiz in eighth grade. In other classes, a bad grade could be overcome. But, in math, each lesson built on what happened before. No matter how hard he tried, he couldn't seem to catch up. It felt like he was getting dumber, and it was humiliating. The next year, he got an F in math.

Math eluded American teenagers more than any other subject. When people talked about the United States' mediocre international scores, they were not really talking about reading. American teenagers scored twelfth in reading on PISA, which was a respectable performance, above average for the developed world. There was still far too big a gap between privileged kids and low-income kids, but the overall average was decent.

In math, the average score placed the United States twenty-sixth in the world, below Finland (third), Korea (second), and Poland (nineteenth). American teenagers did poorly in science, too, but their math results were, statistically speaking, the most ominous.

Math had a way of predicting kids' futures. Teenagers who mastered higher-level math classes were far more likely to graduate from college, even when putting aside other factors like race and income. They also earned more money after college.

Why did math matter so much? Some reasons were practical: More and more jobs required familiarity with probability, statistics, and geometry. The other reason was that math was not just math.

Math is a language of logic. It is a disciplined, organized way of thinking. There is a right answer; there are rules that must be followed. More than any other subject, math is rigor distilled. Mastering the language of logic helps to embed higher-order habits in kids' minds: the ability to reason, for example, to detect patterns and to make informed guesses. Those kinds of skills had rising value in a world in which information was cheap and messy.

America's math handicap afflicted even its most privileged kids, who were *more* privileged than the most advantaged kids in most other countries, including Poland. Our richest kids attended some of the most well-funded, high-tech schools in the world. Yet these kids, including the ones who went to private school, still ranked eighteenth in math compared to the richest kids in other countries. They scored lower than affluent kids in Slovenia and Hungary and tied with the most privileged kids in Portugal.

Our poorest kids did even worse, relatively speaking, coming in twenty-seventh compared to the poorest kids in other developed countries, far below the most disadvantaged kids in Estonia, Finland, Korea, Canada, and Poland, among many other nations.

Why weren't our kids learning this universal language of logic?

As I traveled around the world on this quest, I kept encountering this puzzle. Again and again, the data revealed a startling math deficiency in the United States. Like a lack of nutrition, it started when children were small and took a cumulative toll. Studies had shown that American third graders were being asked easier math questions that required simpler responses than children the same age in places like Hong Kong. By the time our kids graduated from high school, less than half were prepared for freshman-year college math. If our international performance was the mystery, then math held the most important clues.

That morning, in Wrocław, Poland, Tom picked up the chalk. All his old feelings of incompetence came swirling back. He started writing. He knew he could do this; the problem wasn't that hard, and he was older than most of the kids in the class.

Just then, the chalk snapped in half. He let the piece fall and continued writing. But something was wrong; he must have missed a step. Whatever he was doing, it wasn't working, and he knew it. He kept writing anyway. Behind him, one of the Polish students giggled. His hands felt damp with sweat. Finally, the teacher spoke.

"Does anyone else want to try?"

Tom shuffled back to his seat. She didn't call on him again.

As the semester went on, Tom noticed differences between his math class in Poland and his math class in Pennsylvania. Back in America, Tom and all his classmates had used calculators. In his Polish math class, calculators were not allowed. Tom could tell the kids were doing a lot of the math in their minds. They had learned tricks that had become automatic, so their brains were freed up to do the harder work. It was the difference between being fluent in a language and not.

After the first test, the teacher announced the scores in front of the class, so everyone could hear. As a new exchange student, Tom had been exempt from the test himself. But listening to the grade announcements, he felt intensely uncomfortable. Like Eric in Korea, he couldn't imagine such a public reckoning in his American classroom.

Nor could he imagine everyone doing so poorly: In Poland, the lowest grade was always one, and the highest was five. After each test, he waited to see if anyone would get a five; no one ever did. No one seemed surprised or shattered, either. They shouldered their book bags and moved on to the next class. He tried to imagine no one ever getting an A in Gettysburg. Would they give up, or would they try harder?

Kids in Poland were used to failing, it seemed. The logic made sense. If the work was hard, routine failure was the only way to learn. "Success," as Winston Churchill once said, "is going from failure to failure without losing your enthusiasm."

Tom had failed in math, too, back in eighth grade in Pennsylvania. But he hadn't experienced that failure as normal or acceptable. He'd experienced it as a private trauma. Failure in American schools was demoralizing and to be avoided at all costs. American kids could not handle routine failure, or so adults thought.

Like many young people, the lesson Tom had learned from his failure was that he wasn't good at math, and that he should stay away from it whenever possible. He didn't know, back in high school, how central math was to philosophy and music, two subjects he loved. He didn't know that math could be cosmically beautiful, and it was something he could master with hard work, time, and persistence, just the way he'd mastered Chekhov.

the country of minnesota

Of the three American students I followed, Eric was the only one who did not loathe math. Coincidence or not, Eric's home state of Minnesota was one of only two states that came close to achieving world-class math performance. Roughly speaking, Minnesota ranked below just a dozen other countries (including Canada, Korea, and Finland) in math proficiency; only Massachusetts did better in the United States.

When Eric arrived in Korea, he had a solid math background. There were lots of reasons for this: One might have been that his timing was good. Had he been born earlier, things might have turned out differently.

In 1995, Minnesota fourth graders placed below average for the United States on an international math test. Despite being a mostly white, mostly middle-class state, Minnesota was not doing well in math. When Eric started kindergarten two years later, however, the state had smarter and more focused math standards. When he was eleven, Minnesota updated those standards again, with an eye toward international benchmarks. By the time he went to high school, his peers were scoring well above average for the United States and much of the world. In 2007, Minnesota elementary students rocked a major international math test, performing at about the same level as kids in Japan.

What was Minnesota doing that other states were not? The answer was not mystical. Minnesota had started with a relatively strong education system. Then they'd made a few pragmatic changes, the kind of common sense repairs you would make if you believed math was really, truly important—*and* that all kids were capable of learning it.

First, Minnesota officials agreed on a single set of clear, targeted standards. That one change was radical. With that, the state overcame the most glaring problem with America's fragmented system. Until then, Minnesota teachers—like teachers nationwide—had been buffeted by clashing guidance about what to teach. Many American teachers had to contend with both state *and* local district standards, which frequently conflicted with one another. Then, each spring, teachers had to prepare kids for standardized tests, which often had no connection to the various standards or curriculum. Caught in a web of criss-crossing mandates, they had to choose which to ignore and obey.

The purpose of American education was muddled in all kinds of ways. The farther away I got, the more obvious that truth became. There was no better metaphor for this mission confusion than the American textbook.

American teachers taught with textbooks that were written to appease thousands of districts and many states all at once, as education researcher William Schmidt has documented in detail. That meant that American textbooks tended to be far too long—covering (and repeating) way too many topics in too little depth. Internationally, the average eighth grade math textbook was 225 pages long; in the United States, eighth grade math texts averaged 800 pages. That was about 300 pages longer than all thirteen volumes of Euclid's *Elements*.

America's tradition of local control was a nightmare for teachers. They were left to pick and choose between clashing standards as best they could, repeating subjects again and again under the direction of repetitive, sprawling textbooks. Some of the kids who came to them each fall had covered prime numbers; some had not. It was hard to predict.

The end result was that American students ended up learning about, say, fractions every single year, from first to eighth grade, while their peers in smarter countries covered fractions in grades three through six. In a majority of states, American kids learned decimals for six years, until they were nearly catatonic with boredom, while kids in the world's education superpowers covered decimals for three years and moved on. That meant that all the time American kids spent going over—and over—fractions and decimals could not be spent learning other things.

It also meant that different algebra classes within the same school or district covered wildly different material, depending on a given teacher's sampling of the textbook. Geometry textbooks were particularly arbitrary; two American geometry books typically had next to nothing in common with each other. This partly explained the roller coaster of data coming out of schools around the country, the big and unexplained differences in what kids knew.

In Minnesota, a coherent, clear set of standards, which focused on a few important topics each year, rather than dozens, had helped repair this damage. At the same time, elementary students across the state started spending sixty minutes per day on math, up from thirty minutes in 1995. Something else had happened, too. The new standards not only covered fewer topics in more depth; they featured more challenging material. Eric may have been bored at times, but he was nowhere near as bored as he would have been in most other places in the United States. His state had intentionally modeled its math education after the best practices used in the world's education superpowers, and succeeded.

The year that Eric was in Korea, the rest of the United States was considering doing what Minnesota had done. In defiance of a long history of incoherent standards and irrational localism, forty-five states agreed to adopt new, more rigorous standards as to what kids should know in math and reading. Known as the Common Core, they were modeled after standards in the education superpowers. Kids would no longer have to dabble in fractions for eight years; they would dispense with the subject in five years, starting a couple years later than before but going into more depth.

Even still, critics attacked the Common Core Standards as a violation of local authority; others pointed out that if teachers didn't have the math skills or training to bring the standards to life, they would just be words on a piece of paper. Union leaders complained that teachers would be held accountable for higher standards before they'd had enough time to adapt. Texas, Virginia, Alaska, and Nebraska declined to adopt the standards altogether. A handful of other states backed out of plans for new, smarter tests designed around the new goals. It remained to be seen if America would take this one obvious step toward world-class schools or reverse course yet again.

Interestingly, the only class that Eric actually enjoyed in Korea was math. He noticed it on his first day of school. Something was very different about how math was taught in Korea. Something that not even Minnesota had figured out.

The class was ostensibly a geometry class. Since he'd already taken geometry and graduated from high school, Eric understood most of it. He noticed, however, that the students were learning geometry in a totally different way from how he had learned it.

The teacher wove trigonometry and calculus into the lesson, following the thread of the lesson across disciplines, as though geometry were just one solar system in a larger universe of math. Together, the different disciplines could solve problems in the real world, where mathematics was not boxed into neat categories. Geometry was the study of shapes, after all, and calculus was the study of change. To figure out how shapes behaved when they changed—perhaps to design a video game—you needed both.

Eric felt himself waking up. He had not known geometry could be so interesting. Although he'd always done well in math in Minnesota, he had sometimes found it boring. In third grade, his teacher had told his mother he was having problems doing double-digit addition and had done terribly on a test. His mother was surprised; Eric had been doing double-digit addition at home for years. When she'd asked to see the test, she'd noticed that Eric had left many of the problems blank. Then she'd held the paper at arm's length, and she could see that the problems he had answered formed a shape. It was the letter E. Eric had been so bored in math that he'd started carving his initial into the test.

In Korea, math moved fluidly. When the teacher asked questions, the kids answered as if math were a language that they knew by heart. As in Tom's class in Poland, calculators weren't allowed, so kids had learned mental tricks to manipulate numbers quickly.

Eric was impressed to see the equivalent of sophomores understanding the references to calculus. These kids, who were not in any kind of advanced class, were doing math well above the level of the typical sophomore back home. If Minnesota had found kids could rise to high expectations in math, Korea had proven that the ceiling was higher still.

The rest of the country, for the most part, continued to underestimate what kids could do, and the kids themselves knew it. When Kim, Eric, and Tom were growing up, four out of every ten American fourth graders said their math work was too easy. By eighth grade, seven out of ten kids went to schools that did not even offer algebra courses with the kind of content that was standard in most other countries. It was only logical that American kids were behind their peers in the smart-kid countries; they were essentially taking remedial math, whether they needed it or not.

Compared to countries around the world, the typical eighth grade math class in the United States featured sixth or seventh grade content; by the same measuring stick, the highest-performing countries taught eighth graders ninth grade math.

Why were American kids consistently underestimated in math?

In middle school, Kim and Tom had both decided that math was something you were either good at, or you weren't, and they weren't. Interestingly, that was *not* the kind of thing that most Americans said about reading. If you weren't good at reading, you could, most people assumed, get better through hard work and good teaching. But in the United States, math was, for some reason, considered more of an innate ability, like being double-jointed.

The truth was that American adults didn't like math or think it was critical to kids' life chances. In 2009, most American parents surveyed said it was more important to finish high school with strong reading and writing skills than with strong math and science skills. It was almost as though math was optional, like drawing. Half of those parents said that the science and math their children were learning in school was just fine, and they were right, based on a standard from a different era.

But based on the standards of modernity, all decent jobs required some math and science fluency. Contractors needed to be able to factor inflation into cost estimates. X-ray technicians used geometry. In real life, math was not optional, and it hadn't been for some time.

It was widely accepted that young children could learn foreign languages with ease. At ages two and three, their brains absorb and integrate a second or third language at a pace that ten-year-olds could not begin to match. Why hadn't we realized that they could do the same thing with the language of math?

Early childhood programs in America pushed reading, arts and crafts, and behavior—important skills. Yet playing with numbers was still considered taboo, a subject best left to the later years, despite America's obvious and enduring math handicap.

For too long, what American kids learned had been a matter of chance. The problem with chance was that math was a hierarchy. If kids like Tom and Kim missed one rung on the scaffolding, they would strain and slip and probably never get a foothold on the next rung. A child's first algebra course had lasting impact, influencing whether the student would take calculus in high school or give up on math altogether.

part II

winter

From Oklahoma to Finland: Kim in Pietarsaari.

chapter 5

an american in utopia

By late November, Kim's commute to school had become a dark and frigid odyssey. On this particular morning, it was five degrees and windy. The sun would not rise until nine, well into Kim's first class. As she walked, her footsteps crackling in the icy silence, she wondered how Pietarsaari had ever become inhabited. Perched on the west coast of Finland, the town was three hundred miles from Helsinki. How could anyone have endured this winter and thought it was a good idea to stay for another? Pietarsaari had around twenty thousand residents by then, but aside from the occasional car, she saw no other humans for most of her journey.

Up ahead, she could make out the lights of the Pietarsaari *Lukio*, her high school. From the outside, it looked even more depressing than her school back home, a fact that still surprised her three months into her stay. Both schools were low-slung, brick structures, but this one was built out of off-white bricks that had turned gray and dreary with age. A large clock outside the school had stopped working some time ago. This was not the way Finnish schools had looked in her imagination.

She walked inside as groups of laughing boys and pretty girls passed by, ignoring her. The entryway of the school was small and institutional. There were trophies on display, like at Sallisaw High School, but they seemed like an afterthought, dusty and dull. The newest one was ten years old. Had no teams won a single trophy in a decade? She walked on, trying not to bump into anyone.

She sat down in her Finnish class, smiling shyly at the girls next to her. Kim's Finnish teacher seemed even more animated than usual, saying something in Finnish that Kim did not understand. Then the teacher began passing out copies of a heavy book to all the students. Kim recognized the cover. It was *Seven Brothers*, a Finnish classic published in 1870.

Even Kim knew about *Seven Brothers*. When it was written, the Finns were the underclass in their own country. They'd endured five centuries of Swedish, then Russian, domination. Then came *Seven Brothers*, the first major book written in Finnish. The tale of seven rowdy, uncouth, and often delinquent young men who eventually taught themselves to read became a metaphor for Finland, a country that did not even declare its independence until 1917.

Kim felt a knot in her stomach. She knew she could not read *Seven Brothers*. It was written in old Finnish, and she still couldn't understand new Finnish. What would she do? She inhaled and tried to rearrange her face to look mildly curious, like she'd been expecting this all along.

Then the teacher appeared at her side. Kim's teacher, Tiina Stara, was slim and attractive with layered brown hair and a quick smile. She leaned down toward Kim. In her hands, she had a different book. This book was much wider and thinner, with a glossy, shiny cover.

"This is for you," she said quietly in English.

Kim looked at the cover. Instead of seven brothers, it had a cartoon image of seven dogs, all dressed in old-fashioned costume, howling in unison. She translated the title in her head: *Seven Dog Brothers*. Kim laughed. It was a children's book.

"It's in Finnish, but simple Finnish," Stara explained. She looked nervous, as if afraid she might hurt Kim's feelings. "I hope you don't think this is childish. It's just that I would love for you to be able to experience this story, because it is very important for us in Finland. And the plot is the same, so you can follow along with our conversation."

Kim took the book, her eyes full of gratitude. "*Kiitos*," she said. Thank you.

During her three months in Finland, Kim had collected a small catalogue of differences between school here and in Oklahoma. The most obvious were the things that were missing. There were no high-tech, interactive white boards in her classroom. There was no police officer in the hallway. Over time, though, she had begun to notice more important distinctions—the kind that a visiting adult would not see.

Take the stoner kid, as Kim had nicknamed him in her head. He'd walked into class that day looking hung over, with glassy eyes, as usual. He had short blonde hair, icy blue eyes, and a nose that was always a shade redder than the rest of his skin. He didn't talk much in class, but when he was with his friends, smoking cigarettes outside, he was louder.

Kim had seen plenty of kids like him in Sallisaw. Somehow, she hadn't expected to see stoner kids in Finland. But there he was. Every country had its stoner kids, as it turned out. That was lesson one. There was only one major difference, as far as she could tell, and this was lesson two. The Finnish stoner kid was a model student. He showed up to class, and he was attentive. He took notes. When Stara assigned essays, which was often, he wrote them, just like everybody else.

In Oklahoma, the stoner kids didn't do much schoolwork, in Kim's experience. They didn't care. Here, all kids complained about school, too, and they had teachers they liked and disliked. Yet most of them seemed to have bought into the idea of education on some level.

Sometimes Kim found herself staring at this kid and his friends. They didn't fit into any of the boxes she had used to organize the world. It was hard to explain, but there just seemed to be something in the air here. Whatever it was, it made everyone more serious about learning, even the kids who had not bought into other adult dictates.

Kim noticed that some of the teachers seemed more bought-in to school, too. Stara, the Finnish teacher, realized it was probably ridiculous for Kim to even be in a Finnish class for Finnish high-school students, given Kim's primitive grasp of the language. And she had plenty of other students to worry about, students at a range of skill levels themselves. Still, she'd taken the time to come up with an alternative for Kim—a way to include her, despite everything. The children's book was a creative solution. Kim opened it up and began to read about the seven dog brothers.

a tale of two teachers

Like Kim's math teacher back in Oklahoma, Stara was a veteran teacher, approaching two decades in the profession. Both teachers had jobs that were protected by powerful unions, and neither could easily be dismissed. This pattern held true in most developed countries around the world: Teachers' unions held a lot of power, and teachers rarely got fired anywhere.

The similarities ended there. From the moment she had decided to study education in college, Stara had entered a profession completely different from that of Kim's Oklahoma teacher. To become a teacher in Finland, Stara had had to first get accepted into one of only eight prestigious teacher-training universities. She had high test scores and good grades, but she knew the odds were still against her.

She'd wanted to teach Finnish, so she'd applied to the Finnish department at the University of Jyväskylä. In addition to sending them her graduation-exam scores, she'd had to read four books selected by the university, then sit for a special Finnish literature exam. Then she'd waited: Only 20 percent of applicants were accepted.

At that time, all of Finland's teacher-training colleges had similarly high standards, making them about as selective as Georgetown or the University of California, Berkeley in the United States. Today, Finland's education programs are even more selective, on the order of MIT. It was hard to overstate the implications that cascaded from this one fact. Just one out of every twenty education schools was located at a highly selective institution in the United States. Far more than that had no admission standards at all. In other words, to educate our children, we invited anyone—no matter how poorly educated they were—to give it a try. The irony was revealing, a bit like recruiting flight instructors who had never successfully landed a plane, then wondering why so many planes were crashing.

After spending years racking up college loans, teachers-to-be in the United States generally had to pass standardized tests in order to get a teaching position. But the tests were not challenging or particularly relevant to effective teaching. By then, the damage was done: Everyone assumed that the education majors were not the smartest kids in college, generally speaking, and their profession got little respect as a result.

In Finland, *all* education schools were selective. Getting into a teacher-training program there was as prestigious as getting into medical school in the United States. The rigor started in the beginning, where it belonged, not years into a teacher's career with complex evaluation schemes designed to weed out the worst performers, and destined to demoralize everyone else.

A teacher union advertisement from the late 1980s began with this breathtaking boast: "A Finnish teacher has received the highest level of education in the world." Such a claim could never have been made in the United States, or in most countries in the world.

Norway, for example, shares a border with Finland and spends more on education. But Norway is not choosy about who gets to become a teacher, and the quality of preparation varies wildly, just as it does in the United States. Norwegians have fretted about the quality of their teacher-training colleges for decades, and the government routinely interferes in the training to try to make it better. As in many countries, teachers are made to attain ever more amounts of training and education, without much regard for quality. Partly as a result, Norwegian fifteen-year-olds perform at about the same middling levels as teenagers in the United States on PISA, and even the most privileged among them perform poorly in math, compared to advantaged teenagers worldwide.

Back in Finland, Stara still remembers the day she got the letter of acceptance—her mother's excitement, the rush of relief. She didn't celebrate; Finns were much too modest to brag about such things in those days. But she felt very, very lucky.

When she arrived at the University of Jyväskylä, Stara spent the first three years studying Finnish literature. She read intensely and wrote multiple twenty-page papers. She analyzed novels, poems, and short stories—something English trainee teachers do not generally do in the United States. At the same time, she took other required courses, including statistics. In her fourth year (out of six years of study), she began the teacher-training program. All Finnish teachers were required to get a master's degree, which meant something very different than it did in the United States.

For one full year of her master's program, Stara got to train in one of the best public schools in the country. She had three teacher mentors there, and she watched their classes closely. When she taught her own classes, her mentors and fellow student teachers took notes. Afterward, she got feedback, some of it harsh, in much the way medical residents are critiqued in teaching hospitals.

It was hard but exhilarating. She learned she needed to get better at motivating her students at the start of each lesson, before she did anything else. In time, she improved. When Stara wasn't teaching or observing other teachers, she collaborated with her fellow student teachers to design lessons that integrated material from all their subjects, including history and art. Then they practiced teaching those lessons, pretending they were students. Like all Finnish teachers, Stara also had to do original research to get her degree, so she wrote a two-hundred-page thesis on the ways that teenagers' spoken Finnish shaped their written Finnish.

Now, consider Kim's math teacher back home, Scott Bethel. He'd decided to become a teacher mostly so that he could become a football coach. In America, this made sense. As a student at Sallisaw High School, he was an all-state quarterback in 1989. "My dad taught at a school about ten miles from here," Bethel told me. "He was also a football coach, and I was always good at sports, and I thought, 'You know what, I'd like to become a coach.'"

Although Bethel hadn't taken calculus in high school, he'd always been pretty good at math. So, he figured the best way to become a coach was to become a math teacher. Bethel was one of several coaches that Kim had as teachers over the years, a hybrid job that would be considered bizarre in Finland and many countries, where sports lay beyond the central mission of schools.

In Oklahoma alone, Bethel could choose from nearly two dozen teacher-training programs—almost three times as many as in all of Finland, a much bigger place. Oklahoma, like most states, educated far more teachers than it needed. At most U.S. colleges, education was known as one of the easiest majors. Education departments usually welcomed almost anyone who claimed to like children. Once students got there, they were rewarded with high grades and relatively easy work. Instead of taking the more rigorous mathematics classes offered to other students, for example, education majors tended to take special math classes designed for students who did not like math.

Bethel did his training at Northeastern State University, like the Sallisaw superintendent and many Oklahoma teachers, including Kim's mom. The university prepares more teachers than any other institution in the state and has a good reputation. However, it also has a 75 percent acceptance rate, which means that it admits, on average, students with much weaker math, reading, and science skills than Finnish education schools. The university's typical ACT score is lower than the national average for ACT-takers—a pattern that holds true for many teacher-training programs all over America.

To teach in Oklahoma, Bethel did not need a master's degree. He could receive a raise if he got one, and many U.S. teachers did. But, since the typical education college had low standards and little rigor, an advanced degree did not mean much. In many states, teachers were not required to get degrees in their subject area, so they got a master's in teaching instead. A master's degree did not make American teachers better at their jobs, generally speaking, and some research suggested it made them worse.

Nationwide, the United States produced nearly two and a half times the numbers of teachers it needed each year. The surplus was particularly extreme for elementary school teachers. The United States was not exceptional in this regard. The combination of low standards and high supply plagued education systems around the world, dumbing down the entire teaching profession. Oklahomans praised their teachers for doing a hard job, and rightfully so, but they didn't brag about how well educated they were.

Interestingly, Finland's landscape used to be littered with small teaching colleges of varying quality, just like in the United States. That helped explain why the first phase of reforms in Finland were painful, top-down, accountability-based measures. Finland, it turns out, had its own No Child Left Behind moment, one that today will sound familiar to teachers in the United States and many other countries. In the 1970s, Finnish teachers had to keep diaries recording what they taught each hour. National school inspectors made regular visits to make sure teachers were following an exhaustive, seven-hundred-page centralized curriculum. Central authorities approved textbooks. Teachers could not be trusted to make their own decisions.

During the same time period, the Finnish government did something else, too—something that has never happened in the United States or most other countries. The Finns rebooted their teacher-training colleges, forcing them to become much more selective and rigorous. As part of a broader reform of higher education, the government shuttered the smaller schools and moved teacher preparation into the more respected universities. It was a bold reform, and not without controversy. Opponents argued that the new system was elitist and would, as one editorial warned, "block the road to our rural youth when their inner calling beckons them to a [teaching] career." Some university leaders objected, too, fearing that the inclusion of such preprofessional, practical training might dilute academic standards for the rest of the departments and lower their institutions' prestige. Interestingly, these same arguments were also made in the United States whenever anyone tried to make teacher training more selective.

Still, Finland was desperate to modernize, and the country's leaders agreed that education was the only thing that could save their country from being left behind. The more I read the history and talked to Finns who understood it, the more I admired the common sense running through the story. The Finns decided that the only way to get serious about education was to select highly educated teachers, the best and brightest of each generation, and train them rigorously. So, that's what they did. It was a radically obvious strategy that few countries have attempted.

Then, in the 1980s and 1990s, something magnificent happened. Finland evolved to an entirely new state, unrealized in almost any country in the world. It happened slowly, and partly by accident, but it explained more about Finland's success than almost anything else.

With the new, higher standards and more rigorous teacher training in place, Finland's top-down, No-Child-Left-Behind-style mandates became unnecessary. More than that, they were a burden, preventing teachers and schools from reaching a higher level of excellence. So Finland began dismantling its most oppressive regulations, piece by piece, as if removing the scaffolding from a fine sculpture.

The government abolished school inspections. It didn't need them anymore. Now that teachers had been carefully chosen and trained, they were trusted to help develop a national core curriculum, to run their own classrooms, and to choose their own textbooks. They were trained the way teachers should be trained and treated the way teachers should be treated.

In the early 1990s, an economic crisis accelerated this evolution, ironically enough. Because of a deep recession, Finland's local authorities needed to slash spending. Education budgets had to be cut 15 to 20 percent. The only way local officials would agree to deep cuts was if they got something in return. So, national leaders agreed to grant even more autonomy to the locals, more than most other countries had ever dared to do. This liberation worked only because of all the changes that had come before. By then, the Finns had engineered a robust system with highly educated, well-trained teachers and relatively coherent (and high) standards. Once that system was in place, the accountability checks and balances were superfluous. School leaders and teachers were free to write their own lesson plans, engineer experiments within their schools to find out what worked, and generally design a more creative system than any centralized authority ever could.

By the time Kim got to Finland, teachers, principals, union leaders, and politicians routinely worked together to continually improve the education system. They sometimes disagreed, but collaboration was normal, and trust was high. The government conducted standardized testing of targeted samples of students—to make sure schools were performing. But there was no need to test all students, year after year.

Why hadn't that evolution ever happened in the United States— or in most other countries? Had anyone even tried?

The examples were few but revealing. As the new education commissioner in Rhode Island, one of Deborah Gist's first acts was to raise the minimum test scores for teachers-to-be in 2009. At the time, Rhode Island allowed lower scores than almost any state in the nation. She had the power to change this unilaterally, and she did, taking one small step in the direction of Finland by requiring new teachers to score significantly higher on the SAT, ACT, and the Praxis, a teacher certification test.

Immediately, critics called her elitist, lobbing the same accusations critics had used against reformers in Finland in the 1970s. Some argued that a teacher who struggled in school was actually a better teacher, because that teacher could relate to students who were failing. It was a perverse logic. Would a doctor who had botched several surgeries be an ideal medical-school professor?

Others worried that higher standards would lead to a teacher shortage. Yet Rhode Island's teacher colleges already churned out 1,000 teachers a year, about 800 more than the school system needed to hire. Supply, particularly of elementary school teachers, was not a problem. Moreover, the laws of human nature applied: Once it became harder to be a teacher, it could also become more attractive. More people might want to do it, and fewer established teachers might leave the profession.

Because this was America, a diverse country with a long history of racism in colleges, public schools, and every other institution, Gist's efforts were also attacked as discriminatory. Higher education leaders warned that the new standards would prevent minority students, who tended to score lower on tests, from becoming teachers.

In reality, the Rhode Island teaching force was already far too white and far too female; to become more diverse and attract more men, in particular, it could be argued, the profession needed to be more prestigious, not less. More to the point, minority students needed highly educated *and* diverse teachers. It was interesting to note that higher standards were seen not as an investment in students; they were seen, first and foremost, as a threat to teachers.

Rhode Island's teacher-preparation programs produced *five times* more teachers than Rhode Island's public schools actually hired each year. The only institution benefiting from this system seemed to be the colleges themselves, but college leaders still complained that they would lose too many students if the standards were higher. They voiced this concern to newspaper reporters, and reporters quoted them without irony.

"It will disenfranchise too many students," Roger G. Eldridge Jr., interim dean of the School of Education at Rhode Island College told the *Providence Journal*. It was a revealing word choice: Disenfranchise usually means to deprive someone of a sacred legal right, such as the right to vote. And that is in fact how many people viewed the job; most Americans said teaching was a hard and important job, but many of them, including teachers and teaching professors, didn't seem to believe it required serious intellectual heft.

Under the new, higher standards, about 85 percent of Rhode Island College's education students would not make the cut, the dean threatened. Coming from the college that produced more Rhode Island teachers than any other, this was an astounding statistic, one that should have been a source of deep shame, but was not.

Gist did not back down, however. "I have the utmost confidence that Rhode Island's future teachers are capable of this kind of performance," she said. She did agree to phase in the higher cut score gradually over two years and to allow colleges to ask for waivers for highly promising candidates who did not make the cut score. Three years later, she had not received any waiver requests. At Rhode Island College, the percentage of minority students studying to be teachers went from 8.8 percent to 9.24 percent, remaining essentially unchanged despite all predictions to the contrary.

For some American teachers, the lack of serious training didn't matter; they made up for what they didn't know by learning on the job. Some got lucky and had a strong principal or mentor. For other teachers, though, this education gap did matter. As more of their students aspired to attend college, and the economy increasingly rewarded higher-level thinking, more teachers were being asked to teach material they'd never really learned themselves.

Beyond the practical effects, the lower standards sent a demoralizing message: In America and Norway and many other countries, we did not expect our teachers to be the best and brightest of their generation. We told them so in a thousand different ways, and the messaging started the day they went to college.

When Kim was starting kindergarten in 2000, ten out of ten new Finnish teachers had graduated in the top third of their high school classes; only two out of ten American teachers had done so. Incredibly, at some U.S. colleges, students had to meet higher academic standards to play football than to become teachers.

In Finland, the government paid tuition for Stara and all university students. In Oklahoma, Bethel's tuition was paid, too, but his free ride came from a carefully cobbled together safety net of Pell grants, a partial athletic scholarship, and Indian grants. Most students could not manage this feat.

During his sophomore year at Northeastern State University, Bethel had applied to the university's education college. Here was another chance for the university to select its best and brightest to become teachers. But to be admitted, Bethel had to have a grade-point average of just 2.5 or higher (out of 4). He would have needed a higher GPA to become an optometrist at the same university today. To be a teacher, he also had to have at least a C grade in freshman English and a C in speech or a class called the fundamentals of oral communication.

He also needed a score of 19 or higher on the ACT, a standardized test like the SAT. The national average for the ACT back then was 20.6. Let's consider what this meant: It was acceptable to perform *below average* for the country on a test of what you had learned throughout your educational career if you aspired to dedicate your career to education.

At the education college, Bethel discovered that he didn't have to major in math to become a high-school math teacher. So he didn't. Nationwide, less than half of American high-school math teachers majored in math. Almost a third did not even minor in math.

The problem was even worse among students training to teach younger children. "A large majority of elementary education majors are afraid of math," one Oklahoma math department chair said in response to a 2005 survey. "This fear will be passed on to their students." Another estimated that about a quarter of teachers graduating from his or her college actively hated math and showed no interest in improving.

Bethel liked math, but his primary goal was to become a coach, so he majored in physical education and minored in math. When he took the required test for high school math teachers in Oklahoma, he passed easily. Most of the material was at a tenth or eleventh grade level, and he didn't find it difficult. However, if he had, he would have been allowed to retake the test until he passed.

Nationwide, people studying to become math teachers in the United States did not have to actually know that much math compared to teachers in the education superpowers. The deficit was particularly alarming among middle-school math teachers. When researchers tested thousands of aspiring teachers in sixteen countries, they found that future middle-school math teachers in the United States knew about as much math as their peers in Thailand and Oman. They had nowhere near the math competence of teachers-in-training in Taiwan, Singapore, or Poland. So it was not surprising that those same teachers' students would perform just as unimpressively later on. You could not teach what you didn't know.

Still, the most valuable part of any teacher preparation program may be the hands-on practice that student teachers get in a real-life classroom. There is no better way to prepare for teaching than to actually teach—and get meaningful feedback on how to improve.

In Oklahoma, Bethel's student teaching experience helped him learn to plan lessons and manage a classroom. But it lasted just twelve weeks, compared to the year-long residency typical in Finland. Nationwide, U.S. teacher-training colleges only require an average of twelve to fifteen weeks of student teaching, and the quality varies wildly depending on the place.

When Bethel got his first teaching job, he quickly realized that it would have been helpful to major in math. But what was done was done. By the time he taught Kim, he was earning about $49,000 per year, which was more than the typical salary in Sallisaw but still not a lot. Across the Atlantic Ocean, Stara was earning about $67,000. The cost of living was higher in Finland, but Stara's salary was still higher. And her salary was closer to what other college graduates earned in Finland than Bethel's salary was in the United States.

Interestingly, large salaries did not necessarily coincide with greatness worldwide. The world's highest paid teachers lived in Spain, where teenagers performed worse in math, reading, and science than students in the United States. But in higher-functioning education systems, larger salaries could help schools attract better-educated teachers and retain them over time, establishing a baseline of professionalism and prestige. In all the education superpowers, teachers' incomes were closer to the salaries of other college-educated professionals than they were in the United States. In most cases, classes were also larger than they were in the United States, making the cost of the salaries more manageable.

As I listened to teachers like Stara and Bethel, I started to suspect that all these differences interacted, in chronological order. Because teacher colleges selected only the top applicants in Finland and other education superpowers, those schools could spend less time doing catch-up instruction and more time on rigorous, hands-on training; because teachers entered the classroom with rigorous training and a solid education, they were less likely than American teachers to quit in frustration. This model of preparation and stability made it possible to give teachers larger class sizes and pay them decently, since the turnover costs were much lower than in other countries. And, since they had all this training and support, they had the tools to help kids learn, year after year, and to finally pass a truly demanding graduation test at the end of high school.

The subconscious effects were just as powerful. As one U.S. exchange student to Finland explained in the survey conducted for this book:

> "My Finnish school fostered a great deal of respect for the institution and faculty in the students. This can be partly explained by the academic rigors that teachers had to endure in their journeys to becoming educators. The students were well aware of how accomplished their teachers were."

One thing led to another. Otherwise, one thing led to much less. If the rigor didn't start at the beginning, then the most challenging high-school graduation test in the world would not succeed. Federal mandates could only go so far. Without highly educated and well-trained teachers and principals, kids could make only limited progress each year. Realizing that they could never pass the graduation test, many would tune out and give up.

The more time I spent in Finland, the more I started to worry that the reforms sweeping across the United States had the equation backwards. We were trying to reverse engineer a high-performance teaching culture through dazzlingly complex performance evaluations and value-added data analysis. It made sense to reward, train, and dismiss more teachers based on their performance, but that approach assumed that the worst teachers would be replaced with much better ones, and that the mediocre teachers would improve enough to give students the kind of education they deserved. However, there was not much evidence that either scenario was happening in reality.

What if the main problem was not motivation? Was it possible to hammer 3.6 million American teachers into becoming master educators if their SAT scores were below average?

The lesson from Finland had a linear elegance: If we wanted to get serious about education, at long last, we needed to start at the beginning. Following Finland's example, education colleges should only be allowed to admit students with SAT scores in the top third of the national distribution or lose government funding and accreditation. Since 1.6 million U.S. teachers were due to retire between 2011 and 2021, a revolution in recruitment and training could change the entire profession in a short period of time.

Why hadn't this been done in any state in America? Given that colleges already prepared far more teachers than schools needed, this change would not necessarily have led to a teacher shortage. Over time, it might have actually increased the popularity of the profession by making it more prestigious.

It was a bizarre oversight. For all the time and energy that American educators had spent praising Finland, it was remarkable that they did not insist upon this most obvious first step. It was almost as if we wanted the prestige of Finland's teachers—but didn't really believe that our teachers needed to be highly educated and unusually accomplished in order to merit that prestige. But why, then, did Finland?

"why do you guys care so much?"

After class, Kim had a free period—a full seventy minutes with nothing scheduled. This was the other big difference she'd noticed about Finland: the inexplicable stretches of luxurious freedom. She kept finding herself released into the ether, trusted to find her way through long stretches of time. She could even walk out of the school in the middle of the day and go to a coffee shop in the village until her next class began. It was hard to get used to.

Even outside school she felt this freedom. She had learned her way to the Halpa-Halli supermarket by bike and, although it took her an embarrassingly long time to find the simplest ingredients, her host mother didn't seem to worry if she wasn't home on time.

Parents in general seemed to trust their kids more. Kim routinely saw eight-year-olds walking to school alone, wearing reflective vests to keep them visible in the dark. At the high school, she rarely saw parents for any reason. Teenagers were treated more like adults. There were no regularly scheduled parent-teacher conferences. None. If teachers had a problem with the student, they usually just met with the student.

Kim wandered into the central lobby of the school and sat on one of the gray couches. Back home, she'd had five minutes free between classes, and anyone caught hanging out was in trouble. Part of her was still in Oklahoma, waiting for someone to come bust her.

Two girls from her class sat down next to her. They said hello to Kim and started talking about how hard they'd studied for midterm exams last year, lamenting all the work they had ahead of them.

Most of the time, the Finnish students were just as aloof as her guide books had told her they would be. But Kim was still new enough that she could ask them about Finland to make conversation. So, she collected her courage and blurted out the question that had been on her mind.

"Why do you guys care so much?"

The girls looked at her, confused. Kim felt her cheeks flush, but she barreled ahead.

"I mean, what makes you work hard in school?"

It was a hard question to answer, she realized, but she had to ask. These girls went to parties; they texted in class and doodled in their notebooks. They were normal, in other words. Yet they seemed to respect the basic premise of school, and Kim wanted to know why.

Now, both girls looked baffled, as if Kim had just asked them why they insisted on breathing so much.

"It's school," one of them said finally. "How else will I graduate and go to university and get a good job?"

Kim nodded. It was a fair question. Maybe the real mystery was not why Finnish kids cared so much, but why so many of her Oklahoma classmates did not. After all, for them, too, getting a good education was the only way to go to college and get a good job. Somewhere along the way, however, many of them had stopped believing in this equation. They didn't take education very seriously. Maybe because they were lazy, spoiled, or dysfunctional in some other way, or maybe because, in their experience, education wasn't all that serious.

"how is it possible you don't know this?"

Listening to Kim's impressions of Finland, I wondered if she were unique. Kim came from a relatively low-performing state, and no one would say she had an overly generous attitude toward her hometown. Would other exchange students notice the same differences? What about a teenager traveling in the opposite direction? Would a Finnish girl who'd chosen to come to the United States see a mirror image of what Kim had noticed in Finland?

Every year, about four hundred Finnish kids travel to the United States to live and study. Most of them ended up in the Midwest in public high schools. To find out what they thought of their borrowed land, I started tracking them down. It didn't take long to notice a pattern.

Elina came to America from Helsinki when she was sixteen, the same age as Kim. She came because she'd spent much of her life dreaming about the American high schools she saw on television and in movies: the prom, the pep rallies, and all the twinkling rituals of the American teenager.

In America, Elina lived with a host family in Colon, Michigan, a small town named after the punctuation mark, just outside Kalamazoo. At first, Elina's new world looked a lot like home. Colon was surrounded by lakes and trees. The population was 95 percent white and native born. On weekends, men zipped themselves into down jackets and played ice hockey on frozen lakes. The winter lasted most of the year, just like back home.

Early on, however, Elina discovered one important difference about America. Back home, she'd been a good student. In Colon, she was exceptional. She took Algebra II, the most advanced math class offered at Colon High. On her first test, she got 105 percent. Until then, Elina had thought it was mathematically impossible to get 105 percent on anything.

She thought she might have more trouble in U.S. history class, since she was not, after all, American. Luckily, her teacher gave the class a study guide that contained all the questions—and answers—to the exam. On test day, Elina coasted through the questions because, well, she'd seen them in advance.

When the teacher handed the tests back, Elina was unsurprised to see she'd gotten an A. She was amazed, however, to see that some of the other students had gotten Cs. One of them looked at her and laughed at the absurdity.

"How is it possible you know this stuff?"

"How is it possible you *don't* know this stuff?" Elina answered.

I talked to Elina after she had left the United States and gone to college in Finland. She was planning to work in foreign affairs one day. Now that some time had gone by, I wondered if she had a theory about what she'd seen in her American school. Were the students too coddled? Or the opposite—too troubled? Too diverse? Maybe they were demoralized by all the standardized testing?

Elina didn't think so. In her experience, American kids didn't study much because, well, they didn't have to. "Not much is demanded of U.S. students," she said. In Finland, her exams were usually essay tests, requiring her to write three or four pages in response. "You really have to study. You have to prove that you know it," Elina told me about Finnish high school. In the United States, her tests were typically multiple choice.

"It was like elementary school in Finland," she said. In that history class, she remembers, the class spent an inordinate amount of time making posters. "We did so many posters. I remember telling my friends, 'Are you kidding me? Another poster?'" It was like arts and crafts, only more boring. The teacher gave all the students the information for the poster, and the kids just had to cut and glue their way to a finished product. Everybody's poster featured the same subject.

The expectations were lower in America, Elina concluded, and the consequences were, too. She took a journalism class in Colon that was taught by an outstanding teacher. Everyone loved this teacher, including Elina. More important, perhaps, they respected her, and knew they were learning in her class. However, when the teacher told everyone they had to write ten articles by the end of the semester, only Elina actually did all ten stories. The teacher was irritated, but the other students still passed the class.

Elina and Kim's observations were anecdotal to the extreme. How much could we make of a few kids' memories? But it was remarkable how many kids from all different lands agreed on this point. In a large, national survey, over half of American high schoolers echoed Elina's impression, reporting that their history work was often or always too easy. Less than half said they felt like they were always or almost always learning in math class.

In my own survey of 202 foreign-exchange students, an overwhelming majority said their U.S. classes were easier than their classes abroad. (Of the international students who came to America, nine out of ten said classes were easier in the United States; of the American teenagers who went abroad, seven out of ten agreed.) School in America was many things, but it was not, generally speaking, hard.

During her year in America, Elina saw a Broadway show and visited the Washington Monument. She ran track and worked on the yearbook. She was surprised by how involved parents were in the school, much more so than parents back home. However, in the classrooms at Colon High—a school *not* overwhelmed by poverty, immigration, gangs, or any of the blights so often blamed for our educational mediocrity—she did not learn much in the traditional sense.

life after school

When Kim's school day in Finland ended at three forty-five, it was already dark. Her classmates all headed off in different directions. A few boys in a garage band went off to practice; some of the girls went shopping. No one Kim knew went to afterschool tutoring academies. Finnish kids had more free time than American kids, and not just because they did less homework. They were also less likely to play sports or hold down jobs.

As Kim walked through town on the way to the library, she felt hopeful. She spent a lot of time alone with her thoughts. But, she had discovered, to her relief, that life in Finland was different. The distinctions were subtle: the freedom, the freshly cooked food in the cafeteria, the civility. It was hard to describe the cumulative effect of these differences, but it felt, on days like today, as if she'd been paroled for good behavior.

The town felt cleaner and nicer than Sallisaw, like it was built for people instead of cars. As she walked along the brick pedestrian way, she passed boys with Justin Bieber hair, girls with tattoos, and billboards covered with H&M bikini ads. People dressed slightly better than they did back home, but not radically different. There were not nearly as many tall, blonde women as she had expected.

The neighborhood surrounding her school was filled with eighteenth and nineteenth century wooden houses, built after Russians sacked the village and drove out most of the townspeople in the 1700s. Kim had been keeping a mental list of the ordeals Pietarsaari had endured, from famine to communism; it had been fired on by the British Navy and bombed by the allies during World War II. The mystical land of smart children and Nokia, the one she had read about in America, was a relatively recent development.

After the library, she walked to Café Nemo, one of her favorite coffee shops. She'd come so often that the British owner had nicknamed her *Oklahoma*. She ordered in Finnish, proud to have built up a tolerance to the strong Finnish coffee.

Finally, it was time to go back to the apartment. She was out of excuses. Although she adored Susanne, her vivacious host mother, going home was one of the more stressful parts of Kim's day. Despite her best efforts, her five-year-old host sisters had not warmed to her. They resented the attention their busy single mother gave to this strange intruder. It made no sense to them (and indeed sometimes to Kim) that their mom had taken in yet another daughter.

When Susanne was not in the room, the girls called Kim *tyhmä* and laughed. Kim looked it up; it meant "stupid." When she tried to study, they came in and banged on her laptop keyboard. The number four had recently stopped working. Yet her bedroom doubled as their playroom, so Kim didn't feel she had the right to make them leave.

The girls were testing her, as small children will. Kim had never had a younger sibling, and she had no idea how—or whether—to discipline the twins. They were not her children, and she was not really their sister. She blamed herself. Each day, she vowed anew that she would find a way to make them like her.

In many ways, Finland had been the adventure she'd hoped it would be. She'd jumped into a hole in the ice in a frozen lake, an insane tradition in line with the Finns' proud history of endurance. She'd grown to look forward to the warmth of the host family's tiny home sauna after the cold walk home. She'd even made a couple of friends, and not all of them were exchange students.

Her biggest problem was that she herself had not changed very much—not yet, anyway. Most of the time, she felt unsure of herself. At school, she rarely spoke. At home, eager to please her host family, she stifled her frustration. Then she went quiet and sullen when the frustration built up inside her. Kim told herself it was the language barrier; it was hard to find her voice when she literally did not know the words. But this sensation felt unpleasantly familiar, like a bad habit she'd brought with her across the ocean. In her darkest hours, lying awake in her bunk bed in Pietarsaari, she wondered if the feeling would shadow her everywhere.

Accidental Tourist: Jenny at school in Busan, Korea.

chapter 6

drive

Eric got on the crowded No. 80 bus, headed home after Saturday classes. The girls had stopped screaming; Eric's celebrity status had faded. He spent a lot of his time reading *Ulysses* by himself.

"Hi. How's it going?"

Eric looked up. A Korean girl with shoulder-length black hair pushed back behind a headband was talking to him with a pitch-perfect American accent. He'd seen her around Namsan, and he knew she lived in the same apartment complex, but he hadn't heard such a familiar inflection in anyone's voice since he'd left Minnesota.

"My name is Jenny." She had a low voice and a stoic expression. But then she smiled, and her whole face lit up. Eric smiled, too.

"Why is your English perfect?"

Jenny laughed. She explained that although she was born in Korea, she'd lived in Lincoln, Nebraska, and Pittsburgh, Pennsylvania, when she was little. She'd spent much of her childhood in the American heartland, which explained her accent. But then, when she was in middle school, her family had moved back to Korea. Coming back to Korean school had been a traumatic experience, and she knew exactly how Eric was feeling.

"I couldn't believe it when I saw all the kids sleeping in class," she said. "But soon I was one of them."

In the United States, Jenny had taken swimming lessons and played the cello. She'd gone to sleep by ten most nights. Then, in Korea, she'd started attending hagwons like all the other kids she knew. She almost always studied past midnight. Jenny was living proof of something researchers call the peer effect: She behaved differently depending on the kids sitting next to her.

"I just felt the need to study here because all my friends were doing the same thing."

Eric talked with Jenny all the way back to the apartment building. He felt relieved to have a real Korean validate his impressions. He wasn't just a white boy who didn't get it; in fact, Korean high school was objectively terrible. They agreed.

"Kids are the same in both countries," Jenny said. "They're kids! The difference is the way they've been raised. They have this thing, Korean kids; this thing that drives them."

And now Jenny had it, too. She ranked twenty-seventh in her sophomore class at Namsan, out of about four hundred students. She had different standards for herself than she'd had in the States. "I need to do better. I regret not working harder this year," she told Eric, shaking her head. She looked genuinely distressed, despite how well she had done. Eric was perplexed. It was like listening to an Olympic swimmer complain about being out of shape. Jenny was in the top 10 percent of her class, but it wasn't enough. He started to realize that there was a masochism around studying that united Korean students. They berated themselves to keep themselves going.

Like most Koreans he had met, Jenny had high expectations for herself and a low opinion of her performance. He wondered if she would have judged herself differently if she'd stayed in the United

States. Would her standards have slipped down to earth, just the way they'd rocketed to the stars in Korea? Was drive entirely relative?

Jenny was about to find out. Next year, she told Eric, she had to go back to the United States, this time to New Jersey. Her family was moving yet again.

"I don't want to leave my friends," Jenny said, her face darkening. "But they keep telling me how jealous they are—that I'm escaping."

the geography of parenting

Back at the apartment, Eric took out the Nintendo DS he'd brought from home. His younger host brother recognized it like an old friend, and started asking Eric all about the games he played.

"Do you want to play?" Eric offered.

"No, no, I can't," he said, shaking his head.

A while back, his mother had caught his older brother playing his Nintendo DS before he'd finished his homework, so she'd confiscated his game console. That wasn't all; to make her disapproval widely known, she had also taken away the younger brother's Nintendo DS. He was entirely innocent, but months later, he still had not gotten the game console back. He didn't know if he would ever get it back.

When it came to education, Eric's host mother did not send mixed messages. She cooked dinner for her kids every night and worked hard to make every opportunity available to them; but on the subject of studying, she did not negotiate. They had to work hard—especially in English—and school took priority over everything else.

She did not hold the American to the same standards, for which Eric was very grateful. She treated him with patience and kindness, as if he were an adorable grandson. Yet she dealt with her own kids the way a coach might treat his star players. Her job was to train those kids, to push them, and even bench them to prove a point. Her job was not to protect them from strain.

From what Eric had seen, his host mom was not unusual. Most

Korean parents saw themselves as coaches, while American parents tended to act more like cheerleaders. He could tell that Korean kids encountered high expectations very early in their lives, and not just in school.

Parenting, like drive and diligence, was often ignored in international studies of education. The evidence that did exist tended to focus on one country only, and it generally showed what you'd expect: More involved families had children with higher grades, better test scores, improved behavior, and better attendance records. That dynamic held true across all ages, races, and income levels in the United States. But what kinds of parental involvement mattered most? And did parents do different things in different countries?

Andreas Schleicher, the PISA scientist, noticed after the first PISA test in 2000 that a student's home environment dramatically affected scores. He wanted to know more about how families shaped education, so he tried to get all the participating countries to agree to survey parents. Most countries' officials were more interested in the traditional levers of education policy, however: the in-school factors like spending and class size that they felt they could control, which was a pity, since parents could control a lot, too, if they knew what mattered.

By 2009, Schleicher and his colleagues had managed to convince thirteen countries and regions to include parents in the PISA. Five thousand of the students who took the PISA test brought home a special survey for their parents. The survey asked how they had raised their children and participated in their education, starting from when they were very young.

Strange patterns emerged. For example, parents who volunteered in their kids' extracurricular activities had children who performed *worse* in reading, on average, than parents who did not volunteer, even after controlling for other factors like socioeconomic background. Out of thirteen very different places, there were only two (Denmark and New Zealand) in which parental volunteering had any positive impact on scores at all, and it was small.

How could this be? Weren't the parents who volunteered in the school community showing their children how much they valued education? Weren't the mothers who chaperoned field trips and fathers who brought orange slices to soccer games the ones with the most time and energy to devote to their children? The data was baffling. Yet other research within the United States revealed the same mysterious dynamic: volunteering in children's schools and attending school events seemed to have little effect on how much kids learned.

One possible explanation might be that the parents who were volunteering were more active precisely *because* their children were struggling at school. And it is possible that their children would have performed even worse if the parents had *not* gotten involved. Then again, maybe the volunteering parents were spending their limited time coaching basketball and running school auctions, leaving less energy for the kinds of actions that *did* help their kids learn.

By contrast, other parental efforts yielded big returns, the survey suggested. When children were young, parents who read to them every day or almost every day had kids who performed much better in reading, all around the world, by the time they were fifteen. It sounded like a public-service cliché: Read to your kids. Could it be that simple?

Yes, it could, which was not to say that it was uninteresting. After all, what did reading to your kids mean? Done well, it meant teaching them about the world—sharing stories about faraway places, about smoking volcanoes and little boys who were sent to bed without dinner. It meant asking them questions about the book, questions that encouraged them to think for themselves. It meant sending a signal to kids about the importance of not just reading but of learning about all kinds of new things.

As kids got older, the parental involvement that seemed to matter most was different but related. All over the world, parents who discussed movies, books, and current affairs with their kids had teenagers who performed better in reading. Here again, parents who engaged their kids in conversation about things larger than themselves were essentially teaching their kids to become thinking adults. Unlike volunteering in schools, those kinds of parental efforts delivered clear and convincing results, even across different countries and different income levels.

In fact, fifteen-year-olds whose parents talked about complicated social issues with them not only scored better on PISA but reported enjoying reading more overall. In New Zealand and Germany, students whose parents had read to them regularly in their early elementary years performed almost a year and a half ahead of students whose parents had not.

Research from within the United States echoed these findings. What parents did with children at home seemed to matter more than what parents did to help out at school. And yet this finding ran counter to the ideals of modern American parenting.

Stereotypically speaking, American parenting in the early twenty-first century might have been called Parent Teacher Association parenting. PTA parents cared deeply about their children and went out of their way to participate in school functions. They knew education was important, and in fact, American parents tended to be more highly educated than parents in most developed countries.

At the same time, many American parents worried about robbing their children of the joys of childhood through structured learning. They suspected that children learned best through undirected free play—and that a child's psyche was sensitive and fragile. During the 1980s and 1990s, American parents and teachers had been bombarded by claims that children's self-esteem needed to be protected from competition (and reality) in order for them to succeed. Despite a lack of evidence, the self-esteem movement took hold in the United States in a way that it did not in most of the world. So, it was understandable that PTA parents focused their energies on the nonacademic side of their children's school. They dutifully sold cupcakes at the bake sales and helped coach the soccer teams. They doled out praise and trophies at a rate unmatched in other countries. They were their kids' boosters, their number-one fans.

These were the parents that Kim's principal in Oklahoma praised as highly involved. And PTA parents certainly contributed to the school's culture, budget, and sense of community. However, there was not much evidence that PTA parents helped their children become critical thinkers. In most of the countries where parents took the PISA survey, parents who participated in a PTA had teenagers who performed worse in reading.

Korean parenting, by contrast, were coaches. Coach parents cared deeply about their children, too. Yet they spent less time attending school events and more time training their children at home: reading to them, quizzing them on their multiplication tables while they were cooking dinner, and pushing them to try harder. They saw education as one of their jobs.

This kind of parenting was typical in much of Asia—and among Asian immigrant parents living in the United States. Contrary to the stereotype, it did not necessarily make children miserable. In fact, children raised in this way in the United States tended not only to do better in school but to actually enjoy reading and school more than their Caucasian peers enrolled in the *same* schools.

While American parents gave their kids placemats with numbers on them and called it a day, Asian parents taught their children to add before they could read. They did it systematically and directly, say, from six-thirty to seven each night, with a workbook—not organically, the way many American parents preferred their children to learn math.

The coach parent did not necessarily have to earn a lot of money or be highly educated. Nor did a coach parent have to be Asian, needless to say. The research showed that European-American parents who acted more like coaches tended to raise smarter kids, too.

Parents who read to their children weekly or daily when they were young raised children who scored twenty-five points higher on PISA by the time they were fifteen years old. That was almost a full year of learning. More affluent parents were more likely to read to their children almost everywhere, but even among families within the same socioeconomic group, parents who read to their children tended to raise kids who scored fourteen points higher on PISA. By contrast, parents who regularly played with alphabet toys with their young children saw no such benefit.

And at least one high-impact form of parental involvement did not actually involve kids or schools at all: If parents simply read for pleasure at home on their own, their children were more likely to enjoy reading, too. That pattern held fast across very different countries and different levels of family income. Kids could see what parents valued, and it mattered more than what parents said.

Only four in ten parents in the PISA survey regularly read at home for enjoyment. What if they knew that this one change—which they might even vaguely enjoy—would help their children become better readers themselves? What if schools, instead of pleading with parents to donate time, muffins, or money, loaned books and magazines to parents and urged them to read on their own and talk about what they'd read in order to help their kids? The evidence suggested that every parent could do things that helped create strong readers and thinkers, once they knew what those things were.

Parents could go too far with the drills and practice in academics, just as they could in sports, and many, many Korean parents did go too far. The opposite was also true. A coddled, moon bounce of a childhood could lead to young adults who had never experienced failure or developed self-control or endurance—experiences that mattered as much or more than academic skills.

The evidence suggested that many American parents treated their children as if they were delicate flowers. In one Columbia University study, 85 percent of American parents surveyed said that they thought they needed to praise their children's intelligence in order to assure them they were smart. However, the actual research on praise suggested the opposite was true. Praise that was vague, insincere, or excessive tended to discourage kids from working hard and trying new things. It had a toxic effect, the opposite of what parents intended.

To work, praise had to be specific, authentic, and rare. Yet the same culture of self-esteem boosting extended to many U.S. classrooms. In the survey of exchange students conducted for this book, about half of U.S. and international students said that American math teachers were more likely to praise their work than math teachers abroad. (Fewer than 10 percent said that their international teachers were more likely to praise.) That finding was particularly ironic, given that American students scored below average for the developed world in math. It also suggested that whatever the intent of American teachers, their praise was probably not always specific, authentic, and rare.

Adults didn't have to be stern or aloof to help kids learn. In fact, just asking children about their school days and showing genuine interest in what they were learning could have the same effect on PISA scores as hours of private tutoring. Asking serious questions about a child's book had more value than congratulating the child for finishing it, in other words.

Around the world, people who studied parenting usually divided the various styles into four basic categories: Authoritarian parents were strict disciplinarians, the "because I said so" parents. Permissive parents tended to be indulgent and averse to conflict. They acted more like friends than parents. In some studies, permissive parents tended to be wealthier and more educated than other parents. Neglectful parents were just how they sounded: emotionally distant and often absent. They were also more likely to live in poverty.

Then there was the fourth option: *Authoritative*. The word was like a mash up of authoritarian and permissive. These parents inhabited the sweet spot between the two: they were warm, responsive, and close to their kids, but, as their children got older, they gave them freedom to explore and to fail and to make their own choices. Throughout their kids' upbringing, authoritative parents also had clear, bright limits, rules they did not negotiate.

"We're socialized to believe that warmth and strictness are opposites," Doug Lemov writes in his book *Teach Like a Champion*. "The fact is, the degree to which you are warm has no bearing on the degree to which you are strict, and vice versa." Parents and teachers who manage to be both warm *and* strict seem to strike a resonance with children, gaining their trust along with their respect.

When researcher Jelani Mandara at Northwestern University studied 4,754 U.S. teenagers and their parents, he found that kids with authoritative parents had higher academic achievement levels, fewer symptoms of depression, and fewer problems with aggression, disobedience, and other antisocial behaviors. Other studies have found similar benefits. Authoritative parents trained their kids to be resilient, and it seemed to work.

It is perilous to make sweeping generalizations about people based on their ethnic heritage, but the research does suggest patterns. In the United States, European-American parents are more likely to exhibit authoritative styles than Hispanic or African-American parents, who trend toward authoritarian styles of parenting. (Although all ethnicities include all four kinds of parents.) However, the Asian-American parenting style may be the most consistently authoritative.

For example, studies have shown that Chinese-American parents are more hands-on with their children when they are young, training them in the ways of reading, writing, and math, but then they give their kids significantly more autonomy as they get older (a model that sounds eerily similar to the stereotype of the Finnish parent). "In high school, Asian immigrant parents really have a more hands-off approach," says Ruth Chao, who has studied parenting styles for over two decades. "They're not doing direct instruction. They're not managing the child's schoolwork anymore. They feel that if they are still having to do that, then there's really a problem."

After studying the data, Schleicher took his own advice. At his home in Paris, he and his wife were raising three children. They attended public school in a country that, like the United States, did not have strong PISA scores. Before he saw the research, he had always assumed that the ideal parent would spend several hours helping his children do their homework or complete other school projects. But there was a problem: He frequently didn't have several hours free to look over their shoulders. As a result, he did very little.

The data showed that he had more choices than he thought. From then on, even on his most hectic days, Schleicher at least asked his kids how school had gone, what they had learned, and what they had liked most. He talked to them about news and social issues of the day. He still didn't manage to read to his youngest daughter more often, but he at least knew what to feel guilty about—and what not to. Like every parent, he wanted his children to grow up to be thoughtful, curious, and smart. It was a relief to have strategies to influence their learning—regardless of what became of the French school system.

the anxiety olympics

On the eve of the big test, Eric's classmates performed elaborate rituals. The younger students cleaned the classrooms for the seniors. They purged the walls of posters and even covered the flag so that test takers would be able to focus on the college entrance exam without any distractions.

At the supermarket, Eric saw special displays of fancy good-luck candies for parents to buy their test-taking children, amulets to protect them through this ordeal. On the street, parents filed into temples and churches to offer one last prayer.

The whole country obsessed over the test. Korea Electric Power Corp. sent out crew members to check the power lines serving each of the one thousand test locations. The morning of the test, the stock market opened an hour late to keep the roads free for the more than six hundred thousand students headed to the test. Taxis gave students free rides.

That day, Eric took the bus to school as he normally did. But nothing was normal. As he got closer, he heard cheering. Some of his classmates had lined up outside the entrance to hand out tea to the test-takers and wave signs reading, "Hit the Jackpot!" The seniors trudged past them, heads down, like boxers entering a ring for a fight that would last nine hours. Police officers patrolled the school perimeter to discourage cars from honking their horns and distracting the students. Eric ran into a boy he knew, who explained that there was no school for younger students that day. Then he and Eric left to go play video games.

Later that morning, Eric went to Busan's Shinsegae Centum City, the largest department store in the world, to do some shopping. During the English language listening portion of the test, when airplanes were grounded to reduce unnecessary noise, Eric was in a movie theater.

By then, Eric had made a decision. He was going to drop out of Korean high school. He couldn't wait out the rest of the year this way. It felt like he spent every day in a huge cage, watching other kids run on a hamster wheel. The wheel never stopped; it thrummed day and night. And he was tired of sitting quietly in the wheel's shadow, waiting for his life in Korea to begin.

He needed to talk to kids if he was going to learn Korean and stay sane. He knew it was the right thing to do, but he was unsure how to do it. He hoped that leaving high school didn't mean he would have to leave Korea.

That evening, as Eric meandered through the city on his way back to the apartment, trucks delivered late-edition newspapers with the exam questions and answers for families to pore over at dinner. The entire spectacle felt melodramatic to Eric, like some kind of *Hunger Games* of the mind. Why did the whole country have to take the test on the same day? Kids in Minnesota took the SAT multiple times a year without any disruption to normal life.

Still, a child growing up in Korea could not help but get the message: Education was a national treasure. Getting a good one mattered more than stock-market trades or airplane departures. And everyone, from parents to teachers to police officers, had a role to play.

the mystery equation

Listening to the stories of Kim and Eric, I started to notice one fundamental theme. In Korea and Finland, despite all their differences, everyone—kids, parents, and teachers—saw getting an education as a serious quest, more important than sports or self-esteem. This consensus about the importance of a rigorous education led to all kinds of natural consequences: not just a more sophisticated and focused curriculum but more serious teacher-training colleges, more challenging tests, even more rigorous conversations at home around the dining room table. Everything was more demanding, through and through.

In these countries, people thought learning was so important that only the most educated, high-achieving citizens could be allowed to do the teaching. These governments spent tax money training and retaining teacher talent, rather than buying iPads for first graders or mandating small class sizes. It wasn't that public respect for teachers led to learning, as some American educators claimed after visiting Finland; it was that public respect for learning led to great teaching. Of course people respected teachers; their jobs were complex and demanding, and they had to work hard to get there.

One thing led to another. Highly educated teachers also chose material that was more rigorous, and they had the fluency to teach it. Because they were serious people doing hard jobs and everyone knew it, they got a lot of autonomy to do their work. That autonomy was another symptom of rigor. Teachers and principals had enough leeway to do their jobs like true professionals. They were accountable for results, but autonomous in their methods.

Kids had more freedom, too. This freedom was important, and it wasn't a gift. By definition, rigorous work required failure; you simply could not do it without failing. That meant that teenagers had the freedom to fail when they were still young enough to learn how to recover. When they didn't work hard, they got worse grades. The consequences were clear and reliable. They didn't take a lot of standardized tests, but they had to take a very serious one at the end of high school, which had real implications for their futures.

As Kim had noticed, teenagers were expected to manage their own time, and they usually did. Interestingly, this was another difference that exchange students noticed. Six out of ten of those surveyed said that U.S. parents gave children less freedom than parents abroad. (Only one in ten said that U.S. parents allowed more freedom.) One Finnish student who had spent a year in the United States explained this difference this way:

> "In the U.S., everything was very controlled and supervised. You couldn't even go to the bathroom without a pass. You had to turn all your homework in, but yet you didn't really have to think with your own brain or make any decisions of your own."

I'd been looking around the world for clues as to what other countries were doing right, but the important distinctions were not about spending or local control or curriculum; none of that mattered very much. Policies mostly worked in the margins. The fundamental difference was a psychological one.

The education superpowers believed in rigor. People in these countries agreed on the purpose of school: School existed to help students master complex academic material. Other things mattered, too, but nothing mattered as much.

That clarity of purpose meant everyone took school more seriously, especially kids. The most important difference I'd seen so far was the drive of students and their families. It was viral, and it mattered more than I'd expected. Eric and his friend Jenny had reminded me what I'd forgotten in adulthood: Kids feed off each other. This feedback loop started in kindergarten and just grew more powerful each year, for better and for worse. Schools and parents could amp up student drive through smarter, more meaningful testing that came with real consequences for teenagers' lives; through generous grants of autonomy, the kind that involved some risk and some reward; and through higher quality, more challenging work, directed by the best educated teachers in the world. But those policies were born out of a pervasive belief in rigor. Without it, those things just didn't happen.

The question then was not *what* other countries were doing, but *why*. Why did these countries have this consensus around rigor? In the education superpowers, every child knew the importance of an education. These countries had experienced national failure in recent memory; they knew what an existential crisis felt like. In many U.S. schools, however, the priorities were muddled beyond recognition.

Sports were central to American students' lives and school cultures in a way in which they were not in most education superpowers. Exchange students agreed almost universally on this point. Nine out of ten international students I surveyed said that U.S. kids placed a higher priority on sports, and six out of ten American exchange students agreed with them. Even in middle school, other researchers had found, American students spent double the amount of time playing sports as Koreans.

Without a doubt, sports brought many benefits, including lessons in leadership and persistence, not to mention exercise. In most U.S. high schools, however, only a minority of students actually played sports. So they weren't getting the exercise, and the U.S. obesity rates reflected as much. And those valuable life lessons, the ones about leadership and persistence, could be taught through rigorous academic work, too, in ways that were more applicable to the real world. In many U.S. schools, sports instilled leadership and persistence in one group of kids, while draining focus and resources from academics for everyone.

The lesson wasn't that sports couldn't coexist with education; it was that sports had nothing to do with education. In countries like Finland, sports teams existed, of course. They were run by parents or outside clubs. As teenagers got older, most of them shifted their focus from playing sports to academics or vocational skills—the opposite of the typical U.S. pattern. About 10 percent of Kim's classmates played sports in Finland, and they did so in community centers separate from school. Many of them quit senior year so that they would have time to study for their graduation exam. When I asked Kim's Finnish teacher if she knew any teachers who also worked as coaches, she could only think of one. "Teachers do a lot of work at school," she said, "and that's enough I guess."

Wealth had made rigor unnecessary in the United States, historically speaking. Kids didn't need to master complex material to succeed in life—not until recently, anyway. Other things crowded in, including sports, which embedded themselves in education systems, requiring principals to hire teachers who could also coach (or vice versa). The unholy alliance between school and sports pushed student athletes to spend extreme amounts of energy and time in training before and after school.

In isolation, there was nothing wrong with sports, of course. But they didn't operate in isolation. Combined with less rigorous material, higher rates of child poverty and lower levels of teacher selectivity and training, the glorification of sports chipped away at the academic drive among U.S. kids. The primacy of sports sent a message that what mattered—what really led to greatness—had little to do with what happened in the classroom. That lack of drive made teachers' jobs harder, undercutting the entire equation.

I found myself wishing I could travel back in time. Now that I knew what these nations had become, I wanted to see how they had gotten there. *How* did they arrive at a consensus about rigor? How had Finland and Korea done what Oklahoma could not?

In the twenty-first century, Finland was the obvious inspiration, a model for someday. It had achieved a balance and humanity that had eluded Korea. But for most of the world, including the United States, the question was what needed to happen first to make someday possible.

mapping willpower

In the mid-1970s, a small number of economists and sociologists started noticing that academic skills were not all important. It sounded obvious, but in the rush to count and compare IQ and reading scores, this simple truth was easily forgotten. Over the next three decades, more and more studies showed that when it came to predicting which kids grew up to be thriving adults—who succeeded in life and in their jobs—cognitive abilities only went so far.

Something else mattered just as much, and sometimes more, to kids' life chances. This other dark matter had more to do with attitude than the ability to solve a calculus problem. In one study of U.S. eighth graders, for example, the best predictor of academic performance was not the children's IQ scores—but their self-discipline.

Mastery of math never made anyone get to work on time, finish a thesis, or use a condom. No, those skill sets had more to do with motivation, empathy, self-control, and persistence. These were core habits, workhorse traits sometimes summed up by the old-fashioned word *character*.

The problem with the word character was that it sounded like something you couldn't change. But these same researchers discovered something wonderful: Character was malleable, more malleable in fact than IQ. Character could change dramatically and relatively quickly—for better and for worse—from place to place and time to time.

So it was fair to assume that different communities and cultures did more—or less—to promote these traits in their children. In Finland, Kim identified a difference that she thought mattered a lot: a difference, as she put it, in how much kids and teacher cared about school. Eric witnessed this drive, too, albeit the extreme and sometimes dysfunctional Korean version of the trait.

Caring about school was not the most important trait in a human being, to state the obvious. But, around the globe, this particular form of drive had begun to matter more than ever before, at least economically speaking. The research was still a long way off from identifying all the traits that mattered in young people's lives, but could drive be measured between countries? Was there any way to quantify what Kim and Eric had noticed? And could drive be cultivated in places that needed more of it?

Few people had tried to find out. Surveys tended to ask kids to describe their own motivation and attitude, which made it impossible to separate their answers from their own cultural biases. A student in Korea who said he didn't work hard had a very different understanding of *hard* than a typical student in the United Kingdom or Italy.

In 2002, researchers at the University of Pennsylvania had an idea. They thought they might be able to measure students' persistence and motivation by looking not at their answers to international tests, but at how thoroughly students answered the surveys included with those tests.

After the test portion of PISA and other international exams, students typically filled out surveys about their families and other life circumstances. There were no right answers for the questions on the surveys. In fact, the professors, Erling Boe, Robert Boruch, and a young graduate student, Henry May, weren't even interested in the answers. They wanted to track students' diligence in filling out the forms. So, they studied the survey attached to a 1995 test taken by kids of different ages in more than forty countries (called the "Trends in International Mathematics and Science Study").

The researchers encountered several surprises very quickly. First, students around the world were surprisingly compliant. The vast majority dutifully filled out most answers, even though the survey had no impact on their lives. The lowest response rate for any country was 90 percent. There was some variation from within a given country, but the variation didn't seem to reveal much about the students.

Between countries, though, the differences in diligence mattered—a lot. In fact, this difference turned out to be the single best predictor of how countries performed on the actual substantive portion of the test.

This simple measure—the thoroughness with which students answered the survey—was more predictive of countries' scores than socioeconomic status or class size or any other factor that had been studied.

How could this be? When May repeated the analysis with the 2009 PISA data, he found the same dynamic: Half the variation between countries' scores on the PISA math test could be explained by how much of the personal questionnaire students filled out on average in a given country.

In the United States, participants answered 96 percent of the survey questions on average, which seemed very respectable. Yet the U.S. still ranked thirty-third in conscientiousness. Korea ranked fourth. Finland ranked sixth. Kids there answered 98 percent of the questions. Seems virtually the same, right? But small differences in average response rates predicted large differences in academic performance on the same test.

Kids in Finland and Korea answered more of the demographic survey than those in the United States, France, Denmark, or Brazil. The causes of this pattern remain a mystery. May wondered if PISA and other international exams were measuring not skills but *compliance*; some countries had cultures in which kids just took all tests, and authority figures, more seriously. It wasn't a stretch to imagine that those countries included Japan, Korea, and other top PISA scorers. Perhaps that's why those kids answered the survey more thoroughly and did better on the academic questions, too. Those kids were just rule-abiding conformists. Other countries, meanwhile, valued individualism more than compliance. Perhaps those kids simply did not feel compelled to take the survey seriously. "In some nations," May said, "there are a lot of kids who seem like they just couldn't care less. They drag the mean down."

Then why did U.S. students do much better on the reading portion of the test, and so poorly on the math portion? If American kids just didn't care about tests or authority figures, generally speaking, then they would presumably do equally poorly on *all* tests. Likewise, we probably wouldn't see countries like Poland rocket up through the rankings in very short periods of time. It was hard to imagine that Poland had cultivated a culture of conformism in the course of three to nine years.

No one knows the answer for sure, but it's possible that the diligence kids showed in answering the survey reflected their diligence in general. In other words, maybe some kids had learned to finish what they started in school: to persist even when something held no particular gratification. The opposite was also true. Some kids had not learned to persist, and persistence was not valued as much in their school or in their societies at large.

Conscientiousness on a survey seemed like a trifling matter. In life, it was a big deal. Conscientiousness—a tendency to be responsible, hardworking, and organized—mattered at every point in the human life cycle. It even predicted how long people lived—with more accuracy than intelligence or background.

What would a map of conscientiousness look like? Maybe it was less important to find the smart kids, and more important to find the ones who got the job done, whatever the job was. Were there certain cultures that cultivated conscientiousness the way that other cultures cultivated gymnasts or soccer players?

The survey results provided some clues, not all of them obvious. The countries with kids who took the survey most seriously were not necessarily places with the richest kids; affluence does not necessarily lead to persistence, as we all know. In fact, the country with the highest response rate on the survey had nearly the same level of child poverty as that of the United States.

That country was Poland.

The Neighborhood: A child playing in Wrocław, Poland, in 2006, not far from Tom's high school.

chapter 7

the metamorphosis

The children of Breslau, dragging suitcases behind their mothers, watched the slips of paper float toward earth. They squinted up into the bright sky, where they could just make out the silhouette of a Soviet warplane. All around them, the leaflets landed softly on the ground, like snow: "Germans! Surrender! Nothing will happen to you!"

On January 22, 1945, Breslau was an important industrial center in what was then eastern Germany. The city had been largely spared by World War II. The city's eight hundred thousand people, along with its medieval square and its weapons factories, lay just out of reach of allied bombers. For most of Breslau's citizens, it had been possible to believe that life might one day return to normal.

Now, though, the Red Army was pushing west along the Oder River, closing in on the city. Intelligence reports estimated that the approaching Soviet soldiers outnumbered the German soldiers by five to one.

By the time Nazi officials finally allowed Breslau's women and children to leave, it was too late. Families rushed to the train stations and borders, clogging streets already filled with refugees from other German cities. Women pushed strollers full of pots and pans as men, ordered to fight to the death, climbed into church steeples with machine guns. It was three degrees, and many of the fleeing children froze to death before they made it to the next town. Nature finished what man started. Before a single bomb fell, some ninety thousand evacuees died trying to escape Breslau.

On the night of February 13, Soviet tanks encircled the city, churning slowly through the suburbs. The distant artillery fire grew louder each day until it exploded into a street fight in the heart of the city. The Soviets blasted their way through Breslau's historic row houses, wall by wall, occupying the city as they destroyed it.

Retreating Germans threw grenades through windows and set fire to entire neighborhoods as they left, determined to slow the Soviet advance by leveling their own city. The aerial bombardment reached its crescendo just after Easter. By April 30, even Hitler had given up, killing himself in his bunker in Berlin. But, in Breslau, the siege continued, grinding on, defying logic.

Finally, on May 6, Breslau capitulated. Three quarters of the city had been razed in two-and-a-half months. A mere three days later, Europe's long, wicked war came to an end. What was left of Breslau was plundered or burned by Soviet soldiers.

Within months, the allies redrew the map of Europe. Joseph Stalin, Winston Churchill, and Franklin Roosevelt plucked up Breslau like a chess piece. They flicked it over to Poland's side, under the new name Wrocław (pronounced VROTZ-waf). Most of the remaining Germans were run out of town, and hundreds of thousands of traumatized Polish refugees flooded in to take their places—literally—moving into the formerly German houses, sometimes before they'd been abandoned by their owners.

This was the city in which Tom lived. To understand it was to understand this dislocated history, warped by blank spots and confused identities. Over the centuries, the city had been called by more than fifty different names. People that lived there, as in much of Poland, never resided entirely in the present. The place had too many ghosts, too many parallel histories.

The "pioneer" Poles, as they were called, gamely tried to reinvent their adopted city. They renamed Adolf Hitler Street after a Polish poet named Adam Mickiewicz; Herman Göring Stadium became Olympic Stadium. But they were living in a haunted place. Everywhere, in the vandalized statues and the faded outlines left by stripped-away swastikas, they saw reminders of their Nazi persecutors.

The newcomers had precious little time to reflect on those ironies. Soon after the end of World War II, Poland fell under communist rule for forty years. Tens of thousands of Poles, including hundreds of priests and political activists, were imprisoned. Secret police infiltrated every neighborhood. In Wrocław, street names changed once again. One brand of oppression replaced another.

the polish miracle

The defenders of America's mediocre education system, the ones who blamed poverty and dysfunction for our problems, talked as if America had a monopoly on trouble. Perhaps they had never been to Poland.

It is difficult to summarize the tumult that occurred in Poland in the space of a half century. After the fall of communism in 1989, hyperinflation took hold; grocery store shelves were empty, and mothers could not find milk for their children. The country seemed on the verge of chaos, if not civil war. Yet Poland tumbled through yet another transformation, throwing open its institutions to emerge as a free-market democracy. The citizens of Wrocław renamed their streets for a third time. A small Jewish community even returned to the city.

By 2010, when Tom arrived from Gettysburg, Pennsylvania, Poland had joined the European Union. The country still struggled with deprivation, crime, and pathology of all kinds, however. While Tom was there, the local soccer teams started playing in empty stadiums, silent but for the sounds of their feet kicking the ball. There'd been so much violence among the fans that they'd been banned from their own teams' games.

Nearly one in six Polish children lived in poverty, a rate approaching that of the United States, where one in five kids are poor. It is hard to compare relative levels of sadness, but the data suggested that poor children in Poland led jagged lives. In a United Nations comparison of children's material well-being, Poland ranked dead last in the developed world.

Like the United States, Poland was a big country where people distrusted the centralized government. Yet something remarkable had happened in Poland. It had managed to do what other countries could not. From 2000 to 2006, the average reading score of Polish fifteen-year-olds shot up twenty-nine points on the PISA exam. It was as if Polish kids had somehow packed almost three-quarters of a school year of extra learning into their brains. In less than a decade, they had gone from below average for the developed world to *above*. Over the same period, U.S. scores had remained flat.

Tom was living in the transition that Finland and Korea had finished decades earlier. To see this change up close was the next best thing to time travel. Unlike the United States, Poland had dramatically improved its results in just a few years—despite crime, poverty, and a thousand good reasons for why it should fail. It was an unfinished narrative, but one that had turned, quite unexpectedly, in the direction of hope.

from pennsylvania to poland

I met Tom in the center of Wrocław at a grand old hotel where Adolf Hitler, Pablo Picasso, and Marlene Dietrich had all stayed. He wore jeans and a rumpled, button-down shirt, untucked, with the sleeves pushed up above his elbows. He was eighteen, a senior in high school.

Since he'd arrived from Gettysburg, his Polish host mothers had been trying, without success, to fatten his skinny frame.

We walked through the old city, and it looked exactly the way Tom had described it to me months before: an eclectic collage of baroque cathedrals, cobblestone streets, and large, brutalist Soviet-style apartments. In the medieval square, known as the Rynek, tourists drank Piast beer at outdoor cafés underneath a sixteenth century clock that tracked the phases of the moon. *Babcias*, Polish grandmothers, shuffled by, scarves tied under their chins, packages tucked under their arms. The Rynek had been rebuilt and restored many times. This version was slightly too resplendent, the paint a shade more vibrant than it should have been, but still magnificent in its scale and sweep.

We stopped for coffee at Literatka, which represented, as much as anything, the reason Tom had left Pennsylvania. It was a small, cloistered café with smoke purling through the air. A few people sat alone, hunched over books or laptops. No one looked up when we entered.

Tom guided me through the café with the pride other teenagers reserve for showing off their new car. The walls were lined with bookshelves, stacked up to the ceiling. Small volumes about chemistry leaned up against faded tomes about philosophy. When Tom had imagined Eastern Europe back in the States, this was the scene he had pictured. Exactly.

It had been six months since his Polish math teacher had called him up to the chalkboard to solve a problem—and he'd failed. Since that day, his math teacher had not called on him again. He had, however, managed to learn Chopin ("Prelude in E Minor") on the piano, just as he'd imagined he would. His Polish had gotten quite good, too. And even though he didn't hear many references to Nabokov, he'd once overheard two old men arguing about philosophy at one of Literatka's small, marble-topped tables. Tom had stared at them from behind his MacBook, delighted. *"Nie rozumiesz filozofii!"* (You don't understand philosophy!) one man had yelled as he rose to leave. It was perfect.

the bermuda triangle kids

We left Literatka and walked toward Tom's school, LO XIII, known as number thirteen. The ambiance changed abruptly as we walked. The high school was located beside a dodgy neighborhood known as *Trójkąt Bermudzki,* or the Bermuda Triangle. It had earned the nickname years ago, when outsiders who'd wandered into the neighborhood seemed to vanish, never to be heard from again. The crime rate had come down since then, but it remained a complicated place. Just a few weeks before, a friend of Tom's had been mugged at knifepoint there, in broad daylight, as he'd walked home from the school.

The streets in the Triangle were lined with tall, ornate row houses that had survived World War II but were now dilapidated tenements. Blackened statues stared down from the battered facades. The entryways stank of urine, and graffiti was scrawled across the pink, faded frescoes on the walls. Finland felt very far away.

As we walked, a child ran past us, on his way to a small playground tucked behind a stretch of row houses. Until 2007, the spot had been a dirt field, and the children of the Triangle had played there then, too, lacking other options. When an excavator had arrived one day to turn the field into a parking lot, the children had protested, refusing to surrender their square patch of dirt. They'd made signs out of wooden planks: "We demand a playground!" "Excavator Go Away!" The leader among them, a sixteen-year-old named Krystek who would likely go far in life, had called the newspapers. The developers had backed down, agreeing to build a few parking spaces and a modest playground.

The Triangle kids did not have easy lives. Some had fathers in prison; others had mothers who drank too much vodka. On some days, kids came to school tired and hungry. To an outsider, it didn't look all that different from an American ghetto.

Yet something had changed for the Triangle kids rather dramatically in the past decade, something that was hard to see on the street.

These kids spent their days in an education system that had reimagined what was possible. The changes had not been in the margins, where most reforms happened everywhere else on the planet; they had broken through to the core, fundamentally altering the structure and substance of an education in Poland, giving these kids better odds than they would have encountered in many school districts within the United States, a much richer country. These kids still lived in the Triangle, but they were less likely, statistically speaking, to be lost forever.

the alchemist

In 1997, when Mirosław Handke became Poland's minister of education, he was an outsider. A chemist with a white mustache and dramatic, black-slash eyebrows, he looked like an Eastern Bloc version of Sean Connery. Handke was accomplished in his own world at AGH University of Science and Technology in Kraków. He'd published more than eighty papers on the obscure properties of minerals and become the head of the university, one of Poland's best. However, he knew next to nothing about education policy or politics. His cluelessness would serve him well, at least for a little while.

By then, Poland's thirty-eight million citizens had undergone years of economic shock therapy, designed to catapult the country into the West after the fall of communism. So far, deregulation and privatization had worked, making Poland one of the fastest growing economies in the world; unemployment had been steadily falling, along with inflation.

Now the country was on the precipice yet again; without urgent social reforms, the health care, pension, and education systems could suck the life out of the Polish economy, sending inflation soaring again and jeopardizing Poland's trajectory from a Communist backwater to a European power.

Most damning of all, Polish adults did not have the skills to compete in the modern world. Only half of rural adults had finished primary school. The Poles would be relegated to doing the low-skilled, low-wage jobs that other Europeans did not want.

Faced with this existential crisis, Handke studied the education systems of other countries, including the United States, where he had lived for two years. He traveled around Poland meeting with teachers, researchers, and politicians. In the spring of 1998, he and his boss, the new prime minister, Jerzy Buzek (another chemistry professor), announced a series of reforms the likes of which they might never have contemplated if they'd had more experience with the political sensitivities of education.

"We have to move the entire system—push it out of its equilibrium so that it will achieve a new equilibrium," Handke said. He was still teaching chemistry, this time to thirty-eight million people.

To get to the new equilibrium, the country would enter what scientists called a *transition phase*. This phase would, as Handke put it, "give students a chance." It had four main parts, laid out in a 225-page orange book that was distributed to schools all over the country. First, the reforms would inject rigor into the system. A new core curriculum would replace the old, dumbed-down mandates that had forced teachers to cover too many topics too briefly. The new program would lay out fundamental goals, but leave the details to the schools. At the same time, the government would require a quarter of teachers to go back to school to improve their own education.

Along with rigor came accountability. To make sure students were learning, they would start taking standardized tests at regular intervals throughout their schooling—not as often as American kids, but at the end of elementary, junior high, and high school. Those tests would be the same all over the country, for all of Poland's several million children.

For younger kids, the tests would help identify which students—and teachers and schools—needed more help. For older students, the tests would also have consequences, determining which high schools and then universities they could attend. For the first time, all students would take the university entrance exam at the end of high school, and the exams would no longer be graded by local teachers. That way, universities and employers would be able to trust that the results meant the same thing from place to place.

The Poles couldn't know it yet, but this kind of targeted standardized testing would prove to be critical in any country with significant poverty, according to a PISA analysis that would come out years later. Around the world, school systems that used regular standardized tests tended to be fairer places, with smaller gaps between what rich and poor kids knew. Even in the United States, where tests have historically lacked rigor and purpose, African-American and Hispanic students' reading and math scores have gone up during the era of widespread standardized testing.

Why did tests make schools fairer, generally speaking? Tests helped schools to see what they were doing right and wrong, and who needed more help. That insight was a prerequisite, not a solution. Rendering problems visible did not guarantee they would be fixed, as thousands of U.S. school districts had proven under the testing mandates of No Child Left Behind. But identifying problems seemed to be a necessary first step in places with wild variation in what kids knew.

The third reform was the most important one: to literally—not just rhetorically—raise the expectations for what kids could accomplish. To do this, the reforms would force all kids to stay together in the same academic environment for an extra full year, through the equivalent of freshman year in high school. Instead of getting streamed into either vocational or academic programs around age fifteen, a practice known as *tracking*, students would go to the same junior high schools, together, until age sixteen. The difference was only twelve months, but it would have surprising consequences.

In Poland, delaying tracking meant creating four thousand new junior high schools, virtually overnight. There was no other way to accommodate all the students who would normally have gone off to vocational school at fifteen.

Handke might have stopped there. A new core curriculum, a stricter testing regimen, and thousands of new schools would represent a massive disruption, the likes of which no American state had ever seen in such a short time.

But there was an obvious problem. The Poles had recent, traumatic memories of communism. It was politically impossible to impose changes like this from the central government without granting other freedoms in exchange. To extract more accountability, Handke decided to reward schools with more control.

That autonomy was the fourth reform. Teachers would be free to choose their own textbooks and their own specific curriculum from over one hundred approved options, along with their own professional development. They would start earning bonuses based in part on how much professional development they did. In a booming country where people were judged by how much money they made, the cash infusion would telegraph to everyone that teachers were no longer menial laborers. The principal, meanwhile, would have full responsibility for hiring teachers. Local authorities would have full control over budgeting decisions, including where and how to open the new junior high schools.

In other words, the new system would demand more accountability for results, while granting more autonomy for methods. That dynamic could be found in all countries that had dramatically improved their results, including Finland and, for that matter, in every high-performing organization, from the U.S. Coast Guard to Apple Inc.

All this change would happen, Handke declared, in one year.

shock therapy

The orange book provoked extreme reactions. Some Poles applauded the audacity of Handke's plan: "This is our ticket to Europe and the modern world," proclaimed a journalist at *Gazeta Wyborcza,* one of Poland's biggest newspapers. However, the Union of Polish Teachers came out against the reforms, accusing Handke of trying to change too much too quickly with too little funding. In another article in the same newspaper, one principal prophesied disaster: "We can look forward to a deterioration in the standard of education for most young people, a deepening of illiteracy and a widespread reluctance to pursue further education."

The timing, however, was exceptional: Poland had a new government full of so-called reformers. They couldn't easily call themselves reformers and then obstruct reform. More important, there were a lot of distractions. The government was reforming health care and pensions at the same time. The dizzying pace of change gave Handke cover.

On September 1, 1999, four thousand new junior high schools opened their doors across Poland. The metamorphosis had begun. Handke wisely started the day by praying for the best. In the ancient Polish city of Gniezno, he attended a special Mass at the Gothic cathedral. Then he went to the city's new junior high school, a three-story, concrete-and-glass structure known as number three, for an inauguration of Poland's new educational era. He vowed that the new system would be "more creative and safe, not hammering redundant information into the head." Designed for the present world instead of the past, the new system would teach children how to think.

In reality, it was a chaotic day. Many teachers and principals were not ready. Buses failed to show up in many rural towns where students lived far from the new schools. Parents, teachers, and principals complained bitterly about the changes. The orange books were a nice idea, but they had not convinced the public and teachers that the changes were wise. At the end of the school year, 60 percent of Poles surveyed said they did not think the reforms guaranteed equal access to an education. No one, including Handke, knew whether the gamble would pay off.

"we don't want to be left behind."

While Handke the chemist was disrupting the equilibrium in Poland, Schleicher the physicist was trying to persuade countries to participate in the first-ever PISA test. Many countries had signed on, but Poland was not among them.

Poland had little experience with international exams, and many felt that the money could be better spent elsewhere. However, a few officials, like Jerzy Wiśniewski, an adviser in the education ministry and a former high-school math teacher, lobbied for Poland to join the experiment. To them, PISA represented modernity—a rational, sophisticated tool for the first world.

"The only other developed country still opposed is Turkey," Wiśniewski pointed out. "We don't want to be left behind."

The peer pressure worked and, in 2000, Polish fifteen-year-olds took the PISA. No one realized it then, but the timing was perfect. PISA captured, entirely by coincidence, a snapshot of Poland before and after the reforms.

The Polish kids who took the first PISA in 2000 had grown up under the old system. Half had already been tracked to vocational schools, half to academic schools. They were the control group, so to speak.

No one in Poland had expected to lead the world, but the results were disheartening all the same. Polish fifteen-year-olds ranked twenty-first in reading and twentieth in math, below the United States and below average for the developed world. Once again, Poland had found itself on the outside looking in. If the vocational students were evaluated separately, the inequities were startling. Over two-thirds scored in the rock-bottom lowest literacy level.

Three years later, in 2003, a new group of Polish fifteen-year-olds took PISA. They had spent their elementary years in the old system but were by then attending the new gymnasia schools. Unlike their predecessors, they had not yet been tracked. They were the experimental group.

The results were shocking—*again*. Poland, the punch line for so many jokes around the world, ranked thirteenth in reading and eighteenth in math, just above the United States in both subjects. In the space of three years, Poland had caught up with the developed world.

How could this be? Typically, it takes many years for reforms to have any impact, and most never do. But the results held. By 2009, Poland was outperforming the United States in math and science, despite spending less than half as much money per student. In reading and math, Poland's poorest kids outscored the poorest kids in the United States. That was a remarkable feat, given that they were worse off, socioeconomically, than the poorest American kids.

In 2012, Poland officially joined the ranks of the world's education superpowers. That year, its teenagers performed at the same level on PISA as kids in Finland and Canada. The results suggested a radical possibility for the rest of the world: perhaps poor kids *could* learn more than they were learning. Perhaps all was not lost. Most impressively, 84 percent of Polish students graduated from high school in 2011, compared to 77 percent in the United States.

Over the same time period, the United States had undergone its own education reforms, including more testing and public flogging of failing schools under No Child Left Behind. But all the while, PISA scores for American kids remained largely unchanged. The United States had cranked up the pressure on schools but done little else to inject rigor into the system, delay the tracking of students, or grant autonomy to the best teachers.

When Wiśniewski looked closely at the data, he saw that much of Poland's improvement had come from the students who would eventually end up in vocational schools. Their scores had jumped, lifting the entire country. Poland's schools had gotten more consistent, too. The variation in scores from one Polish school to the next had dropped more than in any other developed country. Childhood had become one notch fairer in Poland, almost overnight. And this improvement had *not* come at the expense of Poland's most advanced kids, who also raised their scores. Over one-third of Polish teens scored in the top two levels of literacy, higher than average for the developed world.

What had made the difference in Poland? Of all the changes, one reform had mattered most, according to research done by Wiśniewski and his colleagues: the delay in tracking. Kids who would have otherwise been transferred to vocational schools scored about 100 points higher than their counterparts in 2000, those who had already been tracked at that point. The expectations had gone up, and these kids had met them.

The four thousand newly inclusive schools had, it appeared, jump-started the education system in ways no one had expected. The principals who had volunteered to run the new schools tended to be the more ambitious school leaders, and they were allowed to handpick the teachers who came with them. Quite by accident, the new system self-selected for talent, and the new schools had built-in prestige. To the rest of the education establishment, the new schools sent a message that these reforms were real, not just another political spasm that could be ignored.

Handke was delighted, seeing the PISA scores as vindication for his reforms. "Our youth have begun to think."

But the data also revealed a troubling flip side: Expectations could fall as quickly as they rose. In 2006 and 2009, Poland gave the PISA test to a sample of sixteen- and seventeen-year-olds, to see what happened once they went off to vocational schools. Incredibly, the gains disappeared: The achievement gap from the first PISA returned, one year later. By age sixteen, vocational students were performing dramatically worse than academic students. The reforms had postponed the gap, not eliminated it.

Wiśniewski was mystified. How could the improvements vanish so fast? "It might be motivation," he said. "It needs more research. But the peer effects are somehow very influential." Something happened to kids once they got into the vocational schools with all the other vocational students and teachers. They seemed to lose their abilities, or maybe their drive, almost overnight.

gifted and talented in america

Intuitively, tracking made sense. A classroom should function more efficiently if all the kids were at the same level. In reality, though, second tracks almost always came with second-rate expectations.

Statistically speaking, tracking tended to diminish learning and boost inequality wherever it was tried. In general, the younger the tracking happened, the worse the entire country did on PISA. There seemed to be some kind of ghetto effect: Once kids were labeled and segregated into the lower track, their learning slowed down.

In Pennsylvania, Tom was tracked starting in third grade. A teacher recommended him for testing, and he did well. So, at the age of eight, he was placed in the gifted and talented program in Gettysburg. At first, this distinction had little practical effect. Once a week, he and the other designated kids went to a special class where they got to sample Latin and learn long division early. As he got older, he was gradually eased onto a more explicit track. By age fifteen, his core classes were all considered advanced in some way. He took English, social studies, and science classes on what was called the *accelerated* track, with other higher-achieving students. He only saw the nonaccelerated kids his age in gym, art, or the other nonessential classes.

It was hard to know what effect this sorting had, but it was safe to say that kids who were told they were gifted at age eight probably tended to see themselves that way, and kids who were not probably did not. The word *gifted* alone implied an innate talent that no amount of hard work could change. In a sense, it was the opposite of Confucianism, which holds that the only path to true understanding comes from long, careful study.

When Tom was a freshman, Gettysburg High School had three main tracks. The most rigorous was the accelerated route, which became the Advanced Placement track in junior and senior year. The second level was for all the regular kids. Then there was yet *another* track, euphemistically called the *applied* track. This was for the 10 to 15 percent of Tom's classmates who, for whatever reason, just aimed low. Instead of English, these kids took something called, "English in the Workplace." Everyone had his or her track, regardless of where it was headed.

When most people thought of tracking, they thought of places like Germany or Austria, where students were siphoned off to separate schools depending on their aspirations. Tracking took different forms in places like the United States, the United Kingdom, Canada, Japan, Norway, and Sweden. But that didn't mean it was less powerful.

Tracking in elementary school was a uniquely American policy. The sorting began at a very young age, and it came in the form of magnet schools, honors classes, Advanced Placement courses, or International Baccalaureate programs. In fact, the United States was one of the few countries where schools not only divided younger children by ability, but actually taught different *content* to the more advanced track. In other countries, including Germany and Singapore, all kids were meant to learn the same challenging core content; the most advanced kids just went deeper into the material.

Meanwhile, the enduring segregation of U.S. schools by race and income created another *de facto* tracking system, in which minority and low-income kids were far more likely to attend inferior schools with fewer Advanced Placement classes and less experienced teachers.

By the early twenty-first century, many countries were slowly, haltingly, delaying tracking. When they did so, all kids tended to do better. In most Polish schools, tracking occurred at age sixteen. At Tom's school in Wrocław, the sorting had already happened; only a third to half of the students who applied were accepted. Tom only saw the vocational kids when he came to gym class. They left as his class arrived.

Finland tracked kids, too. As in Poland, the division happened later, at age sixteen, the consequence of forty years of reforms, each round of which had delayed tracking a little longer. Until students reached age sixteen, though, Finnish schools followed a strict ethic of equity. Teachers could not, as a rule, hold kids back or promote them when they weren't ready. That left only one option: All kids had to learn. To make this possible, Finland's education system funneled money toward kids who needed help. As soon as young kids showed signs of slipping, teachers descended upon them like a pit crew before they fell further behind. About a third of kids got special help during their first nine years of school. Only 2 percent repeated a grade in Finnish primary school (compared to 11 percent in the United States, which was above average for the developed world).

Once it happened, tracking was less of a stigma in Finland. The government gave vocational high schools extra money, and in many towns, they were as prestigious as the academic programs. In fact, the more remote or disadvantaged the school, the more money it got. This balance was just as important as delaying tracking; once students got channeled into a vocational track, it had to lead somewhere. Not all kids had to go to college, but they all had to learn useful skills.

In Finland and all the top countries, spending on education was tied to need, which was only logical. The worse off the students, the more money their school got. In Pennsylvania, Tom's home state, the opposite was true. The poorest school districts spent 20 percent *less* per student, around $9,000 compared to around $11,000 in the richest school districts.

That backward math was one of the most obvious differences between the United States and other countries. In almost every other developed country, the schools with the poorest students had *more* teachers per student; the opposite was true in only four countries: the United States, Israel, Slovenia, and Turkey, where the poorest schools had fewer teachers per student.

It was a striking difference, and it related to rigor. In countries where people agreed that school was serious, it had to be serious for everyone. If rigor was a prerequisite for success in life, then it had to be applied evenly. Equity—a core value of fairness, backed up by money and institutionalized by delayed tracking—was a telltale sign of rigor.

plato's cave

After his first year at Gettysburg High School, Tom got a new principal. His name was Mark Blanchard, and he was on a mission. The high school's test scores were lower than they should have been, and he came in looking for the reason. He'd worked at two other higher-performing public schools in Pennsylvania, so he figured he could fix Gettysburg once he identified the problem.

But he couldn't find it.

Gettysburg High School was palatial. It sprawled out across 124 acres, a red brick and glass campus set back behind a manicured lawn. The $40 million facility, built in 1998, included an engineering lab, a greenhouse, three basketball courts, and a sleek 1,600 seat auditorium. The school spent almost twice as much per student as Kim's school spent in Oklahoma, even after adjusting for cost of living and differences in students' needs. Whatever the school needed, it wasn't money.

Blanchard worried the problem might be the teachers; that would be hard to fix. Yet he was surprised to discover many talented, experienced teachers. He also met hundreds of hard-working, creative kids, including Tom. One in five Gettysburg children came from families living in poverty, a relatively manageable level, and most of Tom's classmates lived in middle- or upper-income homes.

In time, Blanchard realized the problem was more insidious. The challenge was not a lack of potential but a failure of imagination. Some parents—including the ones who worked as professors at nearby Gettysburg College—assumed their children would go to college. But most parents just wanted their kids to get through high school, and that was about it, Blanchard realized. Many of these parents worked in agriculture and had never needed more education than that. Their goals were modest to a fault.

In certain other countries, that twentieth century mindset had been disrupted—often by economic crises. Families in Finland, Korea, and Poland had started to assume that their kids would go to college or get technical training after high school, and most of them did.

Yet in Gettysburg and many schools around the world, the status quo had calcified. And it wasn't just the parents and students who settled for less; that same mindset pervaded many of the classrooms. In his conversations with teachers in the hallways, Blanchard noticed a certain resignation. Why should they stand up in front of kids and talk about politics, literature, or advanced math if all their students wanted was to get through high school?

Blanchard started to think of the problem like Plato's Cave. People assumed the familiar shadows they'd seen on the wall in front of them were real, even if they were just reflections of their own imaginations. He needed to make them turn around and discover that the world was different. Things had changed, and they could dream bigger.

First, Blanchard tried to boost the rhetoric. He started talking about Gettysburg becoming the best. He announced a plan to double the size of the AP program. He told the orchestra teacher he wanted to have the strongest music program in the county. "I want to be great at everything, so nobody can say this is the football high school."

Then he tried to lift the academic expectations, just slightly. When he heard about the applied classes, he started asking questions. Neither of his previous schools had needed applied courses. Why should Gettysburg? He started referring to them as "bonehead" classes, and he proposed doing away with them.

"Kids meet the expectations you set for them," he told his staff.

Some teachers and guidance counselors objected. "The students won't pass," they warned him. "They won't graduate."

Blanchard told them it was their job to teach all the kids, not just the ambitious ones. So Tom's sophomore year, the school offered no bonehead courses. Just like that, Gettysburg deleted its lowest track.

Interestingly, nothing happened. No one dropped out because "bonehead English" went away. Soon, teachers stopped talking about it, and it was as if the applied track had never existed.

Gettysburg and other local school districts also got together to build a new technical school, so that kids who wanted vocational training could spend half their days in the program for diesel mechanics or pre-nursing, earning community college credit. They couldn't do it until they were sixteen, though, just like in Poland. Until then, they had to keep taking English, science, and math.

Diesel mechanics needed to know geometry and the basics of physics in order to diagnose and repair modern heavy machinery. They had to be able to read blueprints and technical manuals. They had to understand percentages and ratios in order to measure the gasses found in exhaust. All jobs had gotten more complex, including blue-collar jobs.

Besides these important changes, though, much remained the same at Gettysburg. There were still multiple tracks, and kids got sorted onto them early on. The AP program had grown but not doubled. Most of the teachers remained the same. And, while many were strong, some were not, a veteran Gettysburg teacher told me. "Parents complain about them, and kids complain, too, and yet they are still here."

Overall, the state of Pennsylvania got a D+ for its management of teachers from the National Council on Teacher Quality in 2011 and 2012; it got a flat-out F for its practices regarding the removal of ineffective teachers.

Sports remained the core culture of Gettysburg High School. At each football game, no less than three local reporters showed up. Both local newspapers devoted entire sections to high-school sports. Many games were broadcast on the radio. Student athletes had grueling schedules that left little time or energy for studying. They had to lift weights all summer, but they didn't have to do much math. Blanchard had worked hard to increase the drive and equity quotient at his school, but the rest of the equation remained mostly the same.

In 2011, four out of ten Gettysburg high school juniors still weren't doing math at grade level, according to the state's own test, which wasn't very hard. When Tom's classmates took the SAT, they scored a bit better than the national mean in reading and a little worse in math. Their AP scores were high, but only a third of the students took AP classes. It was almost as if Gettysburg were two different schools, with one set of ideals for the top students and another for the rest. The metamorphosis had stalled.

the fundamentals

Tom liked Principal Blanchard, though he didn't know him well, and he was reluctant to say anything critical about his hometown. But as we walked through Wrocław talking about the differences, he described the problem with Gettysburg this way: "The school is not that concerned with sending people off to do big things." It was one reason he'd wanted to spend his senior year somewhere else. He'd wanted to do big things.

We got to number thirteen just before first period, arriving with a throng of other students. The building was made of deep red and black bricks, with bars covering the windows. Like the rest of the city, number thirteen was a contrast of old and new; half of it was rebuilt after World War II, while the other half dated back to the 1800s. A scowling guard allowed us to pass through the foyer into the main lobby.

Number thirteen was a bilingual German school, considered one of the better high schools in the city. It had hardwood floors, high ceilings, and wooden desks, but it was not in the same league as the facility in Gettysburg. There was no cafeteria, for example. Kids brought sandwiches from home or bought food from a small snack counter inside the school.

There were no high-tech white boards or laptops, either. Back at Gettysburg, half the classrooms had laptops for all students, and the other half used one of five computer labs as needed. As we made our way downstairs, I asked Tom what kinds of things he did with those laptops. "We played Flash games," he said smiling, "or tried to find a way to get on Facebook."

Polish kids wasted time on Facebook, too, of course. They procrastinated by playing World of Warcraft, just like kids back home.

However, they also spent a lot of time studying for their graduation exam, far more than most of Tom's classmates had spent studying for the SAT. When Polish kids took that graduation test, they got dressed up in their nicest clothes—the way high-school football players did on game day in America.

And one other thing: There were no sports at Tom's school in Poland. Sports simply did not figure into the school day; why would they? Plenty of kids played pick-up soccer or basketball games on their own after school, but there was no confusion about what school was for—or what mattered to kids' life chances. Unlike Principal Blanchard back in Pennsylvania, Tom's Polish principal did not have to spend any time worrying about whether her new math teacher could also coach baseball.

When the bell rang at the end of class, I followed Tom outside for one of several daily smoke breaks. We stood beside the school, along with dozens of other students, as a streetcar churned by, shaking the ground around us. He'd picked up the habit soon after he'd arrived. Back in Gettysburg, he would have been suspended for smoking outside school.

Like many American exchange students, Tom relished the freedom he had in his time abroad. After school, he liked to go to one of the twelve islands located on the Odra River that ran through the city. There, with throngs of other Polish teenagers, he and his friends drank beer and smoked. He felt more like an adult who could decide what to do, even if it was bad for him.

That autonomy was not always fun, however. If teenagers were capable of taking care of themselves after school, they were also expected to face facts during school. They were not protected from hard truths. In one class, Tom remembered, the teacher announced the exam scores aloud. He was stunned when he heard the results: Twenty-two out of twenty-six kids had failed, an unimaginable ratio in most U.S. high schools. School didn't necessarily seem better in Poland, in Tom's opinion, but it did seem less forgiving.

Later that day, I asked Tom to introduce me to his principal, Urszula Spałka. He took me to her office, where we sat down underneath a large eagle, the national symbol of Poland, hanging on the pale violet wall. Spałka wore a low-cut black blouse and a brown suit with chunky jewelry. She had started out as a math teacher, but she had been the principal at number thirteen for almost 20 years.

Like the United States, Poland ran its schools on the local level. The country was divided into 2,500 municipalities. On average, Spałka and other principals had about $4,681 to spend on each student each year, compared to $11,000 per student in Gettysburg.

Spałka gave succinct answers to my questions, betraying little emotion. When I asked her about the reforms, the ones that had made the country a role model for the rest of the world, her expression soured.

"We're not too excited about the reforms," she said drily. "Schools don't like radical changes. And these were radical changes."

Despite Poland's higher PISA scores, many Poles still thought it had been a mistake to keep all kids together during the volatile teenage years. Or they were focused on other problems: Many thought the graduation exam had gotten too easy, and the country's teachers were feuding with the government over a move to increase their hours.

Everywhere I went, in every country, people complained about their education system. It was a universal truth and a strangely reassuring one. No one was content, and rightly so. Educating all kids to high levels was hard, and every country—every one—still had work to do.

In the summer of 2000, after seeing through the first phase of reforms, Handke had resigned. He'd failed to secure funds needed to pay for a promised pay raise for teachers, and besides that, he was tired. He went back to chemistry, and soon afterwards, his party was defeated in a landslide.

Poland was more rigorous than it had been; it had a higher level of drive, some measure of autonomy and a dose of equity. But, like

Gettysburg High School, it hadn't changed enough. It still had too many teacher-training colleges of wildly varying quality. The teachers who managed to find jobs still did not get paid enough.

Still, Poland had made a breakthrough. It had proven that even troubled countries could do better for their children in just a few years. Rigor could be cultivated. It didn't have to appear organically. In fact, there was no evidence that it ever had, in any country. Expectations could go up. Bold leaders who didn't know better could help to raise an entire generation of smarter kids.

Before they'd gotten tracked, Polish kids had finished that survey, the one attached to the PISA test, coming in first in the world for conscientiousness. It seemed as if, somewhere along the way, they'd bought into the idea that they should take school seriously. Maybe because they were expected to do so.

When I talked to Handke in 2012, he was convalescing from a heart condition, which he blamed, semiseriously, on the three years he'd spent trying to reform his country's education system. Looking back, he wished he and his colleagues had done a better job selling the reforms. They had focused more on the policy than public relations, when they should have done the reverse. That was another common mistake, lamented too late in every time zone. Politics, history, and fear mattered more than policy, always and everywhere. Still, he consoled himself with the knowledge that controversy was inevitable.

"Every reform hurts. People want peace. When you're used to something, it's better when nothing is happening."

I asked him what he would do if he could go back and push for one last change before he died. He did not hesitate.

"The teachers. Everything is based on the teachers. We need good teachers—well-prepared, well-chosen. I wouldn't change anything else."

part III

spring

The New Finland: Self-portrait by a student
in Espoo, Finland.

chapter 8

difference

One Friday during that long, dark winter, Kim's host mother told her
that she needed to get help. Something had happened to Kim around
the time of her sixteenth birthday that February; she had started crying for no obvious reason, at school and at home. Kim wasn't sure
why. It had been one of the coldest winters in Finland's history, and
the sun was present for just six hours a day. Maybe that explained
it. Or maybe it was the cold war with the twin five-year-olds who
wanted their mother back. Maybe the twins had outlasted her in the
end. All Kim knew for sure was that she felt drained, as if the light
inside her had gone out.

  She confided in her host mother that she sometimes felt hopeless.
Susanne had talked to the exchange program people, and they had
decided that Kim had to go to Helsinki to see a psychologist who
could sort out whether she should go back to America early.

  Kim didn't argue. She took out her grandmother's suitcase and
quietly refilled it with all of her things. She packed up the gloves her

sister Kate had given her, and the Irish sweater from a friend of her aunt, all the things they had thought she would need to survive in Finland. Good intentions, she thought to herself.

She said goodbye to the little girls, surrendering the playroom to the victors at last. She carried everything with her, in case the trip ended in Oklahoma. She felt numb, as if this were happening to someone else. She withdrew into silence, that old familiar place.

As she sat on the high-speed train to Helsinki, flashing past the blue lakes and snow-covered pine trees, Kim closed her eyes. She saw the neatly wrapped Rice Krispies Treats she'd sold to raise money, the bunk beds at her new home in Finland, the children's book her Finnish teacher had given her. She thought about the prospect of leaving Finland several months early, having failed at the only impressive thing she had ever done.

Kim had been warned that this might happen in mass emails from AFS, her exchange program. Teenagers living abroad tended to go through predictable phases, and the one that came in the middle of the year was a dark one. Many felt depressed and isolated. The initial buzz had worn off; the holidays had arrived; and the lark had turned into an occupation, the kind that would end one day but not soon. Still, Kim hadn't thought that this malaise would befall her, not after all she'd done to get here.

Looking out the window on the train, Kim saw her reflection. She felt like two people. One part of her felt resigned to defeat, ready to prove everyone right. Maybe she should have gone to Italy after all, somewhere warm and bright, or maybe she should have stayed right where she was in Oklahoma, just as her mom had said.

There was another part of her, too. That part of her was just waking up, beginning to stir after a long silence. This was the girl who had written to sixty businesses in Sallisaw, Oklahoma, asking them to sponsor her trip to Finland. When no one had responded, she'd sold beef jerky door to door instead. That part of her was still there, somewhere. In her mind, she imagined that girl lacing up her combat boots. She pictured her swiping black grease under her eyes. That girl had no intention of going back to Oklahoma early.

In Helsinki, Kim saw the psychologist. They talked about her reasons for coming to Finland, her parents' divorce, and her adjustment to living abroad. The psychologist ruled out serious depression, and they agreed to meet again.

Between sessions, Kim roamed through Helsinki, visiting museums, riding buses, and watching all the people. After sixteen years in rural Oklahoma and six months in rural Finland, it felt exhilarating to see so many humans in one place. Standing by the harbor one afternoon, Kim was struck by how many children she saw. School had ended for the day, but to see them walking casually all by themselves through the streets of Helsinki was disorienting. There was a boy, not more than ten, sitting on a bench; over there were two girls, playing near a fountain. She'd seen kids on their own in Pietarsaari; even small children walked to school on their own. She hadn't, however, expected to see such a thing in Finland's largest city. She felt jealous of them in a strange way. What would it have been like, she wondered, to grow up with that kind of freedom?

After two weeks, the psychologist told Kim she could stay in Finland. She had been given a second chance. Kim felt a weight lift. It was like getting her passport all over again. AFS found an older couple with a big house in Pietarsaari to host Kim for the rest of the year. She could return to the same town, and she'd have a room of her own.

This time, Kim knew, she needed to speak up. She should have told Susanne that she adored her but she needed a host family with enough mental and physical space for her. She hadn't wanted to offend anyone, so she'd been silent for too long.

There was a word in Finnish, *sisu* [pronounced SEE-su]. It meant strength in the face of great odds, but more than that, a sort of inner fire. Kim first learned about *sisu* when she was researching Finland from Oklahoma. "It is a compound of bravado and bravery, of ferocity and tenacity," *Time* magazine wrote in a story about Finland in 1940, "of the ability to keep fighting after most people would have quit, and to fight with the will to win."

It may have been the one word that encapsulated the Finnish way more than any other. *Sisu* was what it took to coax potatoes out of the soil of the Arctic Circle; *sisu* had helped Finland pull itself back from the brink of irrelevance to become an education superpower. *Sisu* helped explain how a country with fewer citizens than Wisconsin had invented Nokia, Marimekko, and the Linux operating system, not to mention the video game *Angry Birds*. *Sisu* was Finland's version of drive, a quiet force that never quit. English has no word for *sisu*, though the closest synonym might be *grit*.

That day, arriving at the station near Pietarsaari, Kim felt as if she understood what *sisu* was. She didn't know how long the feeling would last, but she hoped she would remember it. As she heaved her suitcase off the train and made her way outside with the rest of the passengers, she felt almost as if she belonged.

virtual reality

I met Kim and both of her host families for dinner in Pietarsaari one night that spring. By then, the snow had finally melted. We gathered at a big, white clapboard restaurant on the sea. Kim had stayed in close touch with Susanne despite having moved out. She wrote a regular column for Susanne's newspaper, and Susanne was working on a Finnish magazine story about Kim.

We ate cod and cloudberries, and Kim sat in the middle, wearing a red jacket and telling stories about her first days in Finland. She seemed more sure of herself than she had just a few months before. That's when she told me she was working on a plan for her return to America.

"I'm applying to virtual high school," she said.

Kim had decided she couldn't go back to Sallisaw High School. She didn't want to be the person she was before, and she was afraid she couldn't change if everything else stayed the same.

"I worry that the indifference will start to affect me again. That I'll just slip back into the views of all my peers."

"What view is that?"

"That 'it just doesn't matter; that school sucks, so why should we be here?' I feel like removing myself from that situation."

She'd researched boarding schools on the Internet, just like she'd once researched Finland. That was the fantasy. Then she'd come across a link for something called Oklahoma Virtual High School. She'd discovered it was a real high school, albeit one that existed online. And it was free, unlike boarding school. She and her mother were going to talk about it some more, but Kim seemed confident she'd found a way to get through her last years of American high school.

Afterward, we emerged into the blue twilight. It was ten o'clock and still light out, the time of year when the Nordic countries paid their debts from the winter. Kim let me take a few pictures of her in front of the sea, then she got on her bike and rode home, like a real Finn.

stress test

Two days later, I accompanied Kim to school. I went to classes with her, and she introduced me to her principal and her teachers. It happened to be the week that the seniors got the results of the big matriculation exam they'd taken earlier that year—the one that determined where they would likely go to college. Kim's Finnish teacher, Tiina Stara, was worried about her students. "They are feeling a lot of pressure. It's not like in Japan or Korea, but still."

The test had been around for more than 160 years and was deeply embedded in the system. The countries with the best education outcomes all had these tests at the end of high school. It was one of the most obvious differences between them and the United States—which had a surplus of tests, few of which had meaningful effects on kids' lives.

Matriculation exams like Finland's helped inject drive into education systems—creating a bright finish line for kids and schools to work toward. Teenagers from countries with these kinds of tests performed over sixteen points higher on PISA than those in countries without them.

Still, Stara worried that this test stressed out her students and drove too much of her lesson planning. "I sometimes want so badly to do something fun with them," she said, clenching her fist in her lap. "I think it's very important that they enjoy studying." In addition to the matriculation exam, Finnish kids still took regular classroom tests and final exams every six weeks at the end of each mini-semester. In surveys, Finnish kids cited the high number of tests as one reason that they didn't like school. Tests were controversial all over the world, another universal truth.

Stara hastened to add that she would not do away with the matriculation test if she could. "It's a very good exam," she said, nodding her head.

Then she described what rigor looked like: Finland's exam stretched out over three grueling weeks and lasted about *fifty hours*. Teachers followed students to the bathroom to make sure they didn't cheat. The Finnish section took two days. On the first day, students read several texts and wrote short essays analyzing each one, over the course of six hours. On the second day, students chose one topic out of fourteen options and wrote a single, very long essay, over the course of another six hours. One recent topic was, "Why is it difficult to achieve peace in the Middle East?" Another was, "I blog, therefore I am."

To do well, students had to be able to structure a long-form essay, communicate complex ideas, and, of course, use proper spelling and grammar. Stara felt a heavy responsibility to help her students do well on this test.

It was hard to think of a test like this in the United States. The SAT and ACT served a similar purpose, but neither was as comprehensive or as embedded in schools themselves. Many states had some kind of graduation test, but kids didn't need much *sisu* to pass them. The New York State Regents exam was considered one of the most challenging. Yet the English portion lasted only a quarter as long as the Finnish portion of Finland's test. It included just one essay and two short responses, each of which only had to be one paragraph long.

The English test used to be six hours, but the New York Board of Regents voted to cut it in half in 2009, citing the logistical challenges of administering a long test, particularly with other distractions, like snow days, a rationale that would have amused the Finns. Altogether, the Regents exam required one-third the time of Finland's test.

In Finland, school was hard, and tests affected students' lives. Snow was not a good excuse. That might explain why only 20 percent of Finnish teenagers said they looked forward to math lessons, compared to 40 percent of Americans. They had to work hard, and expectations were high. About half of Finnish kids said they got good grades in math, compared to almost three-quarters of Americans. (In fact, American fifteen-year-olds were more likely than kids in thirty-seven other countries to say they got good math grades.) The problem with rigorous education was that it was *hard*. Ideally, it was fun, too, but it couldn't always be, not even in Finland.

There was much to be said for American teachers, who, in many schools, worked hard to entertain and engage their students with interactive classrooms. In my survey of 202 exchange students, I was struck by how many of them brought up their affection for their U.S. teachers. One German exchange student surveyed described the difference this way:

> "The teachers in the U.S. are way more friendly. They are like your friends. . . . In Germany, we know nothing about our teachers. They are just teachers. We would never talk to them about personal problems."

This bond between teachers and students mattered, and U.S. teachers deserved credit for connecting with their students. But learning to do higher-order thinking, reading, and math mattered, too. Finland seemed to have found a way to create manageable pressure, something compassionate teachers worried about, but not something that forced millions of kids to study for fifteen to eighteen hours per day. The Finns had gone long on teaching quality, autonomy, and equity, which meant they could ease up a bit on drive. In Finland, kids could have a life *and* an education, too.

black people in finland

The more time I spent in Finland, the more I appreciated the rare balance it had struck. Finland had achieved rigor without ruin. It was impossible not to notice something else, too: During my time in Pietarsaari, I saw exactly one black person. In Kim's classes, everyone looked basically the same. Nationwide, only 3 percent of Finland's students had immigrant parents (compared to 20 percent of teenagers in the United States).

In fact, Finland, Korea and Poland were *all* homogeneous places with few immigrants or racial minorities. Japan and Shanghai, China, two other education superpowers, were similarly bland. Maybe homogeneity was a prerequisite for rigor at scale. Did sameness beget harmony, which somehow boosted learning? If so, was Finland irrelevant to a big, jangling place like the United States?

Diversity was one of those words that got hijacked so often it had lost most of its meaning. Part of the problem was that there were thousands of ways to be diverse. In the United States, conversations about diversity were usually about race. The United States closely tracked the race of students because of its history of institutionalized racism; other countries did not, which made comparisons difficult.

But within the United States, African-American students did poorly on PISA, heartbreakingly so. On average, they scored eighty-four points below white students in reading in 2009. It was as if the white kids had been going to school two extra years, even though they were the same age. The gap between white and African-American students showed itself in dozens of other ways, too, from graduation rates to SAT scores. Generally speaking, up to half the gap could be explained by economics; black students were more likely to come from lower-income families with less-educated parents.

The other half was more complicated: Black parents tended to have fewer books and read less to their children, partly because they tended to be less educated. Then, when black children walked out of their homes and went to school each day, the disparities compounded. African-American kids were more likely to encounter inferior teaching and lower expectations in school, and they were disproportionately tracked into the lowest groups for reading and math lessons.

Each school day, African-American kids got the message in many schools around the country. It was subtle, but it was consistent: Your time is not precious, and your odds are not good. Those kinds of signals took up residence in kids' brains, echoing in the background whenever they contemplated what was possible. In one long-term study of Australian teenagers, researchers found that teenagers' aspirations at age fifteen could predict their futures. Kids who had high expectations for themselves, who planned to finish school and go to college, were significantly more likely to graduate high school. In fact, their parents' socioeconomic status didn't seem to affect their graduation odds, statistically speaking, as long as they held these aspirations.

Still, despite all the insidious disadvantages they faced, African-American kids were not responsible for the lackluster U.S. performance overall. For one thing, five of every six American kids were *not* black. For another, white kids didn't do so great in math, either. On average, white American teens performed worse than *all* students in a dozen other countries, including *all* kids in Canada, New Zealand, and Australia, which had higher ratios of immigrant kids. On a percentage basis, New York State had fewer *white* kids performing at high levels in math than Poland and Estonia had among kids overall.

Nothing was simple. Diversity could raise *or* lower test scores, and it did. One in five U.S. students came from an immigrant background, the sixth highest ratio in the developed world. But U.S. immigrants were, well, diverse: Hispanic students scored higher than blacks on

PISA, for example, and lower than whites, but Asian-Americans did better than everyone.

Overall, the gap between PISA reading scores for native and immigrant students in the United States was 22 points—better than Germany or France, where the gap was 60 points, but not as impressive as Canada, where the gap was zero. Much depended on the education and income of the immigrant parents, which had a lot to do with the history and immigration policies of a given country.

The rest depended on what countries *did* with the children they had. In the United States, the practice of funding schools based on local property taxes motivated families to move into the most affluent neighborhoods they could afford, in effect buying their way into good schools. The system encouraged segregation.

Since black, Hispanic, and immigrant kids tended to come from less affluent families, they usually ended up in underresourced schools with more kids like them. Between 1998 and 2010, poor American students had become more concentrated in schools with other poor students.

The biggest problem with this kind of diversity is that it wasn't actually *diverse*. Most white kids had majority white classmates. Black and Hispanic students, meanwhile, were more likely to attend majority black or Hispanic schools in 2005 than they were in 1980.

Populating schools with mostly low-income, Hispanic, or African-American students usually meant compounding low scores, unstable home lives, and low expectations. Kids fed off each other, a dynamic that could work for good and for ill. In Poland, kids lost their edge as soon as they were tracked into vocational schools; likewise, there seemed to be a tipping point for expectations in the United States. On average, schools with mostly low-income kids systematically lacked the symptoms of rigor. They had inconsistent teaching quality, little autonomy for teachers or teenagers, low levels of academic drive, and less equity. By warehousing disadvantaged kids in the same schools, the United States took hard problems and made them harder.

In Singapore, the opposite happened. There, the population was also diverse, about 77 percent Chinese, 14 percent Malay, 8 percent Indian, and 1.5 percent other. People spoke Chinese, English, Malay, and Tamil and followed five different faiths (Buddhism, Christianity, Islam, Taoism, and Hinduism). Yet Singaporeans scored at the top of the world on PISA, right beside Finland and Korea. There was virtually no gap in scores between immigrant and native-born students.

Of course, Singapore was essentially another planet compared to most countries. It was ruled by an authoritarian regime with an unusually high-performing bureaucracy. The government controlled most of the rigor variables, from the caliber of teacher recruits to the mix of ethnicities in housing developments. Singapore did not have the kind of extreme segregation that existed in the United States, because policy makers had forbidden it.

In most freewheeling democracies, governments did not have that kind of power. Left to their own devices, parents tended to self-segregate. If the class distinctions were less obvious, and the quality of the schools more consistent, this tendency was manageable.

Watching the kids sitting in Kim's classes, some animated, some aloof, but all of them white, I wondered what would happen if Finland's population suddenly changed. Would the Finns still have a shared belief in rigor if students came in all different colors? Or would everything come undone?

"i want to think about them as all the same."

Finland was a homogeneous place, but getting less so. The number of foreigners had increased over 600 percent since 1990, and most of the newcomers had ended up in Helsinki.

To find out how diversity changed the culture of rigor, I went to the Tiistilä school, just outside Helsinki, where a third of the kids were immigrants, many of them refugees. The school enrolled children aged six to thirteen. It was surrounded by concrete block apartment buildings that looked more communist than Nordic.

In a second-floor classroom, Heikki Vuorinen stood before his sixth graders. Four were African; two wore headscarves. An Albanian boy from Kosovo sat near a Chinese boy. There was a smattering of white kids born in Finland. Vuorinen gave the class an assignment and stepped out to talk to me.

Wearing a purple T-shirt, jeans, and small, rectangular glasses, Vuorinen proudly reported that he had kids from nine different countries that year, including China, Somalia, Russia, and Kosovo. Most had single parents. Beyond that, he was reluctant to speculate.

"I don't want to think about their backgrounds too much," he said, running his hand through his thinning blonde hair. Then he smiled. "There are twenty-three pearls in my classroom. I don't want to scratch them."

When pressed, he told me about one of his students in particular. She had six brothers and sisters; her father was a janitor and her mother took care of other people's children. Money was very tight. But she was, he said, the top student in his class.

Vuorinen was visibly uncomfortable labeling his students. "I don't want to have too much empathy for them," he explained, "because I have to teach. If I thought about all of this too much, I would give better marks to them for worse work. I'd think, 'Oh, you poor kid. Oh, well, what can I do?' That would make my job too easy."

He seemed acutely aware of the effect that expectations could have on his teaching. Empathy for kids' home lives could strip the rigor from his classroom. "I want to think about them as all the same."

I'd never heard a U.S. teacher talk that way. To the contrary, state and federal laws *required* that teachers and principals think about their kids as different; they had to monitor their students' race and income and report that data to the government. Schools were judged by the test scores of kids in each category. Most principals knew their ratios of low-income and minority kids by heart, like baseball players knew batting averages. There were important reasons for all this labeling; the U.S. government was trying to highlight injustice in order to fix it. Still, I wondered how much that raised consciousness had suppressed expectations along the way.

Diane Ravitch, one of the most popular education commentators in the United States, had insisted for years that Americans should think about our students' backgrounds *more,* not less. "Our problem is poverty, not schools," she told a roaring crowd of thousands of teachers at a D.C. rally in 2011. Kids were *not* all the same, in other words, and their differences preceded them.

In Finland, Vuorinen said the opposite of what Ravitch was saying in America.

"Wealth doesn't mean a thing," he said. "It's your brain that counts. These kids know that from very young. We are all the same."

The more time I spent in Finland, the more I started to think that the diversity narrative in the United States—the one that blamed our mediocrity on kids' backgrounds and neighborhoods—was as toxic as funding inequities. There was a fatalism to the story line, which didn't mean it was wrong. The United States *did* have too much poverty; minority students were *not* learning enough. Parents *did* matter, and so did health care and nutrition. Obviously.

But the narrative also underwrote low aspirations, shaping the way teachers looked at their students, just as Vuorinen feared. Since the 1960s, studies have shown that if researchers tested a class and told teachers that certain students would thrive academically in the coming months, teachers behaved differently toward the chosen kids. They nodded more, smiled more, and gave those kids more time to answer questions and more specific feedback.

In fact, the kids had been chosen at random. The label was fictional, but it stuck. At the end of the school year, teachers still described those students as more interesting, better adjusted, and more likely to be successful in life. As for other kids who had done well in the classroom, but were not chosen? The same teachers described them as less likely to succeed and less likable. The human brain depends on labels and patterns; if a researcher (or cultural narrative) offers teachers a compelling pattern, they will tend to defer to it.

What did it mean, then, that respected U.S. education leaders and professors in teacher colleges were indoctrinating young teachers with the mindset that poverty trumped everything else? What did it mean if teachers were led to believe that they could only be expected to do so much, and that poverty was usually destiny?

It may be human nature to stereotype, but some countries systematically reinforced the instinct, and some countries inhibited it. It was becoming obvious to me that rigor couldn't exist without equity. Equity was not just a matter of tracking and budgets; it was a *mindset*.

Interestingly, this mindset extended to special education in Finland, too. Teachers considered most special ed students to have temporary learning difficulties, rather than permanent disabilities. That mindset helped explain why Finland had one of the highest proportions of special education kids in the world; the label was temporary and not pejorative. The Finns assumed that all kids could improve. In fact, by their seventeenth birthday, about *half* of Finnish kids had received some kind of special education services at some point, usually in elementary school, so that they did not fall farther behind.

During the 2009 to 2010 school year, about one in four Finnish kids received some kind of special education services—almost always in a normal school, for only part of the day. (By comparison, about one in eight American students received special education services that year.)

As I watched Vuorinen talk with his students, I thought back to a Washington, D.C., public school at which I'd spent time a few years before. The school was in a poor part of the city, and many of the families were struggling. One veteran teacher I met had a warm manner and a bright, tidy classroom. She'd paid for classroom supplies with her own money.

However, when she'd talked about her fourth grade students' backgrounds, she'd stressed their disadvantages above all else. She'd talked about her kids' families as if they were a lost cause: "Our parents on this side don't have the know-how to raise their children," she'd said. "They're not sure what it takes for their child to make it."

She'd felt genuinely sorry for her students, but what good had come from her sympathy? After a year in her class, her students were farther below grade level in reading than they'd been when they'd first met her. They'd performed worse than other low-income kids who'd started the year at the same level in the very same city. Yet she'd seemed oddly sanguine about those results. The diversity narrative explained everything, even when it didn't.

fear and the marketplace

At Vuorinen's school, all fifth graders had been tested in math two years earlier. It was one way that the Finnish government made sure that schools were working. Unlike in the United States, the account-ability tests were precision targeted; the government tested only a sample of students. It usually took just one hour.

Compared to the rest of Finland, the Tiistilä kids performed above average. That was impressive: Better than average in Finland meant better than average just about anywhere.

Tiistilä students were diverse *and* good at math. The school was inspiring. It was also different from most U.S. schools in almost every way. First, it was *truly* economically and ethnically diverse. The school's three hundred children came from poor families, who lived in tiny, crowded apartments, and from rich families, who lived by the sea. Second, the Finnish government gave the school extra money for its immigrant students, to help pay for intensive language instruction.

The other difference was that Tiistilä had highly educated teach-ers. Vuorinen did not get into education college on his first try. Or his second. His test scores weren't high enough.

Finally, after spending years gaining experience as a substitute teacher, Vuorinen was accepted on his third try. He didn't find his university experience nearly as helpful as substitute teaching, but he didn't begrudge the process, either. When I asked him if he had any advice for the United States, he said: "You should start to select your teachers more carefully and motivate them more. One motivation is money. Respect is another. Punishing is never a good way to deal with schools." Autonomy mattered as much to Vuorinen as cash.

Vuorinen had worked at ten schools in fifteen years, but he liked Tiistilä the best. His reason was the same reason happy teachers cited everywhere:

"I like the principal. She knows what to do," he said. "I feel like I am trusted. And every time I need help, I can trust she will help me."

The principal, Mirja Pirinen, had worked at the school for fifteen years, going back to when it was much less diverse. She gave me a tour that ended at the playground, where a group of Muslim girls in pink headscarves jumped rope in the sunshine.

In her eight years as principal, Pirinen hadn't dismissed any of Tiistilä's permanent, full-time teachers. As in the United States, Finnish teachers almost never lost their jobs due to their performance. They were protected by a strong union contract. However, it was easier to manage inflexible workforces if employees arrived at work well-educated, rigorously trained, and decently paid from day one.

To me, Tiistilä seemed like a model school. Pirinen was smart and organized. She was the only principal I met on any continent who could actually tell me how much money her government spent per student. (In most schools, this was a mysterious figure that required many phone calls to uncover.) By all indications, Pirinen had successfully led Tiistilä through a major transition, adapting to a surge in families who couldn't speak a word of Finnish.

But not everyone in the neighborhood had such confidence in the school.

"Some parents in this area say that they would never want their children in this school," Pirinen told me matter of factly. The parents who did enroll their kids sometimes had to defend their decision to their neighbors.

Why? The parents were worried about the immigrant children. They'd been worried when there were 6 percent immigrants, and they were more worried now that there were 30 percent. Pirinen had to work hard to convince them that the school was good, despite its diversity.

There were virtually no private schools in Finland, nor any vouchers or charter schools. However, school choice took many forms, I was discovering. The kids who lived near the Tiistilä school could apply to attend special international, science, music, or foreign language schools, which were public schools that took only the higher performers (a practice that sometimes favored upper-income or savvier parents).

Finland's teenagers could also choose to go to job-training high schools, and about half of them did. The Finnish government had recently lavished vocational schools with funding and performance bonuses, so regular academic high schools like Kim's had to work even harder to keep their students.

Normally, Finnish schools did not publicize test results, but Pirinen had posted her school's scores on the web site to help reassure parents. With more diversity, test data had become more valuable, not just to track the school's effectiveness, but to assuage parental anxieties.

In every country, parents tried to get their children into the best schools. That was another universal truth, and who could blame them? The problem was defining *best*. Lacking good information, parents tended to judge schools based on hearsay, or the skin-color, ethnicity, or income level of the students and their families.

If everyone agreed that all schools met certain baseline standards, as in Finland, then the competition was mostly friendly. However, as more immigrants arrived, parents became less trusting. Even in Finland, with its long history of equity, there were reports of parents moving to other parts of Helsinki to avoid schools with just 10 percent immigrant children.

"Undoubtedly, we all want to live in a multicultural and tolerant atmosphere," one Finnish mother told the newspaper *Helsingin Sanomat* in 2011, explaining one reason why her child attended school outside of her neighborhood. "But the fact is that if there are many children who do not speak Finnish, the teacher's time is spent on them." The mother did not know any children at the local school, but she had heard stories.

I wondered what would happen in a true free market in which parents had real insight into the rigor of a school and the quality of its teachers, not just the aesthetics of the building or the ethnicity of the students. Some U.S. education reformers and politicians were convinced that more competition would lead to just this kind of scenario, pushing schools to get better results, or shut down.

At the time, 11 percent of children in the United States were enrolled in private schools—less than average for the developed world. According to PISA data, private schools did not add much value; private-school students did better on PISA than public-school students, but not better than would have been expected if they'd been in public school, given their socioeconomic status. Charter schools (a more autonomous type of public school available in some U.S. cities) accounted for another 5 percent of students. But here, too, the benefits varied widely depending on the charter school.

Competition existed almost everywhere, even if it was sometimes hard to see. Across the developed world, three-quarters of kids attended high schools that competed for students one way or another. But in the United States and most other countries, the competition was modest and distorted by a lack of information. As far as I could tell, there was really only one place in the world with a true free market for education, where supply and demand determined prices, and customers had closer-to-perfect information. That place was not the United States. Nor was it likely to ever be found in any public-school system on the planet.

Now that I appreciated the importance of rigor, I wanted to see if it could be jumpstarted by competition. To find out, I had to go into the shadows of South Korea's hagwons, a laboratory for the best and worst of everything, all at once.

chapter 9

Celebrity Teacher: Andrew Kim teaches at a Megastudy hagwon in the Daechi-dong neighborhood of Seoul.

the $4 million teacher

When Andrew Kim taught English, he spoke quietly into a tiny hands-free microphone that protruded from under his right ear. He wrote on an old-fashioned chalkboard. He didn't seem to be doing anything remarkable, but in his class, unlike so many Korean classes, the students did not sleep.

Andrew Kim earned $4 million in 2010. He was known in Korea as a *rock-star teacher*, a combination of words that I'd never heard before. He'd been teaching for over twenty years, all of them in Korea's private afterschool tutoring hagwons. That meant that he was paid according to the demand for his skills, unlike most teachers worldwide. And he was in high demand.

I interviewed Kim in his office in a luxury high-rise building in Seoul in June 2011. One of his employees greeted me at the door and offered me bottled water. We gathered around a table, and Kim explained that he worked about sixty hours per week, although he only taught three in-person lectures. The Internet had turned his classes into commodities. Each lecture he did went online, where kids could purchase his teaching services at the rate of $3.50 per hour. The rest of the time, he responded to students' online requests for help, developed lesson plans, and wrote textbooks and workbooks. He'd written about two hundred books. "The harder I work, the more I make," he said. "I like that."

He didn't seem overly proud of his salary, but he didn't seem embarrassed by it either. Most of his earnings came from the 150,000 kids who watched his lectures online each year. Kim was a brand, I came to realize, with the overhead that entailed. He employed thirty people to help him manage his teaching empire. He ran a publishing company to produce his books.

To call this *tutoring* was to wildly underestimate its scale and sophistication. Megastudy, the online hagwon that Kim worked for, was listed on the Korean stock exchange. Three of every four Korean kids participated in the private market. In 2011, their parents spent almost $18 billion on cram schools, which was more than the federal government spent fighting the drug war in the United States. The so-called tutoring business was so profitable that it attracted investments from places like Goldman Sachs, the Carlyle Group, and A.I.G.

The involvement of multinational bankers in education was, generally speaking, ominous. Still, there was something thrilling about meeting Andrew Kim. For the first time, I was in the presence of a teacher who earned the kind of money professional athletes earned. Here was a teacher—*a teacher*—who was part of the 1 percent. Someone with his ambition and abilities might have become a banker or a lawyer in the United States, but in Korea, he'd become a teacher, and he was rich anyway.

The idea was seductive. What better way to guarantee that the best and brightest went into teaching than to make the greatest teachers millionaires? Maybe Korea offered a model for the world after all.

Still, the world of hagwons was mysterious. It was hard for an outsider to understand how this industry functioned—and boomed.

To learn how the business worked, I met with Lee Chae-yun, who owned a chain of five hagwons in Seoul called Myungin Academy. We had lunch in a traditional Korean restaurant, sitting on pillows and wielding metal chopsticks.

Lee understood the private and public worlds unusually well. She had been a teacher for almost two decades in public schools and in a university. But now, she sounded like a CEO.

"Students are the customers," she said.

She was speaking literally. To recruit students, hagwons held open houses, sent out mass mailings, and posted their graduates' test scores and university acceptance figures outside their entrances. In the Korean marketplace, results mattered more than anything else.

Once students enrolled, the hagwon employees did not wait for parents to get involved, then complain if they didn't; the hagwon embedded itself in their lives. Parents got text messages when their children arrived at the hagwon; then they got another message relaying students' progress. Two to three times a month, the teachers called home with feedback. If parents were not engaged, that was considered a failure of the hagwon, not the family. I had seen few U.S. schools go to such lengths to serve their so-called customers.

The most radical difference was that students signed up for specific teachers, not just hagwons, so the most respected teachers got the most students. Andrew Kim had about 120 students per lecture, though the typical teacher's hagwon classes were much smaller. The Korean private market had unbundled education down to the one in-school variable that mattered most: the teacher.

It was about as close to a pure meritocracy as it could be, and just as ruthless. In hagwons, teachers were free agents. They did not need to be certified. They didn't have benefits or even a guaranteed base salary; their pay was determined by how many students signed up for their classes, by their students' test-score growth, and, in many hagwons, by the results of satisfaction surveys given to students and parents.

To find star teachers, hagwon directors like Lee scoured the Internet, reading parents' reviews and watching teachers' lectures. Competing hagwons routinely tried to poach one another's star teachers. But, like movie stars and first-round draft picks, the big-name teachers came with baggage.

"The really good teachers are hard to retain—and hard to manage. You need to protect their egos," she said smiling.

Still, most hagwon teachers were not rock stars. Foreigners who came to teach English in Korea told stories of working exorbitant hours in unreasonable conditions for low pay. Most hagwon instructors earned much less than public-school teachers, and since Korean education colleges produced far too many would-be teachers, the competition for jobs was intense.

At Lee's hagwons, about one in five applicants made it to the in-person interview. There, she asked the candidates to teach two mock lessons while she watched, something U.S. teachers were rarely asked to do before being hired. That way, she could get a sense of whether they would be able to teach. It was a radically logical hiring strategy.

Once teachers got hired, Lee tracked their performance. If student test scores or enrollment figures dropped for a particular teacher, she put that teacher on probation. If the numbers remained low after six months, she let the teacher go. Each year, she fired about 10 percent of her instructors. (By comparison, U.S. schools dismissed about 2 percent of teachers annually for poor performance.)

In Lee's opinion, this flexibility made all the difference. She could undo hiring mistakes and motivate the rest of her teachers to work hard. Normal public-school teachers, by contrast, lacked such incentives, she said, which made them less effective and drove parental demand for hagwons. "Without hagwons, Korea would nosedive on PISA."

highest, inc.

When Eric's friend Jenny had moved back to Korea from the United States, she'd enrolled in a hagwon, like all her friends in eighth grade.

There, she'd repeated virtually everything she was supposedly learning in school during the day: Korean, math, science, and social studies. On most nights, she'd stayed at the hagwon until ten; before tests, she'd stayed until midnight.

Jenny said she'd learned more at her hagwon than she did at school. When I asked her why, she had a simple explanation: "I think they're better because they teach more effectively."

Most Korean teenagers preferred their hagwon instructors to their normal teachers. In a survey of 6,600 students at 116 high schools, Korean students gave their hagwon teachers higher scores across the board: hagwon teachers were better prepared, more devoted to teaching, and more respectful of students' opinions, they said. The hagwon teachers did best of all, students said, when it came to treating all students fairly, regardless of their academic performance.

The free-market incentives seemed to be working, at least in the opinion of the students. Teachers treated students more like customers. Was Korea proof that the burgeoning American charter-school market could work? Competition had clearly led to profits and customer-friendly practices. But did kids actually learn more in hagwons?

It was very hard to isolate what was causing Korea's PISA scores; were the regular public schools helping kids do well or the hagwons? Statistically speaking, private tutoring did seem to lead to higher test scores, especially in math, but the benefit diminished for reading as students got older. PISA data for the entire world suggested that the quality of afterschool lessons mattered more than the quantity. Outside North America and Europe, private tutoring was pervasive and, on every continent, the quality varied—a lot.

As in many free markets, price was loosely related to quality. And that was the problem.

There was a hierarchy in tutoring. Jenny's most affluent classmates went to expensive private tutors for one-on-one help. That was considered the premium service. Jenny went to a large hagwon chain called Highest, along with some of her classmates. These outfits offered tutoring for the masses. They weren't cheap, but even many poor Korean parents scraped together the money for the fees. Then there were some kids whose parents could not afford either option; they studied on their own or in after-hours programs at their schools. Eight out of ten Korean parents said they felt financial pressure from hagwon tuition costs. Still, they kept paying the fees, convinced that the more they paid, the more their children learned.

That inequity nagged at Andrew Kim. Even though this system had made him a millionaire, he didn't see it as a model for anyone. "I don't think this is the ideal way," he said. "This leads to a vicious cycle of poor families passing on poverty to their children."

He, too, thought the demand for hagwons reflected a failure of normal public schools—a popular belief that was hard to prove or disprove. Clearly, parents believed the schools were inadequate, but it was hard to know if they were right. In any case, just like Korea's minister of education, Kim believed that Finland was a much better model for the world.

In the meantime, he was making a lot of money from the vicious cycle, and he planned to continue until 2017, when his contract with Megastudy expired. After that, he wanted to give back to society, he said, maybe by helping train public-school teachers. He had a six-year-old son and didn't want him to grow up inside a pressure cooker.

the war on hagwons

I didn't meet anyone in Korea who praised the education system, not even people who were getting rich off it. The lesson seemed to be that without *equity*—meaningful opportunities for everyone, not just the elite—the system would be gamed and distorted. Parental anxieties would lead to an education arms race. The rewards for an education had gotten too great and too rare in Korea, based on metrics that were too rigid. Every year, Korean newspapers ran stories about cheating scandals involving hagwon instructors, students, and sometimes parents. In 2007, some 900 Korean students had their SAT scores canceled because of leaked test questions.

For decades, the Korean government had been trying to tame the country's culture of educational masochism. Politicians had cajoled and threatened, even going so far as to ban hagwons altogether during the 1980s, when the country was under a dictatorship. Each time, though, the hagwons came back stronger. After the government capped hagwon tuition fees, about half of hagwons flouted the rules, charging double and sometimes quintuple the allowable rates.

Nothing worked because the most powerful incentives remained the same. Korean kids gorged themselves on studying because they wanted to get into one of the country's top universities. And who could blame them? In 2007, nine out of ten Supreme Court and high court justices were alumni of Seoul National University, one of the top three. Four out of ten CEOs of major Korean companies came from the same place.

To change those incentives, Korean employers needed to change, not just Korean schools. The raw meritocracy that ruled the lives of children did not, it seemed, extend to the lives of adults.

It was impossible to say for sure, but that hierarchy may have helped explain the suicide rate in Korea, which followed an unexpected pattern. Despite all that studying, Korean teenagers did not have a high suicide rate. In fact, Korea's suicide rate for fifteen- to nineteen-year-olds was lower than that of Finland, Poland, and the United States, along with at least fourteen other countries. However, Korean adults *did* commit suicide at a very high rate. Korea's overall suicide rate was one of the highest in the world. The reasons behind a country's suicide rate were mysterious and complex, but it did seem that the worst choke points in the Korean system were in the workplaces and universities of adults, not just the classrooms of children.

Until the rest of society changed, Korean politicians would keep launching quixotic attacks against the twenty-four-hour study culture. It was like an endless game of Red Rover in which government bureaucrats repeatedly charged a wall of Korean mothers and fathers ten times as strong.

When I arrived in Korea, the government's latest maneuver was to enforce a curfew on hagwons, raiding the cram schools in the middle of the night and sending children home to bed. It was impossible to imagine government enforcers winning this round of Red Rover, but I wanted to see them come over.

on patrol with the study police

On a rainy Wednesday evening in June, Seoul's late-night study squad gathered for a patrol. The preparations for the raid were subdued. We had tea and rice crackers in a fluorescent-lit conference room, surrounded by government cubicles.

The squad leader was Cha Byoung-chul, a midlevel bureaucrat at Seoul's Gangnam district office of education. He had small oval glasses and wore a pinstriped blazer over a yellow and white shirt.

At about ten-twenty, Cha smoked a cigarette in the parking lot. "We don't leave at ten sharp," he explained, as thunder rolled across the sky. "We want to give them twenty minutes or so. That way, there are no excuses."

Hagwons caught operating after ten got three warnings. Then they had to shut down for a week. If the violation happened after midnight, the hagwon had to close immediately for two weeks. To find violators, the government had begun paying citizen tipsters. One Korean informer had reportedly earned a quarter of a million dollars just by ratting out various hagwons. Meanwhile, always quick to sense an opportunity, hagwon entrepreneurs were offering new classes on how citizens could find and report hagwon violations. On and on went the cycle of punishment and profit. So far, the government had paid out $3 million in bounties.

Finally, we piled into a silver Kia Sorento and head into Daechi-dong, one of Seoul's busiest hagwon districts. The streets were clogged with hundreds of parents picking up their children from all the hagwons that had closed in time for the curfew. The six inspectors walked along the sidewalk, staring up at the floors where hagwons were located, looking for telltale slivers of light behind drawn shades.

Around eleven, they headed toward an establishment they'd gotten calls about in the past. They climbed the dingy stairs, stepping over an empty chip bag. On the second floor, the unit's only female member knocked on the door. "Hello? Hello!" she called. A muted voice called from within: "Just a minute!"

The inspectors glanced at each other. Cha signaled to one of his colleagues to go back downstairs and block the elevator.

A moment later, a stooped, older man opened the door. He had a worried look on his face, but he let the inspectors in. They took off their shoes and walked briskly through the place.

The establishment was an after-hours self-study library, not technically a hagwon. In a den of rooms with low ceilings and fluorescent lights, about forty teenagers sat at small carrels, hard at work. When we walked through, they looked up, only half-interested, with a slightly glazed look in their eyes. The place felt claustrophobic, like a postmodern sweatshop, one that mass produced knowledge instead of T-shirts.

Self-study libraries were allowed to stay open past the curfew, but something didn't look right to Cha. The students were all studying from the same worksheets, and there were a handful of adults milling about. He suspected this was a hagwon in disguise, in a clever attempt to circumvent the curfew.

One of the adults, a middle-aged woman wearing a green T-shirt, began arguing with Cha. "We are just doing our own work here. We didn't teach," she said, frowning. Cha shook his head.

"I saw you with the students," he said.

Just then, a chubby boy, who appeared to be about fourteen, wandered out of one of the rooms. He looked around at the inspectors, cocking his head to the side. Then, shuffling along in his indoor flip-flops, he walked up to the woman in green, holding up his worksheet and starting to ask a question. She shushed him and corralled him back into the room.

Cha informed the older man that the library would likely be suspended, and directed him to come to the government office the next day. The man listened quietly, with the same pained expression on his face.

Afterward, the squad made a few more stops at other self-study libraries, but nothing seemed out of place. Around midnight, Cha stood on the corner and lit one last cigarette, staring out at the neon lights of a city that was still very much awake. Then he headed home and went to sleep, taking comfort in the satisfaction that comes with liberating forty teenagers out of 4 million.

escape from the hamster wheel

Eric would have gone anywhere, done almost anything, to get out of Korean high school. In order to comply with the requirements of his exchange program, however, he needed to remain in school. So, when he heard about a vocational college that would take foreigners, he pleaded with his exchange-program handlers to let him go. To get a spot, he would have to major in Chinese for business, but he didn't hesitate. He wanted out of the pressure cooker, and he would have studied Chinese for bowling to get there.

His first day was in March. The college was on a hill, built around a large fountain that worked intermittently. The buildings were institutional, not unlike his high school. He walked into the Chinese-for-business class and found students talking and laughing with each other. One guy was wearing skinny jeans and boots. They sat around a table and waited for the professor. A young woman named Go-un introduced herself to Eric and asked him about what he'd been doing since he'd arrived in Korea.

"I was in high school."

She looked at him for a moment. "For how long?"

"Six months."

Her eyes widened. Then she tilted her head in sympathy. "Oh, I'm so sorry. No one should have to go to Korean high school."

After class, the students lingered, chatting with each other. They asked for Eric's cell-phone number and entered it into their phones. They walked leisurely to lunch. In college, Korean students had time to talk to the American kid. They thought about things other than their test scores. They had lives, and now Eric did, too.

chapter 10

The United States Revisited: If states were countries, which countries would they be? (Map derived from analysis of math performance across states and countries in Peterson et al., Globally Challenged.)

coming home

It was snowing when Tom got the email. He was staying at a youth hostel in Poland. He read the words over and over. "We hope you will celebrate your admission to Vassar College in grand style."

Vassar was his first choice, the same school his grandmother and his brother had attended. He imagined himself studying great literature there, just as he'd pictured himself learning Chopin in Poland. He wanted to study English, and Vassar offered a freshman seminar on Virginia Woolf, his favorite author. In Poland, that spring, he re-read *Mrs. Dalloway* and *To the Lighthouse*. He couldn't wait to get to college.

In the summer of 2011, the American field agents headed home. It was a strange time in their lives, an ellipse before adulthood. Kim, Eric, and Tom had much to look forward to, assuming they went to college and graduated. When they returned to America, the cash prize for a college education was bigger in the United States than almost anywhere in the world. It might take a while, but if they got a degree, the odds were good that they would eventually get a decent job. That summer, the unemployment rate for college graduates was a temperate 4 percent. The world was big and alight for Americans with college degrees and the ability to adapt to change.

If they didn't go to college, they would earn half as much money. They would encounter an unemployment rate that was twice as high. They might still find a way into a decent job, though it was unlikely. When they went home at night, they would keep paying the price: Americans who did not graduate from college were more likely to get divorced and raise children on their own. They even died younger than college graduates.

If they walked out on high school altogether, they would enter a world of perpetual struggle, with low wages, vanishing benefits, and 14 percent unemployment. It was an unlikely fate for Kim, Eric, and Tom, but a foregone conclusion for about a quarter of their peers. By the time Kim turned twenty, there would be some six million more Americans without high-school diplomas than there would be jobs for them.

Depending on what happened next, in other words, Kim, Eric, and Tom could essentially be living in different countries than kids they'd sat next to in kindergarten. So much remained unknown about their futures, but it was becoming harder to change one's destiny in America. The tracks that had begun sorting kids in elementary school ran on and on into adulthood. Without dramatic changes in the way the country operated, the paths would not intersect.

as american as polish pie

As Tom left Poland, another American was arriving. Paula Marshall came from Oklahoma, not far from where Kim lived. She didn't come to study or sightsee, however; she came to open a factory.

Marshall ran the Bama Companies, an Oklahoma institution. Her grandmother had started selling homemade pies to local restaurants in the 1920s. Then, Paula's father had pitched a brilliant idea to McDonald's: Portable pies customers could eat in their cars. It was a profoundly American success story: a young man who turned deep-fried apples into gold.

Decades later, Paula had taken over, opening new factories in Oklahoma and China. The company had grown exponentially, supplying breadsticks to Pizza Hut and biscuits to McDonald's. Most of its one thousand employees still worked in Oklahoma.

But now, she'd come to Poland to open her next plant. There were lots of reasons, one of which was that modern factory jobs required skilled workers who knew how to think critically. The locals had assured her that she wouldn't have trouble filling jobs in Poland. "We hear that educated people are plentiful," she said.

When I met Marshall for coffee, she spoke in very practical terms about the challenge of filling jobs in the United States. Take maintenance jobs, she said. Those jobs paid twenty-five to thirty dollars per hour, but they required more skill than the title implied. Today, maintenance techs had to be able to understand technical blueprints; communicate in writing what had happened on their shifts; test possible solutions to complex, dynamic problems; and, of course, troubleshoot and repair major mechanical systems.

The Bama Companies had trouble finding enough maintenance techs in Oklahoma. Some years, they even had trouble filling their lowest-skilled line jobs, because even those workers had to be able to think and communicate. Marshall was willing to pay for employees' technical training, but she'd discovered that many people came to her unable to read or do basic math. She found that she couldn't trust a high-school diploma; graduates from different high schools within the same Oklahoma school district knew wildly different things. (The military had found the same thing, interestingly. A quarter of Oklahoma high-school graduates who tried to enlist could not pass the military's own academic aptitude test.)

To backstop the diploma, Bama's human-resources people

learned to have applicants fill out documents in front of them, so that they could see if the person really understood the questions. Then they asked candidates to respond to hypothetical scenarios to see if they could articulate their thoughts and solve problems. Finally, they administered a drug test, a background check, and a physical test and, by the time that was over, not many people were left.

In 2012, Marshall started hiring two-hundred people for a dough-making facility in Poland. She sounded optimistic. "Poland seems to me what it might have been like here in the 1800s," she said. "You get the same feeling in Shanghai. People are busy."

day one

After her year in Finland, Kim went back to Oklahoma full of complicated emotions. This time, she reminded herself, she would be different, even if everything else stayed the same. On her first day back in American high school, she wore fuzzy dog-shaped slippers. She drank a cup of the coffee she'd brought back to Oklahoma from Finland. Then she settled into an easy chair with her cat George to start online biology.

Kim loved the idea of Oklahoma Virtual High School. This way, she thought, she could recreate the autonomy she'd had in Finland. She could decide when to wake up and when to do geometry. And she could eat lunch with real forks and knives from her kitchen, just as she had in the school cafeteria in Finland.

The freedom would help motivate her, she hoped. She couldn't control things like teaching quality or equity, but she might be able to conjure autonomy and drive. And, if so, she'd be halfway to Finland, theoretically speaking.

That first day at virtual school, Kim logged in and checked her progress on a dashboard. So far, the bar graphs were all green, which meant she was on track. She had 149 days left to fall behind. She watched twenty minutes of video lectures on the basics of geometry.

Teachers were available five days a week, twenty-four hours a day. She could communicate with them over email, phone, or instant message. It was a new day, and not a terrible one.

For eight hours, she had zero live, face-to-face interactions. At three-thirty or so, her mom got home from her teaching job. At midnight, Kim was still awake, reading about colleges in Ireland, her latest dream. It didn't seem nearly as inconceivable as Finland once had. At one in the morning, she studied Mesopotamia for her World History class.

"I really, really like it," she told me on the second day, shortly after writing a report on carrier pigeons. "I don't miss people at all."

"Aren't you worried you'll be isolated?" I asked.

"People always say that," she said. "But what people forget is that I was very isolated in my American high school anyway."

This way, I began to understand, Kim was lonely on her own terms. The only downside she'd noticed so far was that she tended to personify the cat and dog. "You talk to them a lot," she admitted. "Everything they do becomes adorable."

She mitigated against insanity by joining a writer's club that met at a coffee shop in the next town. And she signed up for Irish dance lessons one evening a week. Her mom faithfully drove her there and back, grateful to have her daughter back and unsure how long she would stay. In this way, Kim still saw people on a regular basis. She missed Finland, but for now, for her, virtual reality was better than bricks and mortar.

Kim's school was run by Advanced Academics, a for-profit company headquartered in Oklahoma City that offered online courses in thirty states. That company was itself owned by DeVry, a publicly traded corporation that posted $2 billion in revenue in 2011. For Kim, virtual school was free, just like public school; most of the state money that would have normally gone to Sallisaw High School went to Advanced Academics instead.

In three years, the number of Oklahoma public-school students participating in some form of online education had grown 400 per-

cent. No one, though, knew whether the virtual schools were any better or worse than regular schools. It felt a little like the early days of
the Korean hagwon industry. Without the cultural obsession with
results, however, the analogy broke down. Was a free market really
free if no one knew the quality of the product, or even agreed as to
what the product should be?

That school year brought another milestone for Kim's state: After
decades of debate, Oklahoma had finally decided to require an end-
of-school test, just like Finland, Poland, and Korea. For the first time,
high-school seniors had to pass four out of seven tests in math, English, biology, or history to get a diploma. The *Oklahoman* newspaper
supported the move, which had been planned for seven long years: "It's
not too much to expect Oklahoma students to have a working knowledge of basic math, science and English content."

The tests were not hard. Nine out of ten Oklahoma high school
seniors were expected to pass. Those who failed could retake any of
the tests at least three times per year, take an alternate test, or complete a project instead. Special education students did not have to
score as high as other students.

Nevertheless, Oklahoma lawmakers fought over the exam all
year long. Some deemed even this baby step toward a more rigorous
education system too harsh. Democratic legislator and teacher Jerry
McPeak introduced a bill to repeal the mandate, likening the test to
child abuse: "We're going to brutalize and bully those children because they don't have the intellectual capacity of another child?"

Finland had required a matriculation test for 160 years; it was a
way to motivate kids and teachers toward a clear, common goal, and
it made a high school diploma mean something. Korea rerouted air
traffic for their graduation test. Polish kids studied for their tests on
nights and weekends, and they arrived for the exam wearing suits,
ties, and dresses.

In America, however, many people still believed in a different
standard, one that explained a great deal about the country's endur-

ing mediocrity in education: According to this logic, students who passed the required classes and came to school the required number of days should receive their diplomas, regardless of what they had learned or what would happen to them when they tried to get a job at the Bama Companies. Those kids deserved a chance to fail later, not now. It was a perverse sort of compassion designed for a different century.

This time, Oklahoma state superintendent Janet Barresi held fast. "If we keep rolling these limits back, students are not going to take this seriously," she said. "I'm more concerned with a student's ability to get a job than about their ability to walk across the stage with their buddies."

That spring, fewer than 5 percent of Oklahoma's 39,000 high school seniors failed to meet the new graduation requirements, far fewer than many superintendents had predicted. Oklahoma's kids had been wildly underestimated. (Interestingly, the failure rate resembled the roughly 6 percent of seniors who did not pass Finland's far more rigorous graduation exam.)

In Oklahoma, some students appealed their results, and their local school boards granted them diplomas, citing extenuating circumstances of one kind or another. Flexibility was built into the system. Still, school boards across Oklahoma protested the tests, passing resolutions and calling for mercy. "There are some kids that just can't test well. And this is terribly unfair to them," the Owasso school board president told the *Tulsa World*. The fact that students had many different options, including completing a project instead of taking a test, did not assuage her concerns.

When Kim finished her first school year back in America, the United States was ranked number seven in the World Economic Forum's list of global competitiveness. That was a very high ranking indeed, though it had fallen for four consecutive years. The country that ranked number three? A small, remote Nordic land with few resources, aside from something the locals called *sisu*.

a freshman in america

When Tom returned to Gettysburg from Poland, he put himself on a strict regimen of reading one hundred pages per day. That summer, he pushed through Michel Foucault, just to see if he could. He quit smoking. Still, he missed being able to wander the streets of a sprawling city and drink lukewarm Polish beer with his friends as the sun set over Wrocław. Back in Gettysburg, he wanted to have his friends over at midnight the first night he came home, and his parents wondered if he'd lost his mind. He wanted to linger at coffee shops; Gettysburg's cafés closed at dusk. He asked his mother, Gettysburg's chief public defender, to buy him beer; she said no.

That fall, he packed up his books and his indie band t-shirts and moved to Poughkeepsie, New York. When he got to Vassar, he moved into an old, red brick dormitory with a peaked roof, located right on the grassy quad. It was quintessentially collegiate in all the right ways. His roommate decorated the walls with Christmas lights and Tibetan prayer flags. Tom signed up for the Virginia Woolf seminar, just as he'd planned, and started seeing a girl who lived two doors down from him.

When classes started, however, he had an uncomfortable sensation. Sitting in the Woolf seminar, he realized he wasn't quite as prepared as he'd expected. Four out of ten Vassar students had attended private schools, including elite boarding schools in the Northeast. They seemed to have a fluency in analyzing literature that he didn't possess. They made casual references to Greek mythology that Tom didn't catch. One student described *Jacob's Room* as starting *in media res,* as if everyone knew what that meant. They'd read Virgil, but he had not. It was unnerving.

At the same time, eight hundred miles away, Eric was experiencing the opposite sensation.

He'd moved to Chicago to attend DePaul University. He knew from his year in Korea that he felt most alive in the clamor of a big city, a place where he knew he could eat sushi at four in the morning—

whether or not he ever chose to. He was looking forward to studying politics and philosophy. But, that fall, when he sat down in the writing course required of all freshmen, he'd discovered something surprising. He was actually *over*prepared.

It was not like the Virginia Woolf seminar at Vassar. This class was taught by graduate students and designed to bring all students up to a baseline level of competence. Eric was bored. It was just like elementary school math class all over again, when he'd amused himself by answering addition problems in the shape of his initials.

Eric had already learned how to formulate a thesis and conduct basic research in his high school back in Minnesota; he'd assumed everyone else had learned those things, too. Sitting in the DePaul class, his notebook empty, he felt himself deflate, like a freshman balloon drifting back to earth.

In college, Eric and Tom were witnessing firsthand the same variation that defined schools across the United States and the world, the reason for this book. When the students edited each other's work, Eric got to read his classmates' writing. He discovered that many did not know how to structure an essay, develop an argument, or clearly communicate an idea. The writing was disjointed, and the grammar shabby. It wasn't that these students were unwilling or unable to do better; it was that they'd never learned how.

Eric found other, smaller classes that he liked better. He explored Chicago. And he started thinking about transferring to a different college. It had worked in Korea, so maybe it would work in America, too.

In Tom's case, he adapted easily; he read Virgil. He looked up *in media res* and discovered it was a Latin phrase that referred to starting a story in the middle of the plot. He caught up quickly, and by spring, he could toss off his own allusions to Greek mythology in his English classes. He figured out that a lot of the banter had been bullshit, but he'd needed to learn the vernacular. By the end of his freshman year, he was working on a paper with his classics professor about the Roman poet, Catullus.

But he had a glimpse of what might have been. If his mom and dad hadn't taken him to Barnes & Noble as a regular Friday night ritual, if he hadn't devoured literature on his own, he might not have gotten into the habit of reading deeply every day. Without that practice, he realized, he would have certainly been overwhelmed at Vassar. It wouldn't have mattered that he'd taken AP English at Gettysburg High School; it wouldn't have mattered that he'd gotten good grades. He needed more rigor than his schools had to offer. Luckily for him, he had found it on his own.

a korean in new jersey

Like Kim, Jenny was still in high school back in America. They both had two more years until graduation. Jenny had bounced back and forth between Korea and the United States before, so she had some idea what to expect when her family moved to central New Jersey in the summer of 2011. She figured school would be much more humane than it was for her and Eric back at Namsan High School, and she was correct. Her classes were easier; her teachers and her classmates were more relaxed.

Still, there were surprises.

During the first Algebra II test that fall, the girl sitting next to her complained that she didn't understand one of the problems. Jenny had answered it quickly, probably because she'd learned the material two years earlier. But the girl kept saying she needed help. Then something amazing happened: The teacher came over to help her! Right there in front of everyone he walked her through the solution—*during the test*.

Jenny watched, speechless. She wondered what would happen when that girl took the SAT without the teacher there to help. Later, a boy in her class did the same thing and, again, the teacher came over to help. Jenny rolled her eyes. She wished her Korean friends could see this; she looked forward to telling them the story on Skype when she got home.

Not everything was easier in American high school. That was

another surprise. That spring, Jenny discovered that kids at schools across America took something called the Presidential Fitness Test in gym class. It had been around for decades, and all that time, the standards had been impressively, almost inexplicably, high.

To meet the award benchmarks, Jenny and her classmates had to run an eight-minute mile and do forty-four sit-ups in sixty seconds. Bouncing off the floor between sit-ups was strictly prohibited; there were no short cuts in presidential fitness, unlike in algebra. The boys had to do thirteen pull-ups, and the girls had to do twenty-five push-ups. It didn't count toward her gym grade, but a lot of the students, and the gym teacher, took it seriously, as if they were training for a real test.

Jenny couldn't believe it. Twenty-five push-ups was not a joke. Why were the expectations so high? And why, given these expectations, did America have such an obesity problem?

Back in Korea, Jenny had taken a similar physical test in gym class, but the standards were lower. Instead of eight minutes to run a mile, kids were allotted nine-and-a-half minutes. And none of them cared about it anyway; they just walked around the track. They were worried about their math tests.

The irony was not lost on Jenny, who told her friends back home about the crazy intense American gym test. "For physical things, the standards are higher here. For studying, the standards are higher in Korea!"

Luckily, she felt confident she would pass the fitness test in New Jersey. She'd been training for it, after all, just like she used to train for math in Korea. She knew by then that meeting high expectations was mostly a matter of hard work.

hamster wheels and stoner kids

When I got back to the States at the end of the school year, I spent a long time trying to make sense of what I'd seen. I was amazed by how many of our problems were universal. Everywhere I'd gone, teachers had complained about tests, principals, and parents; parents, in turn, had agonized over their children's education, relying on fear and emotion when they could not get facts. Politicians had lamented unions, and union leaders had lamented politicians.

Kids, meanwhile, were kids, as Jenny had told Eric on the bus that day in Busan, Korea. They had teachers they liked and teachers they didn't. They played video games, texted in class, and watched television in every country I'd visited. What was different, more than anything else, was how seriously they took their education. That dedication fluctuated like an EKG line, depending on where children lived.

Why did they care? Kim had asked the question in Finland, distilling this quest down to one sentence. After visiting her, I started to suspect that the answer was fairly straightforward: They took school more seriously because it *was* more serious. And it was more serious because everyone agreed it should be.

There was a consensus in Finland, Korea, and Poland that all children had to learn higher-order thinking in order to thrive in the world. In every case, that agreement had been born out of crisis: economic imperatives that had focused the national mind in a way that good intentions never would. That consensus about rigor had then changed everything else.

High school in Finland, Korea, and Poland had a purpose, just like high-school football practice in America. There was a big, important contest at the end, and the score counted. Their teachers were more serious, too: highly educated, well-trained, and carefully chosen. They had enough autonomy to do serious work; that meant they had a better chance of adapting and changing along with their students and the economy. The students had independence, too, which made school more bearable and cultivated more driven, self-sufficient high school graduates. The closer they got to adulthood, the more they got to act like adults.

In the United States and other countries, we'd put off this reckoning, convinced that our kids would always get second and third chances until well into adulthood. We had the same attitude toward teachers: Anyone and everyone could become a teacher, as long as they showed up for class, followed the rules, and had good intentions. We had the schools we wanted, in a way. Parents did not tend to show up at schools demanding that their kids be assigned more challenging reading or that their kindergarteners learn math while they still loved numbers. They did show up to complain about bad grades, however. And they came in droves, with video cameras and lawn chairs and full hearts, to watch their children play sports.

That mindset had worked alright for most American kids, historically speaking. Most hadn't needed a very rigorous education, and they hadn't gotten it. Wealth had made rigor optional in America. But everything had changed. In an automated, global economy, kids needed to be driven; they need to know how to adapt, since they would be doing it all their lives. They needed a culture of rigor.

There were different ways to get to rigor, and not all of them were good. In Korea, the hamster wheel created as many problems as it solved. Joyless learning led mostly to good test scores, not to a resilient population. That kind of relentless studying could not be sustained, and there was evidence that Korean kids' famous drive dropped off dramatically once they got to college.

Still, if I had to choose between the hamster wheel and the moon bounce that characterized many schools in the United States and other countries—a false choice, needless to say—I think I'd reluctantly choose the hamster wheel. It was relentless and excessive, yes, but it also felt more honest. Kids in hamster-wheel countries knew what it felt like to grapple with complex ideas and think outside their comfort zone; they understood the value of persistence. They knew what it felt like to fail, work harder, and do better. They were prepared for the modern world.

In the moon bounce, kids were being misled. Too much of the time, they were being fed a soft diet of pabulum by middling professionals. If they failed, there were few obvious consequences. Only later, after high school, would they discover they'd been tricked. The real world did not always give second and third chances; the real world didn't give credit just for showing up. When things were hard, your math teacher didn't materialize to give you the answer.

Learning had become a currency, the kind that bought freedom. It wasn't all that mattered in life, but it mattered more than ever. In that sense, countries like Finland—and Canada and New Zealand— had tapped into the ultimate natural resource. Their children were freer in some ways than kids in the hamster-wheel countries, because they'd gotten smarter without sacrificing the rest of their lives.

When it came to happiness, Finland ranked second (after Denmark) in the 2012 World Happiness Report commissioned by the United Nations. The Finns had many reasons to be happy, including the fact that education increased income, and income increased happiness. "If you want the American dream," United Kingdom Labour Party leader Ed Miliband said at a social mobility conference in 2012, "go to Finland." In the twenty-first century, it was easier for a poor person to get a great education in Finland than in almost any country in the world including the United States (number eleven in happiness).

When I thought about the future of education, I worried about kids like Kim, kids who had been underserved and underinspired by the system for years. I wondered what would happen to the stoner kids in Finland—and Oklahoma. I also felt more hopeful, though, than before I'd left. It was obvious that no country had figured this problem out; everyplace had problems, most of them fixable.

One thing was clear: To give our kids the kind of education they deserved, we had to first agree that rigor mattered most of all; that school existed to help kids learn to think, to work hard, and yes, to fail. That was the core consensus that made everything else possible.

I came back to a country humbled by recession and splintered by politics. Did this moment represent enough of a crisis for America? Would this be our Finland hour? Our Korean revelation? When we would decide once and for all that a real education is a *hard* education for everyone, including teachers, rich kids, and poor kids? Top-down policy changes, from No Child Left Behind under President George W. Bush to Race to the Top under President Barack Obama, had tried to impose rigor on the U.S. system, to inject it forcibly into faltering schools and homes across the country. That could lift the floor but not the ceiling. People had to believe in rigor; they had to decide, maybe under duress, that it was time to get serious. They could be nudged into this revelation, but they had to experience it.

But would they?

When I returned, most Americans seemed to feel the urgency, the unsettling proximity of change and competition. That wasn't enough, historically speaking. After all, most countries experiencing economic distress had not done what Korea, Finland, and Poland had. They had lacked the leadership or the luck to see that economic and social well-being depended on the combined intellectual health of regular citizens and that the *only* way to get smart was to work hard and learn well.

In 2014, Oklahoma was scheduled to roll out a set of more rigorous, coherent, and clear standards, called the Common Core. The standards, which had been adopted in forty-four other states, were designed to teach kids to think. They were shaped by international benchmarks as to what children should know. Yet this change, too, had come under attack by Oklahoma lawmakers. "The Common Core State Standards are federalization of education and this violates local control," Republican state representative Sally Kern told her fellow lawmakers, urging them to reject the standards.

As Kim, Eric, and Tom finished their first school year back in America, no one could say there was a consensus around rigor. In a culture plagued by distractions, from digital white boards to self-esteem building to high school football, that clarity of purpose was hard to find. But not impossible.

boys without backpacks, girls without f's

William Taylor taught math in a traditional public school in Washington, D.C. He had grown up in D.C, and he'd always loved math. As a brand-new teacher, he'd happened to land in a school with a principal who understood the importance of rigor. She was not perfect, but she taught him important things; she taught him, for example, never to send misbehaving students into the hallway as a form of punishment. Find another way to get them to behave.

School was not a good-behavior factory; it was a learning factory. That was her vision, and it was clear. If kids were in the hallway, they were not learning.

She also taught him never to let a child leave school without a backpack. Where was their work? School was about learning; work mattered. These little boys and girls lived in a neighborhood where one of every five adults was unemployed; every student at that school was African-American, and most were poor or close to it. These children had to do a lot of learning if they were going to make it. Their backpacks were like lifejackets, and they would surely drown without them.

After a couple of years, Taylor became an exceptionally strong math teacher. Year after year, his students' knowledge advanced more than one grade level in his class. When they left, they were at or above grade level. They had also learned about hard work, which was just as important.

Will Taylor believed in rigor and embedded it in his classroom. He wasn't a hero; he just believed that kids were smarter and tougher than other people assumed, and he acted accordingly. He was also good at his job, and he had a boss who made him better. Under D.C.'s complex teacher evaluation scheme, Taylor was even paid according to his value, a rarity in schools worldwide. He had been rated highly effective three times in a row, an unusual and mighty feat. Thanks to controversial bonus schemes put into place under former Chancellor

Michelle Rhee, Taylor was earning six figures. He had just bought his first house.

In 2011, Taylor transferred to a new public school in an equally troubled corner of D.C. He was excited to be there. The principal was warm and supportive, the teachers were enthusiastic, and the parents seemed relatively involved. It took him a while to discover the airless void where the rigor should have been.

Taylor did what he'd always done: He taught his students all kinds of games, hand gestures, and systems to help them learn without wasting time. He used tricks to make sure he was calling on all of them, and he grouped the kids together strategically, so that they could help each other when he could not.

In the first few weeks, he had to spend more time than usual getting his students to take his class seriously and control their behavior. But once he got their respect, he didn't have to ask for it again.

Then, one day, a little girl who rarely spoke walked up to him and said something important.

"My mother wants to know why you gave me an F."

Taylor looked down at her over his tiny wire-frame glasses, unblinking.

"I didn't give you an F," he said. "You earned an F."

"Well, I try," she said quietly.

"I don't grade you on effort. I grade you on results."

Taylor did not change the girl's grade. He did not believe in setting kids up for failure. He believed in telling kids the truth.

He asked around and found out that some of his colleagues were basing 60 percent of students' grades on effort alone. *Sixty percent.* Who was going to tell these kids that effort didn't count on the SAT? Math counted, and there *was* a right answer.

Soon, he started hearing other complaints from parents. He was sending kids home with books, and they didn't like it. The books were too heavy, and the homework was too hard. He asked the other teachers why they didn't send books home, too. They told him the kids wouldn't take care of the books. Taylor raised his eyebrows. How could they learn without books?

He started noticing other things. When he walked the halls, he routinely saw students standing outside classroom doors doing nothing. Usually they were boys, young African-American boys who reminded him of himself. He asked them what they were doing, and they told him they'd been ejected for misbehaving.

One afternoon, watching the students shuffle, slink, and run out the front doors of the school into the world, Taylor noticed something that made his heart sink. Most were not wearing backpacks at all.

The little girl got an F on her report card that semester. But after that, it was as if she woke up. She started to do the homework. She made fewer excuses. She formed a study group with some of the other kids and came into the classroom at lunchtime to work. The next semester, she got a D. By the end of the year, she had a C in math.

When Taylor told her the grade, she started crying. "I cannot believe I did this," she said. And he could tell her, in total honesty, "You did."

desert warriors

There are teachers like Taylor all over America. There are even whole schools built around the ideals of rigorous learning and telling children the truth. These are countercultural places, though, with leaders who spend a lot of time convincing parents that their children are tougher than they think.

At BASIS public charter schools in Arizona and Washington, D.C., teachers train students for academic conquests the way most American high schools train football players for Friday night games. On the day of Advanced Placement exams, each student files into the classroom to the *Rocky* theme song, "Eye of the Tiger."

In 2012, teenagers at two Arizona BASIS schools took a special new version of the PISA test designed to compare schools to international benchmarks. Until then, PISA had only shown nationwide or statewide results, not individual school outcomes.

The results were breathtaking. The average BASIS student not only outperformed the typical U.S. student (by nearly three years in reading and science and *four years* in math) but outscored the average student in Finland, Korea, and Poland, as well. These kids even did better than the average student from Shanghai, China, the region that had ranked number one in the world on PISA in 2009.

Without a doubt, American teenagers can perform at the top of the world on a sophisticated test of critical thinking. Students at traditional public high schools that took the test in Fairfax, Virginia, also trounced teenagers around the world.

On the same test, however, students from another U.S. high school in a western state performed worse than teenagers in twenty-three countries in math. The PISA organizers did not release the name of this school, but it had no obvious excuses. The school was mostly white and middle class; only 6 percent of its students were living anywhere near the poverty line. Its home state had just awarded it an A letter grade. And yet fewer than one in ten students performed at a high level of critical thinking in math, compared to six in ten students at BASIS. Teenagers at that school scored below teenagers in Finland, Korea, and Poland, not to mention the Slovak Republic and Estonia.

The parents at that school may never know about these results, but the students will find out, one way or another. If not as freshmen in college, when they are placed in remedial math or struggle to follow a basic physics lecture, then in the workforce, when they misinterpret a graph at the bank where they work or miscalculate a drug dosage at a hospital nursing station. This revelation—that they lack tools that have become essential in the modern economy—will in all likelihood arrive privately, a kind of sinking shame that they cannot entirely explain. They may experience it as a personal failing, though I hope they don't.

I hope they experience it as an outrage instead. Maybe, unlike generations before them, these young Americans will decide that their own children, like children in Finland, deserve to be taught by the best-educated, best-trained professionals in the world. They might realize that if Korean kids can learn to fail and try again before leaving high school, so can their kids. Perhaps they will conclude that Poland is not the only place where change is possible.

History shows us that great leaders matter, and so does luck. Politics are critical, as is power. All major shifts, though, also require a feeling that spreads among people like a whispered oath, kitchen table by kitchen table, until enough of them agree that something must be done.

The stories of Finland, Korea, and Poland are complicated and unfinished. But they reveal what is possible. All children must learn rigorous higher-order thinking to thrive in the modern world. The only way to do that is by creating a serious intellectual culture in schools, one that kids can sense is real and true. As more and more data spills out of schools and countries, and as students themselves find ways to tell the world how much more they could do, these counternarratives will, I hope, become too loud to bear.

author's note

Writing this book was a blatant escape attempt. In the early twenty-first century, the debates about education in the United States had become, in my opinion, so nasty, provincial, and redundant that they no longer led anywhere worth going. I wanted to wander off, as far away as I could, and see if the conversation changed.

The data gave me the perfect excuse: A small number of countries had taught almost all of their children higher-order thinking. How had that happened? What was stopping it from happening elsewhere? I didn't care deeply about charter schools, vouchers, tenure, or other policy hang-ups. The grown-ups were looking inward, sniping at one another in hotel ballrooms and city halls, while billions of children were learning to reason and solve problems—*or not*—all around the world. So, I thought, I'll just slip out the back door and go investigate this other mystery for a while.

It took about six months before I realized I was nuts. Writing about one foreign country is hard; writing about three is borderline fraudulent. A stranger who parachutes into a faraway country ends up, as the Koreans would say, "licking the outside of a watermelon," unable to get beneath the surface into what matters.

I needed a lot of help: about as many people, in front and behind the scenes, as a Broadway musical. Only I didn't have a Broadway budget. And even though I had little to offer them, people did remarkable things. I think they did it because they thought the mystery mattered. Or maybe it was pity. They could see that I would never be able to navigate the labyrinth of data and other countries' bureaucracies without them. In the end, more than a hundred people around the world—researchers, teachers, translators, fixers, politicians, business people, diplomats, students, and parents—helped me find my way.

From beginning to end, I relied most of all on Kim, Eric, Tom, and Jenny, the young people who took me inside their schools and homes on three continents and patiently explained what they knew—again and again. Without them, I never would have glimpsed the ordinary lives of kids and families, the scenes that make it possible to understand why policy works or, more often, misses the mark totally. They answered thousands of tedious and sometimes foolish questions, by Skype, phone, email, Facebook, text message, and in person. They sat patiently outside of Buddhist temples, in high-school hallways, and in hotel lobbies while I recorded them talking about their experiences (in video snippets now archived on www.AmandaRipley.com). They let me talk to their families, their teachers, and their friends. I am sure I embarrassed them in ways I will never realize. I kept waiting for them to roll their eyes and storm off, but they never did.

I visited Kim, Tom, Eric, and Jenny in person in Finland, Poland, and Korea. I also visited Kim and Tom's hometowns in the United States. Whenever I was not able to witness a scene in person, I used interviews, newspaper clips, and other historical documents to help me reconstruct it as accurately as I could. I owe a particular debt to Kim and Tom for their richly detailed, thoughtfully written blogs, which filled in any holes left over from our conversations. (Kim's blog is cited in the bibliography under Kim; Tom's blog is not cited because the url includes his last name.)

One lesson from this experience was that reporting about young people has become alarmingly easy; many teenagers (though not all) leave a long, meandering trail of digital footprints that they may one day come to regret. I, for one, am very glad that the VHS tape my friend made of me pretending to be a newscaster when I was twelve is not on YouTube.

For this reason, I decided not to include the last names of the teenagers featured in this book. They exhibited levels of self-awareness and modesty that I don't see in most of the adults that I interview. But, just in case, I wanted to give them a chance to change their minds, to reinvent themselves and tell their own stories one day.

The parents of these young informants took a risk in letting them talk to me. I am so grateful for their trust. In some cases, they spent hours talking to me about their children and their own theories about parenting and education in America and abroad. My sincere thanks, as well, to everyone at AFS, Youth for Understanding, the Rotary Clubs, and CSIET, who graciously connected me to exchange students all over the world.

Arranging for young people to live and study thousands of miles from home is a complicated, risky business; the people who do it well are dedicated to the simple idea that the world is a big and wondrous place, and the sooner we teach our children about it, the better off we all will be.

For believing that it was possible to write a not-boring book about education and never giving up on that radical idea, I want to thank my longtime editor and friend, Priscilla Painton, along with Jonathan Karp, and the rest of his team at Simon & Schuster. Thank you for making it possible to go on far-flung quests and share the treasures with the rest of the world.

My longtime agent, Esmond Harmsworth, wisely insisted that I find characters before I did anything else. Thank you, Esmond, for saving me from years of suffering, and for supporting this idea from beginning to end. The very talented and wise Dan Baum rescued me from a writing quagmire, reminding me that stories matter most of all.

To make a living as a long-form writer today requires a crowd of sponsors. Without the support of the Bernard L. Schwartz Fellowship, Laurene Powell Jobs, Stacey Rubin, and the Emerson Collective, and all the advice and encouragement of Steve Coll, Andrés Martinez, Faith Smith, and Caroline Esser at the New America Foundation, this book would never have gotten off the ground. Special thanks are due to Marie Lawrence, a smart and meticulous researcher at New America, who made the AFS survey happen and contributed reams of valuable analysis on child poverty and the primacy of high-school sports in America. Thank you as well to Rebecca Shafer, a former teacher and New America staffer, who helped make sense of the research into special education around the world.

The seeds of many of these stories came from magazine articles, the kind that take a long time to write, a lot of effort to edit, and significant real estate when they get published. Thank you many times over to Michael Duffy, Nancy Gibbs, and Rick Stengel at *Time* magazine, and to James Gibney, Scott Stossel, Corby Kummer, and James Bennet at *The Atlantic* for helping me tell the stories of kids, teachers, and parents around the world, before and after this book came out.

The data gurus at the OECD, including Andreas Schleicher, do vitally important work that is not easy to understand. I thank them for helping me all along the way. At times of great confusion, I also got valuable guidance from the good people at the Education Trust, AIR, the U.S. Department of Education, and the Embassies and Ministries of Education of Finland, Poland, and South Korea.

School leaders in Seoul and Busan, Korea; Wrocław and Warsaw, Poland; Helsinki, Espoo, and Pietarsaari, Finland, as well as in Gettysburg, Pennsylvania, Washington, D.C., and Sallisaw, Oklahoma, graciously allowed me to see their schools up close. Many teachers in many countries, including Binh Thai from New York City, Lynn Hommeyer and Will Taylor from Washington, D.C., and Sung Soon Oh from Busan, Korea, spent precious time explaining their worlds to me, complicating the picture in critical ways.

For translation and research in Poland, I relied heavily on the intrepid and insightful Mateusz Kornacki. In Korea, Stephen Kim, an outstanding translator and agile reporter, led me through schools, hagwons, and government offices in two cities at all hours. I also received translation and research assistance from Justine Jablonska and Theresa Buchstätter in Washington, D.C., Jenni Santaholma in Helsinki, Finland, and Sarah Zarrow in Warsaw, Poland. For fact checking a fact-dense book, I thank the indomitable Rachael Brown for her conscientious and smart work.

For the second time, Kaitlyn Andrews-Rice, a woman who can do damn near anything, helped me brainstorm, research, and refine this book. Thank you, Kaitlyn, for telling me straight up what was boring and what was not.

No one finishes a book, as far as I can tell, without friends, colleagues, and family who listen to them talk about it ad nauseam. Romesh Ratnesar, Lesley Chilcott, Michael Schaffer, Dave Ripley, Ben Ripley, Ta-Nehisi Coates, Robert Gordon, Lisa Green, Rachel Dolin, Steven Farr, Karen Marsh, Lennlee Keep, and Courtney Rubin each helped me figure out what this book was about and why it mattered. Kate Walsh at the National Council on Teacher Quality provided generous and helpful guidance on the preparation of American teachers. Timothy Daly from TNTP helped me translate what I'd seen for U.S. consumption. My dear friend Catherine Brown spent many years and jogging miles brainstorming, commiserating, and guiding me toward the finish line. Thank you, Catarina.

John, my husband and best friend, helped imagine this book, and he made it better at every stage along the way. He has listened to more rants about education dysfunction than any human should have to endure. And he did me the enormous twenty-first century favor of telling me I could work for myself, and showing me how it was done (with grace, grit, and a habit of literally knocking on wood). My son, Max, drew cover-jacket mock-ups, rejected many titles, researched countries on his globe, and understood what I was trying to do better than most people well over the age of six.

My mom, Louise Ripley, died while I was writing this book. Many years ago, she taught elementary school in Iowa—a job she loved. She believed that education was a serious pursuit, never to be left to chance. She believed it fiercely. This book is dedicated to her spirit—one part empathy, two parts fight.

appendix I

how to spot a
world-class education

Like most reporters, I'd rather not give advice; I prefer to just relate other people's stories and let you form your own conclusions. That is better for everyone.

And yet. Everywhere I go, parents ask me for specific action items that they can actually use in real life. They ask me at the supermarket, they ask me at the playground. It's as if they live in the real world, where prose is not all that matters.

In most countries, most parents have some choice as to where to send their children to school. It is a very hard choice, however, and useful information is shamefully hard to find. So, here is my best attempt to deliver what the people want.

Every child is different. An outstanding school for one child would be hell on earth for another. Still, when it comes to finding a school that is both rigorous and alive, full of spirit and learning, there are a few reliable questions to ask. Here is my cheat sheet to finding a world-class school based on what I have seen from visiting schools on four continents, listening to kids, teachers, and parents and studying the research of other, smarter people than myself. It is incomplete, but it is a start.

watch the students

If you are trying to understand a school, you can ignore most of the information you are given. Open houses? Pretty much useless. Spending per student? Beyond a certain baseline level, money does not translate into quality in education anywhere. The smartest countries in the world spend less per pupil than the United States.

Average class size? Not as important as most people think, except in the earliest years of schooling. In fact, the highest-performing countries typically have larger classes than the United States. The research shows that the quality of the teaching matters more than the size of the class.

Test data? More helpful, but very hard to decipher in most places. How good is the test? How much value is the school adding beyond what kids are already learning at home? More and more U.S. school districts have this kind of information, but do not make it public.

Instead, the best way to gauge the quality of a school is to spend time—even just twenty minutes—visiting classrooms while school is in session.

When you get there, though, it's important to know where to look. Parents tend to spend a lot of time staring at the bulletin boards in classrooms. Here is a better idea: Watch the students instead.

Watch for signs that *all* the kids are paying attention, interested in what they are doing, and working hard. Don't check for signs of order; sometimes learning happens in noisy places where the kids are working in groups without much input from the teacher. Some of the worst classrooms are quiet, tidy places that look, to adults, reassuringly calm.

Remember that rigorous learning actually looks rigorous. If the kids are whizzing through a worksheet, that's not learning. That's filling out a form. Kids should be uncomfortable sometimes; that's okay. They should not be frustrated or despairing; instead, they should be getting help when they need it, often from each other. They should not spend long, empty stretches of time getting in line for lunch, sitting down for circle time, or handing out papers. There should be a sense of urgency that you can feel.

Resist the urge to focus on the teacher. In the best classrooms in the world, the teacher might be quiet. Or charismatic or even a tiny bit crazy (as most of us remember from our own school days). What you think of the teacher during a short visit is not as important as what the kids think after watching her all year.

I did this in every nation I visited. How interested were the students in my arrival? Engaged kids didn't take much notice; they had more important things to do. Bored kids looked back and smiled, offered a shy wave, and handed me a tissue if I sneezed. Their time was being wasted, and they were desperate for a distraction.

I saw bored kids in every country. Boredom is the specter that haunts children from kindergarten to graduation on every continent. In American classrooms, I watched a girl draw a beautiful rose tattoo on her arm with a ballpoint pen; she did it slowly, meticulously, as though she were serving a life sentence. I saw a young boy dance silently in his bright white high-tops under his desk. His upper body never moved.

In Finland, I saw a teenage boy take unusual interest in the cord of the window blinds next to him, as if it were a ripcord that might parachute him into another place. In Korea, I saw rows of students sleeping—flat-out REM sleeping—with their heads upon the desks. Some had pillows. Korea was where boredom went to sleep, and got up later to study all night.

Boredom varied wildly from one classroom to the next, usually within the same school. In the best schools, though, boredom was the exception rather than the norm. You could walk into five classrooms and see just one or two students who had drifted away, mentally or physically, rather than eight or ten. That's how you know that you are in a place of learning.

talk to the students

People, including reporters, rarely ask students for their insight. Everyone focuses on the teacher, the principal, the building, or the bulletin boards. Young kids are thought to be too small to understand; older kids are presumed to be too jaded. Neither is true, in my experience. As long as you ask intelligent questions, students are the most candid and helpful sources in any school.

Don't ask, "Do you like this teacher?" or "Do you like your school?" What if a tall, smiling stranger came to your office and asked, "Do you like your boss?" You'd wonder if he was a consultant brought in to fire you. Kids have the same reaction. And in any case, liking a teacher is not the same as learning from a teacher. Instead, ask questions that are specific, respectful, and meaningful.

The first thing I usually ask is straightforward: *What are you doing right now? Why?*

You'd be amazed how many kids can answer the first question but not the second. The second question is imperative, however. To buy into school, kids need to be reminded of the purpose all day, everyday.

In 2011, an epic Gates Foundation research study found that kids' answers to specific questions were surprisingly predictive of student test-score growth and more reliable over time than classroom observations by trained observers. Tens of thousands of students of all ages were asked to agree or disagree with thirty-six different items on that particular survey (the Tripod Survey designed by Ronald Ferguson at Harvard). When you are visiting a school, you obviously cannot conduct a scientifically valid survey like this. But the questions that most correlated with student learning in that study might help shape questions that would be worth asking anyway. For example:

1. In this class, do you learn a lot every day?
2. Do students in this class usually behave the way your teacher wants them to?
3. Does this class stay busy and not waste time?

Those are the kinds of questions that students—and only students—can answer.

Some schools have started using variations of this same survey to help teachers improve, a smart and relatively cheap idea. If a principal or teacher uses this kind of classroom-level survey *and* spends significant time studying the results and learning to do better, that is a promising sign.

And here's one more question to ask students, this one supplied by Dwan Jordon, former principal of John P. Sousa Middle School in Washington, D.C.: *If you don't understand something, what do you do?*

In rigorous classrooms, kids know the answer.

listen to the parents

In 2011, I took a tour of a Washington, D.C., private school that was hard to get into and cost about $30,000 a year. I really couldn't afford the school, but I'd already visited many public schools and charter schools, and I wanted to know what my child might be missing.

Sunlight streamed through the skylights. As I walked down the hall, the sound of kids learning in different languages filtered out into the hallway. There were muffins in the principal's office. It felt like a learning spa—a parent's dream.

But strange things happened on this visit. When the head of the school talked, nothing she said made sense to me. There was a lot of jargon about the curriculum and vague promises of wondrous field trips and holistic projects. All the visiting parents nodded; I got the sense that no one wanted to say anything off key that might hurt a child's admission chances.

Then a parent with three children at this school took us for a tour. We saw gleaming floors, bright, colorful walls, beautiful, framed art projects, and other seductive tokens. Finally, one visiting father asked a good question:

"Every school has its weaknesses. What is this school's weakness?"

I lifted my head, straining to hear what our tour guide would say.

"You know, I'd have to say the math program is weak."

I was speechless. Imagine visiting a tony private hospital that only admitted healthy patients who could afford its services, and finding out the surgery practice was weak. What did it mean if the math program was weak at a school that made small children take I.Q. tests before they were even accepted? That particular parent wrote a check each year for about $90,000 to this school to cover the tuition for her three children. Wouldn't she demand decent math classes in exchange?

But no one said anything. Maybe all the parents were stunned, as I was. Then the tour guide parent added one more thing:

"Oh, and I wish the football program was stronger."

Suddenly, the parents perked up.

"Really, what do you mean? Is there not a football team? What age does it start?"

I wandered out into the parking lot, mystified. Perhaps this explained why our most affluent kids scored eighteenth in math compared to affluent kids worldwide: Even wealthy American parents didn't care about math as much as football.

That was a big difference between America and Finland, Korea, and Poland. In the world's education superpowers, parents agreed that a rigorous education was critical to their kids' life chances.

Wherever you live, if you can find a community or school where parents and educators share this baseline belief, then you have found something more valuable to more children than the best football program on earth.

As you search for a world-class school, ask parents at each place to talk about the school's weaknesses. Listen carefully. If parents say they are very involved in the school, ask them *how*. American parents tend to be more involved in school than parents in the education superpowers, but not, generally speaking, in ways that lead to learning.

Raising money, going to soccer games, and serving on teacher-appreciation committees are wonderful things to do. They do not, however, tend to impact the quality of your child's education, as documented throughout this book.

Around the world, parents have dramatic influence on how their children learn. But Parent Teacher Association meetings are not where that learning happens. The research shows that parents who are most active in their children's schools do not tend to raise smarter children. The real impact happens mostly at home.

Parents who view themselves as educational coaches tend to read to their children every day when they are small; when their children get older, they talk with them about their days and about the news around the world. They let their children make mistakes and then get right back to work. They teach them good habits and give them autonomy. They are teachers, too, in other words, and they believe in rigor. They want their children to fail while they are still children. They know that those lessons—about hard work, persistence, integrity, and consequences—will serve a child for decades to come.

For different cultural and historical reasons, most parents in the world's smartest countries seem to understand the importance of academic resilience—the same way American parents understand why coaches bench their sons and daughters when they've missed practice. World-class principals keep parents focused on what matters, even if it means five hundred dollars in lost bake-sale revenue per semester.

ignore shiny objects

Old-school can be good school. Eric's high school in Busan, South Korea, had austere classrooms with bare-bones computer labs. Out front, kids played soccer on a dirt field. From certain angles, the place looked like an American school from the 1950s. Most of Kim's classrooms in Finland looked the same way: rows of desks in front of a simple chalkboard or an old-fashioned white board, the kind that was not connected to anything but the wall.

Tom's school in Poland didn't even have a cafeteria, let alone a state-of-the-art theater, like his public school back home in Pennsylvania. In his American school, *every* classroom had an interactive white board, the kind that had become ubiquitous in so many American schools. (In fact, when I visited Tom's American high school in 2012, these boards were already being swapped for next-generation replacements.) None of the classrooms in his Polish school had interactive white boards.

Little data exists to compare investments in technology across countries, unfortunately. But the anecdotal evidence suggests that Americans waste an extraordinary amount of tax money on high-tech toys for teachers and students, most of which have no proven learning value whatsoever. As in all other industries, computers are most helpful when they save time or money, by helping to sort out what kids know and who needs help. Conversely, giving kids expensive, individual wireless clickers so that they can vote in class would be unthinkable in most countries worldwide. (In most of the world, kids just raise their hands and that works out fine.)

"In most of the highest-performing systems, technology is remarkably absent from classrooms," Andreas Schleicher, the OECD international education guru, told me. "I have no explanation why that is the case, but it does seem that those systems place their efforts primarily on pedagogical practice rather than digital gadgets."

In the survey conducted for this book, seven out of ten international and American exchange students agreed that U.S. schools had more technology. Not one American student surveyed said there was significantly less technology in U.S. schools.

The smartest countries prioritize teacher pay and equity (channeling more resources to the neediest students). When looking for a world-class education, remember that people always matter more than props.

ask the principal the hard questions

When you meet a principal, ask the questions you might ask a potential employer. Get a sense of the school's priorities and the culture. Don't be afraid to be as assertive as you might be when buying a car or taking a job.

When searching for a school, the leader matters more than any other factor. Yes, the teachers are critically important, too, but you can't pick your child's teacher in our system. So, you have to rely on the principal to do that for you.

How do you choose your teachers?

Finland, Korea, and all the education superpowers select their teachers relatively efficiently, by requiring students accepted to teacher colleges to be in the top third of their graduating high school classes. This selectivity is not enough by itself, but it ensures a level of prestige and education that makes other world-beating policies possible.

Since most countries do *not* take this logical step, the principal is even more important. That leader acts as the filter instead of the education college or the teacher certification system, which is not robust in most places. Nothing matters more than the decisions the principal makes about whom to hire, how to train, and whom to let go. "Great vision without great people is irrelevant," as Jim Collins wrote in his classic book, *Good to Great*.

Find out if the principal can choose which candidates to interview and hire. That kind of common-sense autonomy is rare in many schools. Then ask if the principal actually watches the job applicant *teach*. That, too, is almost unheard of in many countries including the United States—even though it is an obvious way to see whether a person has the extraordinary leadership abilities required to be a great teacher, one of the most demanding and complex jobs in the modern age. Even if candidates pretend to teach—to an adult audience—as part of the hiring process, that is far better than nothing.

How do you make your teachers better?

The more specifics you hear in response to this question, the better. Most teachers operate without meaningful feedback, in isolation. That is indefensible today. Professional development, which is jargon for training in the education world, should be customized to the strengths and weaknesses of the individual teacher. It should not feature hundreds of teachers sitting through a lecture in an auditorium.

No country has figured this out. But some countries do it better than others. In Finland, teachers are more likely to watch each other teach—in training and throughout their careers. Many countries give teachers more time to collaborate and plan together; the United States ranks poorly in this respect. American teachers work relatively short school years, but they have little time to share ideas and get feedback in most schools. Ask principals how they help teachers collaborate and what kind of leadership roles they give to their top teachers.

How do you measure your success?

Strong leaders can clearly explain their vision. If you hear a long, vague answer, full of many disparate parts, you may have found yourself in a school without a mission—which is to say, an average school. In the United States, most principals will mention test-score data as one measure of success, which is fair but insufficient. They might also mention graduation rates or parental satisfaction surveys.

Fine. But how do they measure the intangible outcomes that matter just as much? How do they know if they are training students to do higher-order thinking and solve problems they have never seen before? Most standardized tests do not capture those skills. How do they judge if they are teaching kids the secrets behind the world's greatest success stories, skills like persistence, self-control, and integrity?

Do they ask their students what needs to be improved? Do those opinions change the way the school works in fundamental ways—every semester? World-class educators have a vision for where they are going, tools to determine if they have lost their way, and a culture of perpetual change in order to do better.

How do you make sure the work is rigorous enough? How do you keep raising the bar to find out what kids can do?

At the Success Academy charter schools in New York City, students spend an hour and a half reading and discussing books each day. Then they spend another hour and a half writing. Kids start learning science every day in kindergarten. That's what rigor looks like. In most New York City public schools, kids don't learn science daily until middle school.

That's not all. Success Academy students also take music, art, and dance; they learn to play chess. They almost never skip recess, even in bad weather—a policy they share with Finland. They call their strategy "joyful rigor."

Does this work? All fourth graders at Success Academy schools are proficient in science, according to New York City's test, and 95 percent perform at advanced levels. Success Academy Harlem I, where the mostly low-income students are randomly admitted by lottery, performs at the same level as gifted-and-talented schools across New York City.

Teachers at these schools are expected to be intellectually fascinating and hyper-prepared; they are trained to overestimate what kids can do, rather than worrying about kids' self-esteem. At these schools, kindergarten teachers are forbidden from speaking to children in a singsong voice. It's hard to respect children when you are talking down to them.

"It's an insult to the scholars' intelligence," writes founder and CEO Eva Moskowitz and her co-author Arin Lavinia in their 2012 book, *Mission Possible*. "What the teacher is saying should be so interesting that the kids are sitting on the edge of their seat, hanging on every word. It's intellectual spark that holds and keeps their attention, not baby talk."

Parental involvement means something different at Success Academies; parents are not asked to bake cookies or sell gift wrap. Instead, they are asked to read to their kids six nights a week. They are expected to help speed the learning at home to get their students ready for college, just as Korean parents do. Parents have the cell phone numbers of their kids' teachers and principal.

In 2011, Success Academy opened a new school on the Upper West Side of Manhattan, a far richer neighborhood than its previous locations. Unlike most schools in America, including the best public charter schools, these new schools were actually *diverse*, in the literal sense. Moskowitz wanted a true mix of white, Asian, African-American, and Hispanic students at a range of income levels, and she got it. That is how kids learn best—together, with a mix of expectations, advantages, and complications—according to the hard-earned lessons of countries around the world.

There are stories like this all over the country: Success Academy charter schools in New York City, the closest thing to Finland in the United States; William Taylor, a public-school teacher who has almost Korean expectations for his low-income students in Washington, D.C.; and Deborah Gist in Rhode Island, a leader who has dared to raise the bar for what teachers must know, just like reformers in Finland and Korea.

These world-class educators exist, but they are fighting against the grain of culture and institutions. That fight drains them of energy and time. If they ever win, it will be because parents and students rose up around them, convinced that our children cannot only handle a rigorous education but that they crave it as never before.

appendix II

AFS student
experience survey

introduction

No country has figured out how to help all children reach their full learning potential. Like health care systems, education systems are dazzlingly complex and always in need of change. To improve, countries can learn from each other; the trick is figuring out which of our differences matter most.

Tests can measure skills, and surveys within a country can measure attitudes. It is hard, however, to compare survey results across different countries, since the surveyed populations live in unique cultural contexts.

However, people who have lived and studied in multiple countries can transcend some cultural barriers and identify meaningful distinctions. Their voices, in combination with quantitative research, can help us chip away at this mystery.

Each year, tens of thousands of enterprising teenagers from

around the globe leave home to live and learn on exchange programs. During the 2011–2012 academic year, 1,376 Americans went abroad and another 27,688 international students came to the United States. Immersed in new cultures, families, and schools, these young students could compare education systems in ways no adult researcher ever could.

survey design

In May 2012, Amanda Ripley and New America Foundation researcher Marie Lawrence collaborated with AFS Intercultural Programs, one of the world's oldest and most respected exchange organizations, to try to learn from this corps of young travelers. AFS (formerly the American Field Service) is a nonprofit that facilitates exchanges in more than fifty countries.

We conducted an online survey of all AFS exchange students who were sent abroad from the United States or sent to the United States from other countries during the 2009-2010 academic year. (We chose that year in part because all the students would be over eighteen and able to participate without parental permission.)

The primary goal of the survey was to understand whether differences observed by the exchange students featured in this book were also noticed by a larger number of students. We also wanted to discover whether students' opinions had changed since a previous survey was conducted in 2001 and 2002, before a decade of reforms to the U.S. education system. Last, we were curious to investigate, to the extent possible, whether differences in student experiences might be associated with differences in PISA performance.

Students have been shown to be highly reliable observers of their teachers and classroom environments. The Measures of Effective Teaching Project, an effort by the Bill & Melinda Gates Foundation to understand good teaching, has found that student ratings are consistent across different groups of students taught by the same teacher and strongly related to gains in academic achievement. It only makes sense to ask students what they know.

To begin the survey, AFS-USA sent an email invitation to 242 U.S. students who had studied abroad in thirty-three countries, and AFS-International sent the invitation to 1,104 students who had traveled to the United States from nineteen different countries.

The survey included thirteen questions. (The full text appears at the end of this appendix.) Most questions evolved from dozens of conversations the author has had with other exchange students over the course of several years. Two questions, regarding the overall difficulty of school abroad and the importance of sports, were reconstructed from the Brookings Institute surveys of international and U.S. students in 2001 and 2002. The survey also included two opportunities for open-ended responses to capture observations that might not otherwise have been drawn out by the close-ended survey questions. For privacy reasons, none of the questions collected identifying information about participants.

To analyze the responses, we divided them into two groups based on home country (United States versus international students) and, among international students, by high-achieving country (HAC) and lower-achieving country (LAC). Each sending country was categorized based on its average PISA math score rankings. We chose math because math performance is more easily comparable across countries and because math skills tend to better predict future earnings and other economic outcomes than other subjects.

Countries with PISA math scores significantly above average for developed nations were classified as high-achieving countries; those with math scores not significantly different than average or significantly below average were classified as lower-achieving countries. Of the sending countries participating in this project, the high-achieving countries were Denmark, Finland, Germany, Hong Kong, Iceland, Japan, Netherlands, New Zealand, and Switzerland. The lower-achieving countries were Brazil, Colombia, Costa Rica, France, Honduras, India, Italy, Latvia, Philippines, and Russia.

limitations of the data

Of the 1,346 students invited, a total of 202 completed the survey (see Table 1), a response rate of 15 percent. There were various possible reasons why more students did not participate, including the fact that many had changed email addresses since AFS had last heard from them. Still, the response rate was high enough to form broad conclusions about students' perceptions, with some caveats.

Of U.S. respondents, a significant number (19 percent) had studied in Italy. Of international respondents, a large group (37 percent) had come to the United States from Germany. Those ratios mirrored the distribution of AFS students generally, but the results should be considered with those biases in mind.

Germany, for example, was counted among the high-achieving countries because German teenagers scored above average in math on PISA. That meant that 54 percent of our international high-achieving sample came from Germany. However, Germany is not in the same league as Finland or Korea—two countries that perform at the very top of the world in math, reading, and science on the PISA test.

Moreover, international exchange students in general are not necessarily representative of their peers back home, of course. Some exchange students (though not all) come from higher-income families and from higher-achieving schools. They may also possess higher levels of motivation and adventurousness than those who did not participate in an exchange program. In their host countries, these students are not treated in the same way as their classmates; that distinction, combined with the obvious language barriers, may limit their abilities to assess other countries' education systems and cultures.

Despite these caveats, the observations by these 202 students show intriguing patterns. They agreed more often than they disagreed. We are grateful to the students and to AFS for helping us collect wisdom from the one stakeholder group rarely consulted in education debates around the world—the students themselves.

Table 1. Response Rates from U.S. and International Students

Host /Home Country	U.S. Students			International Students		
	N	n	%	N	n	%
Argentina	16	0	0.0%			
Austria	9	1	11.1%			
Belgium	12	1	8.3%			
Brazil	4	2	50.0%	47	4	8.5%
Chile	3	0	0.0%			
China	5	0	0.0%			
Columbia				19	2	10.5%
Costa Rica	3	0	0.0%	5	0	0.0%
Czech Republic	2	0	0.0%			
Denmark	4	0	0.0%	51	6	11.8%
Dominican Republic	2	0	0.0%			
Ecuador	6	1	16.7%			
Egypt	3	0	0.0%			
Finland	4	2	50.0%	38	10	26.3%
France	29	3	10.3%	62	14	22.6%
Germany	16	3	18.8%	334	61	18.3%
Honduras				4	0	0.0%
Hong Kong	2	1	50.0%	22	3	13.6%
Hungary	1	0	0.0%			
Iceland	1	0	0.0%	11	4	36.4%
India	1	1	100.0%	15	0	0.0%
Italy	33	7	21.2%	234	30	12.8%
Japan				136	6	4.4%
Latvia				5	1	20.0%
Netherlands	8	3	37.5%	24	4	16.7%
New Zealand	1	0	0.0%	3	1	33.3%
Norway	5	0	0.0%			
Panama	4	0	0.0%			
Paraguay	9	4	44.4%			
Peru	1	0	0.0%			
Philippines				14	0	0.0%
Portugal	8	0	0.0%			
Russia	2	1	50.0%	7	0	0.0%
Spain	28	4	14.3%			
Sweden	7	1	14.3%			
Switzerland	10	2	20.0%	73	19	26.0%
Thailand	2	0	0.0%			
Turkey	1	0	0.0%			
HAC Total				692	114	16.5%
LAC Total				412	51	12.4%
TOTAL*	242	37	15.3%	1104	165	14.9%

*Excludes four student responses. Three students reported the U.S. as neither the
home nor host country. One reported the U.S. as both the home and host country.

High-achieving countries that sent students to the U.S.

Lower-achieving countries that sent students to the U.S.

N= the total number of students who were invited to participate in the survey.
n = the total number of students who completed the survey.
Serbia and Canada also agreed to participate in the survey, but they sent no
students to the U.S. via the relevant AFS program in the 2009–2010 academic year.

results and discussion

For clarity, we inverted the questions and answers for the different populations. For example, international students were asked: "Compared to school in your home country, how much technology (computers, laptops, digital white boards, etc.) did you see in use in your U.S. school?" U.S. students were asked the same question, phrased in the opposite way: "Compared to school in the United States, how much technology (computers, laptops, digital white boards, etc.) did you see in use in your school abroad?" In order to easily compare the results, however, we have expressed all responses in terms of students' opinions of the U.S. education system vis-à-vis their experience abroad.

Technology

International and U.S. students agreed there was more technology in U.S. schools. In all, 70 percent of international students and 73 percent of U.S. students said so; though compared to international students, U.S. students were more likely to say there was a little more rather than much more technology (see Chart 1). Not one U.S. student said there was much less technology in U.S. schools.

To date, there is remarkably scant research comparing the relative investments in technology in schools around the world. We know precious little about how much money countries spend on technology,

Chart 1. U.S. and international students saw more technology in use in U.S. schools.

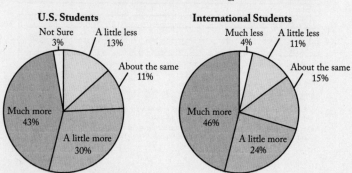

let alone whether those expenditures actually lead to student learning.

Our results suggest that the United States invests more heavily in technology in classrooms than even high-performing countries. (In our survey, 61 percent of students from HACs said the United States had more technology in its classrooms.) That does not necessarily mean that technology is negatively correlated with education performance, of course; many things interact to lead to education outcomes, and our results suggest that lower-performing countries use even less technology than high-achieving countries. (Almost three-quarters of students from LACs said the United States had "much more" technology compared to a third of students from HACs.)

Still, this difference might help explain (in part) why the United States spends more money per student than almost any country in the world. Our romance with educational technology has been expensive, distracting, and one-sided for a very long time.

Difficulty

International and U.S. students agreed that school in the United States was easier than school abroad. In all, 92 percent of international students and 70 percent of U.S. students said school in the United States was easier than school abroad. U.S. students were more likely to say school in the United States was a "little easier" rather than "much easier" (see Chart 2).

Chart 2.   U.S. and international students said that U.S. classes were easier.

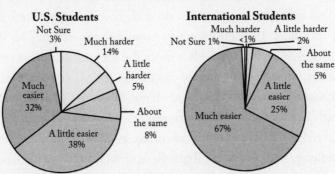

These results corroborate the findings from the 2001 and 2002 Brookings Institute surveys of international and U.S. exchange students. In those surveys, 85 percent of international students and 56 percent of U.S. students found U.S. classes easier.

The similarity in the findings suggest that the intervening ten years of education reforms under the federal No Child Left Behind Act did not, in the estimation of our sample, render U.S. schools any harder compared to schools abroad.

Another interesting finding points to a lack of rigor in U.S. coursework. International students from both high- and lower-achieving countries agreed that U.S. school was easier. However, international students from high-achieving schools were more likely to say that U.S. school was "much easier" than school at home. Specifically, 73 percent of students from high-achieving countries said U.S. school was "much easier," compared to just 53 percent of students from lower-achieving countries. This finding is consistent with the hypothesis of this book: In countries with strong education systems, school is actually harder. Rigor runs through those countries' approaches to learning and parenting, shaping everything from teacher training to the make-up of standardized tests.

It is interesting to note, however, that even students from lower-achieving countries overwhelmingly reported that U.S. school was easier. There may have been a bias toward defending the rigor of one's home education, but that wouldn't explain why U.S. students also said that their home classes were easier.

This difference may have to do with how students perceive difficulty in school. In many countries around the world, high-achieving and lower-achieving, school is a more formal and structured environment than school in the United States. The codes of conduct are more rigid, and the consequences for academic failure are more serious, particularly in high school. In some cases, students might have been reacting to those differences of school culture as opposed to the actual level of challenge in the material. Regardless, given other research showing a lack of rigor in U.S. textbooks, curricula, and teacher training, this difference in perceived rigor is important and worthy of further research.

Parental Freedom

International and U.S. students also agreed that U.S. parents gave their children less freedom than parents abroad. Of all respondents, 63 percent of international students and 68 percent of U.S. students agreed with this assertion (see Chart 3).

Interestingly, international students from high-performing countries were much more likely than students from lower-performing countries to report that the U.S. parents gave their children much less freedom. Specifically, 70 percent of international students from high-performing countries said U.S. parents gave their children less freedom compared to 45 percent of students from lower-performing countries.

These findings support existing literature suggesting that United States children lead highly structured lives. The reasons for this difference are complex and hard to disentangle. American parents might be more protective of their children due to pervasive concerns about crime and violence, for example. In some areas of the United States, particularly low-income neighborhoods, these concerns could be based in hard facts; in other, higher-income areas, crime may be low but parental anxiety about crime may still be high.

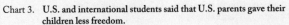

Chart 3.   U.S. and international students said that U.S. parents gave their children less freedom.

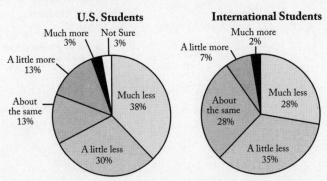

Regardless of the reasons, what does it mean for education outcomes if U.S. parents really *do* grant their children less autonomy? It is, again, difficult to speculate, but the existing literature on raising resilient children suggests there is great value in allowing them to be free to make decisions and mistakes (within limits) while they are still children. Otherwise, teenagers raised in highly controlled high schools and homes only discover the perils and thrills of independence when they are grown, and largely on their own.

Importance of Sports

International and U.S. students agreed on the importance of sports in the lives of U.S. teenagers. Of all students, 91 percent of international students and 62 percent of U.S. students said U.S. students placed more importance on doing well in sports than did students abroad (see Chart 4). International students were more likely to say U.S. students cared "much more" about athletic achievement.

These findings corroborate results from the Brookings Institute surveys. In those surveys, 85 percent of international students and 82 percent of U.S. students said that U.S. students placed higher importance on doing well in sports than did students abroad.

It is not at all clear that placing a high importance on athletic achievement is negatively associated with academic performance. Of interna-

Chart 4. U.S. and international students said U.S. students placed more importance on doing well in sports.

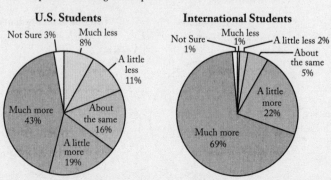

tional students, 88 percent of those from high-achieving countries said U.S. students place more importance on doing well in sports than students abroad; whereas nearly all students (96 percent) from lower-achieving countries said U.S. students placed more importance on success in sports. This suggests that students from high-achieving countries cared more about sports than students in lower-achieving countries—although none of them cared as much as American students, it seems.

In any case, the unparalleled importance of athletic achievement at U.S. high schools should be the subject of serious debate. Sports, for all the value they offer, also siphon money and attention from classroom learning. It is their relative importance—not their absolute existence—that is worrisome.

Praise

International and U.S. students agreed that U.S. math teachers were more likely to praise student work than math teachers abroad. Roughly half of international *and* U.S. students said their U.S. math teachers were more likely to praise student work; about a third thought that their math teachers did about the same amount of praising in both countries; and less than 10 percent of both groups thought their math teachers abroad were more likely to praise student work (see Chart 5).

Note that this question was asked of a slightly smaller sample. We

Chart 5. U.S. and international students said U.S. math teachers gave their students more praise than did teachers abroad.

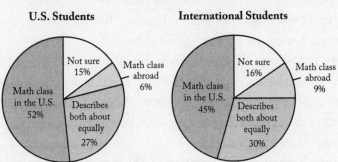

U.S. Students

- Math class in the U.S. 52%
- Not sure 15%
- Math class abroad 6%
- Describes both about equally 27%

International Students

- Math class in the U.S. 45%
- Not sure 16%
- Math class abroad 9%
- Describes both about equally 30%

asked students specifically to compare their experiences in their math class at home and abroad. Of the international students who filled out the survey, 82 percent took a math class in the United States, allowing them to answer this question. Of the U.S. respondents, 89 percent took math and completed this question.

The results beg the question: Are U.S. teachers warranted in praising their students to the extent reported in this survey? The United States is solidly among the lower-achieving countries in math, and yet U.S. kids are much more likely to report getting high grades in math, as discussed elsewhere in this book.

What are the effects of praising students for work that does not reach the average performance of students in other developed nations? How does pervasive praise impact the learning environment and students' expectations for themselves? Is praise related to the tendency (also suggested by this survey) of U.S. parents to grant their children less freedom? Do U.S. teachers and parents treat their children as if they are more fragile than they are? Or do other countries handle their children with too *little* care?

Praise is not all bad, to state the obvious. Indeed, the results show a complex relationship between praise and results: Students from lower-achieving countries were much more likely than students from high-achieving countries to say that U.S. teachers gave more praise. Of international students, 38 percent of those from high-achieving countries said their U.S. teachers praised students more often; by comparison, 62 percent of students from lower-achieving countries said so. Praise might not lead to learning, but the absence of praise does not necessarily do much good either.

In fact, some of the students in this survey explicitly celebrated the positive classroom culture of their American classrooms in their responses to the open-ended questions. As one Italian exchange student to the U.S. put it: "[U.S.] teachers believe in you, in your potential, and never put you down."

One French student contrasted the two experiences this way:

"In France, the teachers put way more pressure on the students—for homework, grades. In the United States, the teachers usually congratulate students [on] their work."

That said, praise is a risky currency. To work, praise must be specific, sincere, accurate—and used in moderation. These results suggest that the praise commonly deployed in U.S. classrooms may not meet those requirements. Excessive, vague, or empty praise has corrosive effects, as multiple studies have shown, incentivizing kids to take fewer risks and give up more easily. Self-esteem is important, but it comes from hard work and authentic accomplishment, not flattery.

Mixed or Inconclusive Results

The results of U.S. and international student responses to four questions were mixed or inconclusive. These focused on:

Importance of doing well in school. Most international students said that students in the United States and abroad placed a similar importance on doing well in school, while most U.S. students said their peers placed *less* importance on doing well in school. The only point of clear agreement was that U.S. students did *not* care "much more" about doing well in school. Just 4 percent of international students and 3 percent of U.S. students chose this response. It is not immediately clear why U.S. and international students did not agree on this question, though it is possible that students had difficulty assessing how much other students cared about school in a cross-cultural context.

Challenge of classwork in math class. U.S. student responses were mixed on this question, but international students showed a clearer preference for one answer over the others. Specifically, 58 percent of international students said that their math classes abroad were more challenging than in the United States.

Tendency of math class to "stay busy and not waste time." Both U.S. and international students were mixed on this question. For both groups, about one-third said they stayed busy in math class in the U.S., one-third chose "abroad," and one-third reported that their experience of busy classrooms was about equal in the U.S. and abroad.

Tendency of math teachers to "accept nothing less than our full effort." As in the case immediately above, U.S. and international students showed no strong preference for any of the answer choices. It seems likely that the question was unclear since a significant number of respondents in both groups chose "Not sure." In all, 18 percent of international students and 12 percent of U.S. students chose "Not sure."

Survey

At the start of the survey, participants were tracked into two separate groups—U.S. students and international students—following the question: "What was your host country?" That way, the questions could be phrased more clearly for each group, a critical concern for non-native English speakers.

Questions asked of international students appear below in Roman typeface; questions asked of U.S. students appear below in *italic*. Where no italic text appears, the question's wording was not changed.

Additionally, students were asked whether they took a math course during their exchange. Students who answered "yes" were directed to the next page of questions to compare their math classes at home and abroad; students who answered "no" were automatically directed to the final page of questions regarding their overall educational experience.

WELCOME

Thank you for your help with this survey!

The following 12 questions should take about 5 minutes to complete. Please answer as many questions as you can. If you don't know an answer, choose "Not Sure." Choose "Previous Page" to go back.

The purpose of this survey is to learn from your educational experiences in your home and host countries. The results will appear in a book on international education by Amanda Ripley, a *Time* magazine contributing writer and a fellow at the New America Foundation, a non-partisan policy research organization in the U.S.

Clicking on the "Next" button confirms that you agree to participate in this survey, and you authorize AFS and Amanda Ripley to collect and process the answers. The results of this survey will be completely anonymous, and AFS will not disclose your e-mail or name to any third party in connection with this survey. If you wish to stop participating at any time, just click "Exit this survey" in the top right corner of your browser window.

After the study is completed, AFS will contact you to share the findings. You may also read about the results in Ms. Ripley's book when it is published in early 2013.

Questions or technical problems? Please e-mail lawrence@ newamerica.net.

This survey will close on Friday, May 4, 2012 at 11:59 pm EDT.

You may view Survey Monkey's privacy policy here: http://www. surveymonkey.com/mp/policy/privacy-policy/.

basic information

1. Did you graduate high school before leaving for your exchange program?

   Yes, No

2. Did you receive academic credit for your exchange year?

Yes, No

3. What was your home country at the time of your exchange?

Brazil, Canada, Colombia, Costa Rica, Denmark, Finland, France, Germany, Honduras, Hong Kong, Iceland, India, Italy, Japan, Latvia, Netherlands, New Zealand, Philippines, United States, Russia, Switzerland

4. What was your host country?

Brazil, Canada, Colombia, Costa Rica, Denmark, Finland, France, Germany, Honduras, Hong Kong, Iceland, India, Italy, Japan, Latvia, Netherlands, New Zealand, Philippines, United States, Russia, Switzerland, Other (please specify)

student experience

1. Compared to school in your home country, how much technology (computers, laptops, digital white boards, etc.) did you see in use in your U.S. school?

Much more technology in the U.S., A little more technology in the U.S., About the same technology in both places, A little less technology in the U.S., Much less technology in the U.S., Not sure

2. Compare your classes in your school at home and in the U.S. Were classes . . .

Much easier in the U.S., A little easier in the U.S., About the same in both places, A little harder in the U.S., Much harder in the U.S., Not sure

3. Compared to parents back home, how much freedom did U.S. parents generally give their children?

Much more freedom in the U.S., A little more freedom in the U.S., About the same freedom in both places, A little less freedom in the U.S., Much less freedom in the U.S., Not sure

[QUESTIONS IN ITALICS WERE DIRECTED TO U.S. STUDENTS.]

1. *Compared to school in the U.S., how much technology (computers, laptops, digital white boards, etc.) did you see in your school abroad?*

Much more technology abroad, A little more technology abroad, About the same technology in both places, A little less technology abroad, Much less technology abroad, Not sure

2. *Compare your U.S. classes to your classes abroad. Were classes . . .*

Much easier abroad, A little easier abroad, About the same in both places, A little harder abroad, Much harder abroad, Not sure

3. *Compared to parents in the U.S., how much freedom did parents abroad generally give their children?*

Much more freedom abroad, A little more freedom abroad, About the same freedom in both places, A little less freedom abroad, Much less freedom abroad, Not sure

student experience (continued)

1. Compared to students in your home country, how important did your friends in the U.S. think it was to do well in SCHOOL?

Much more important in the U.S., A little more important in the U.S., About the same importance in both places, A little less important in the U.S., Much less important in the U.S., Not sure

2. Compared to students in your home country, how important did your friends in the U.S. think it was to do well in SPORTS?

Much more important in the U.S., A little more important in the U.S., About the same importance in both places, A little less important in the U.S., Much less important in the U.S., Not sure

1. *Compared to students in the U.S., how important did your friends abroad think it was to do well in SCHOOL?*

Much more important abroad, A little more important abroad, About the same importance in both places, A little less important abroad, Much less important abroad, Not sure

2. *Compared to students in the U.S., how important did your friends abroad think it was to do well in SPORTS?*

Much more important abroad, A little more important abroad, About the same importance in both places, A little less important abroad, Much less important abroad, Not sure

student experience (continued)

1. Did you take a MATH class during your exchange?

Yes, No

student experience—math class

1. Think about your U.S. math class and the last math class you took at home before the exchange. For each statement, choose which class best fits the description.

Our classwork was challenging.

Math class at home, Math class in the U.S., Describes both about equally, Not sure

Our class stayed busy and did not waste time.

Math class at home, Math class in the U.S., Describes both about equally, Not sure

Our teacher accepted nothing less than our full effort.

Math class at home, Math class in the U.S., Describes both about equally, Not sure

Our teacher regularly praised students' work.

Math class at home, Math class in the U.S., Describes both about equally, Not sure

1. *Think about the math class you took abroad and the last math class you took in the U.S. before your exchange. For each statement, choose which class best fits the description.*

Our classwork was challenging.

Math class at home, Math class in the U.S., Describes both about equally, Not sure

Our class stayed busy and did not waste time.

Math class at home, Math class in the U.S., Describes both about equally, Not sure

Our teacher accepted nothing less than our full effort.

Math class at home, Math class in the U.S., Describes both about equally, Not sure

Our teacher regularly praised students' work.

Math class at home, Math class in the U.S., Describes both about equally, Not sure

student experience (continued)

1. What was the biggest difference between the school you attended in the U.S. and the school you attended at home just before the exchange?

   [Open ended]

2. During your exchange, where did most of your learning take place?

   Inside the classroom, Outside the classroom, Not sure

   Optional: Please explain your response.

1. *What was the biggest difference between the school you attended abroad and the school you attended at home just before the exchange?*

   [Open ended]

2. *During your exchange, where did most of your learning take place?*

   Inside the classroom, Outside the classroom, Not sure

   Optional: Please explain your response.

thank you

Thank you for completing the survey! Please click "Done" to submit your answers.

selected bibliography

ACT. *The Condition of College & Career Readiness 2011*. August 2011.

ACT. *Crisis at the Core: Preparing All Students for College and Work*. 2005.

ACT. *2010 ACT National and State Scores: Average Scores by State*. http://www. act.org/newsroom/data/2010/states.html.

Adcock, Clinton. "Sallisaw: A Blue Town." *Tulsa World*, June 21, 2010.

Afdal, Hilde Wågsås. "Constructing Knowledge for the Teaching Profession: A Comparative Analysis of Policy Making, Curricula Content, and Novice Teachers' Knowledge Relations in the Cases of Finland and Norway." Ph.D. diss., University of Oslo, 2012.

Aho, Erkki, Kari Pitkänen, and Pasi Sahlberg. *Policy Development and Reform Principles of Basic and Secondary Education in Finland Since 1968*. Washington, DC: The World Bank, 2006.

Almlund, Mathilde, Angela Lee Duckworth, James Heckman, and Tim Kautz. "Personality Psychology and Economics." In *Handbook of the Economics of Education, Volume 4*, edited by Eric A. Hanushek, Stephen Machin and Ludger Woessmann, 1-182. Amsterdam: North-Holland, 2011.

America Achieves. *Middle Class or Middle of the Pack?* April 2013.

Archer, Kim. "Bill Would Lift Required Graduation Testing." *Tulsa World*, December 28, 2011.

Archer, Kim. "Owasso Board Joins High-Stakes Testing Protest." *Tulsa World*, August 14, 2012.

Arenson, Karen W. "South Korea: 900 SAT Scores Canceled." *New York Times*, March 13, 2007.

Arum, Richard, and Josipa Roksa. *Academically Adrift: Limited Learning on College Campuses*. Chicago: The University of Chicago Press, 2011.

Aud, Susan, Mary Ann Fox, and Angelina KewalRamani. *Status and Trends in the Education of Racial and Ethnic Groups*. Washington, DC: The National Center for Education Statistics, 2010.

Aud, Susan, William Hussar, Grace Kena, Kevin Bianco, Lauren Frohlich, Jana Kemp, and Kim Tahan. *The Condition of Education 2011 (NCES 2011-033)*.

U.S. Department of Education, National Center for Education Statistics. Washington, DC: U.S. Government Printing Office, 2011.

Auguste, Byron, Paul Kihn, and Matt Miller. *Closing the Talent Gap: Attracting and Retaining Top-Third Graduates to Careers in Teaching.* McKinsey & Company, September 2010.

Barber, Michael, and Mona Mourshed. *How the World's Best-Performing School Systems Come Out on Top.* McKinsey & Company, September 2007.

Bernanke, Ben. "The Level and Distribution of Economic Well-Being." Speech before the Greater Omaha Chamber of Commerce, Omaha, NE, February 6, 2007.

"Bildungsstudie - Durchweg schlechte Noten." *FOCUS,* December 3, 2001. Translation by Theresa Buchstätter.

Bill & Melinda Gates Foundation. *Learning about Teaching: Initial Findings from the Measures of Effective Teaching Project.* Measures of Effective Teaching Project, December 2010.

Boe, Erling, Henry May, and Robert Boruch. *Student Task Persistence in the Third International Mathematics and Science Study: A Major Source of Achievement Differences at the National, Classroom, and Student Levels.* Philadelphia: Center for Research and Evaluation in Social Policy, 2002.

Boe, Erling, and Sujie Shin. "Is the United States Really Losing the International Horse Race in Academic Achievement?" *Phi Delta Kappan,* 86, no. 9 (2005): 688-695.

Borgonovi, Francesca, and Guillermo Montt. "Parental Involvement in Selected PISA Countries and Economies." OECD Working Papers No. 73. OECD Publishing, Paris, 2012.

Boser, Ulrich, and Lindsay Rosenthal. *Do Schools Challenge Our Students? What Student Surveys Tell Us about the State of Education in the United States.* Washington: Center for American Progress, July 10, 2012.

Boser, Ulrich. *Return on Educational Investment: A district-by-district evaluation of U.S. educational productivity.* Washington: Center for American Progress, January 2011.

Bowles, Samuel, and Herbert Gintis. *Schooling in Capitalist America: Educational Reform and the Contradictions of Economic Life.* New York: Basic Books, 1976.

Bracey, Gerald W. "Another Nation at Risk: German Students Scores in Academic Tests." *Phi Delta Kappan,* 84, no. 3, November 1, 2002.

Bronson, Po, and Ashley Merryman. *NurtureShock: New Thinking about Children.* New York: Hachette Book Group, 2009.

Bureau of the Census. *State & County Quick Facts, Sallisaw, Oklahoma.* Washington, DC: Bureau of the Census. http://quickfacts.census.gov/qfd/states/40/4065000.html. Accessed 2012.

Bureau of Labor Statistics. "The Employment Situation: December 2011." Bureau of Labor Statistics press release, January 6, 2012.

Catholic Information Agency. "Gniezno: Nationwide Launch of the School Year." September 1, 1999. Translation by Justine Jablonska.

Cavanagh, Sean. "Out-of-School Classes Provide Edge." *Education Week,* April 22, 2009.

Center for Research in Mathematics and Science Education. *Breaking the Cycle: An International Comparison of U.S. Mathematics Teacher Preparation.* East Lansing: Michigan State University, 2010.

Center on Education Policy, George Washington University. *State High School Exit Exams: A Policy in Transition.* Washington, DC: Center on Education Policy, 2012.

Chae, S., J.-H. Hong, and T.J. Lee. "Anatomy of the Rank Structure of Korean Universities: Toward a Design of Integrated Policies for Education Reform in Korea." *AP-EPRI/ KEDI Publications,* 2005.

Chao, Ruth. "Beyond Parental Control and Authoritarian Parenting Style: Understanding Chinese Parenting through the Cultural Notion of Training." *Child Development 65* (1994): 1111-1119.

Chao, Ruth. "Chinese and European American Mothers' Beliefs about the Role of Parenting in Children's School Success." *Journal of Cross-Cultural Psychology 27,* no. 4 (July 1996): 403-423.

Choi, Álvaro, Jorge Calero, and Josep-Oriol Escardíbul. *Hell to Touch the Sky: Private Tutoring and Academic Achievement in Korea.* Barcelona: Barcelona Institute of Economics, 2011.

College Board, *2011 College-Bound Seniors: Total Group Profile Report,* 2011.

Collins, Jim. *Good to Great: Why Some Companies Make the Leap . . . and Others Don't.* New York: HarperCollins, 2001.

Conn, Steven. "In College Classrooms, the Problem Is High School Athletics." *The Chronicle of Higher Education,* April 15, 2012.

Coolahan, John, Paula Santiago, Rowena Phair, and Akira Ninomiya. *Attracting, Developing and Retaining Effective Teachers: Country Note – Korea.* Paris: OECD Publishing, 2004.

"Current Expenditure per Pupil in Average Daily Attendance in Public Elementary and Secondary Schools, by State or Jurisdiction, Selected Years, 1959-60 through 2007-08." National Center for Education Statistics. Accessed 2012.

Czajkowska, Agnieszka. "Kids Revolt." *Gazeta Wyborcza*, September 19, 2007. Translation by Mateusz Kornacki.

Daily Oklahoman. "Past Out: School Officials Should Keep Moving Forward." July 8, 2012.

Darling-Hammond, Linda. *The Flat World and Education*. New York: Teachers College Press, 2010.

Davidson, Adam. "Making It in America." *The Atlantic*, January/Feburary 2012.

Davies, Norman, and Roger Moorhouse. *Microcosm: Portrait of a Central European City*. London: Jonathan Cape, 2011.

Denhart, Matthew, and Christopher Matgouranis. *Oklahoma Higher Education: Challenging the Conventional Wisdom*. Oklahoma City: Oklahoma Council of Public Affairs, 2011.

Dervarics, Chuck, and Eileen O'Brien. *Back to School: How Parent Involvement Affects Student Achievement*. Alexandria: The Center for Public Education, 2011.

District of Columbia Department of Employment Services. "District of Columbia Strategic Workforce Investment Plan: For the Period of July 1, 2009 – June 30, 2010." July 10, 2009.

Duckworth, Angela L., and Martin E. P. Seligman. "Self-Discipline Outdoes IQ in Predicting Academic Performance of Adolescents." *Psychological Science* 16, no. 12 (2005): 939-944.

Dweck, Carol S. "Caution—Praise Can Be Dangerous." *American Educator*, Spring 1999.

The Economist. "How to Be Top." October 18, 2007.

Education Trust. "Not Good Enough: A Content Analysis of Teacher Licensing Examinations." *Thinking K-16* 3, no. 1 (Spring 1999).

Eger, Andrea. "www.school.com." *Tulsa World*, August 15, 2011.

Fenty, Adrian, Joseph Walsh, and Bill Dean. "District of Columbia Strategic Workforce Investment Plan." 2010.

Finnish National Board of Education. *Performance Indicator for Initial Vocational Training in Finland 2011*. Helsinki: Finnish National Board of Education, 2011.

Fleischman, Howard L., Paul J. Hopstock, Marisa P. Pelczar, and Brooke E. Shelley. *Highlights From PISA 2009: Performance of U.S. 15-Year-Old Students in Reading, Mathematics, and Science Literacy in an International Context* (NCES 2011-004). U.S. Department of Education, National Center for Education Statistics. Washington, DC: U.S. Government Printing Office, 2010.

Friedman, Thomas L. "How about Better Parents?" *The New York Times*, November 19, 2011.

Gamerman, Ellen. "What Makes Finnish Kids So Smart?" *The Wall Street Journal*, February 29, 2008.

Glenn, David. "Writing Assignments are Scarce for Students in Two Majors at Texas Colleges." *The Chronicle of Higher Education*, Jan. 18, 2011.

Gove, Michael. "The Benchmark for Excellence." *The Independent*, Jan. 6, 2011.

Greenberg, Julie, Laura Pomerance, and Kate Walsh. *Student Teaching in the United States*. Washington, D.C.: National Council on Teacher Quality, 2011.

Greene, Jay P., and Josh B. McGee. "When the Best Is Mediocre." *Education Next* 12, no. 1 (2012): 35-40.

Greene, Wayne. "Graduation Testing Bill Advances." *Tulsa World*, May 18, 2012.

Hakkarainen, Pentti. "Learning and Development in Play." In *Nordic Childhood and Early Education: Philosophy, Research, Policy, and Practice in Denmark, Finland, Iceland, Norway, and Sweden*, edited by Johanna Einarsdottir and Judith T. Wagner. Greenwich, CT: Information Age Publishing, 2006.

Hancock, LynNell. "Why Are Finland's Schools So Successful?" *Smithsonian*, September 2011.

Hanushek, Eric A., and Ludger Woessmann. *Does Educational Tracking Affect Performance and Inequality? Difference-in-Differences Evidence Across Countries*. Stanford: Stanford University, 2005.

Hanushek, Eric A., and Ludger Woessmann. *Do Better Schools Lead to More Growth? Cognitive Skills, Economic Outcomes, and Causation*. NBER Working Paper No. 14633. National Bureau of Economic Research, Cambridge, January 2009.

Hanushek, Eric A., Paul E. Peterson, and Ludger Woessmann. "Teaching Math to the Talented: Which Countries and States are Producing High-Achieving Students?" *Education Next* 11 no. 1 (Winter 2011): 11-18.

Hanushek, Eric A., and Ludger Woessmann. *The Knowledge Capital of Nations*. Forthcoming.

Hanushek, Eric A., Paul E. Peterson, and Ludger Woessmann. *U.S. Math Performance in Global Perspective: How Does Each State Do at Producing High-Achieving Students?* PEPG Report No. 10–19. Harvard University's Program on Education Policy and Governance and *Education Next*, Cambridge, November 2010.

Heckmann, Carsten. "Schlechte Schüler wegen schlecht gebildeter Lehrer?" *Der Spiegel*, December 4, 2001. Translation by Theresa Buchstätter.

Helliwell, John, Richard Layard, and Jeffrey Sachs, eds. *World Happiness Report*. New York: Earth Institute, 2012.

Henderlong, Jennifer, and Mark R. Lepper. "The Effects of Praise on Children's Intrinsic Motivation: A Review and Synthesis." *Psychological Bulletin* 128, no. 5 (2002): 774-795.

Henderson, Anne, and Karen Mapp. *A New Wave of Evidence: The Impact of School, Family, and Community Connections on Student Achievement.* Austin: National Center for Family and Community Connections with Schools, 2002.

Henry, Brad. *FY-2011 Executive Budget.* Oklahoma City: Oklahoma Office of State Finance, 2010.

Herrold, Kathleen, and Kevin O'Donnell. *Parent and Family Involvement in Education, 2006–07 School Year, From the National Household Education Surveys Program of 2007.* Washington, DC: National Center for Education Statistics and U.S. Department of Education, 2008.

Hinton, Mick. "Legislature Junks High School Grad Test Requirement." *Daily Oklahoman,* May 21, 1992.

Hinton, Mick. "Governor to Require 'Literacy Passports.'" *Daily Oklahoman,* March 29, 1995.

Hofferth, Sandra L. "Changes in American Children's Time, 1997-2003." *International Journal of Time Use Research* 6, no. 1 (2009): 26-47.

Homel, Jacqueline, Astghik Mavisakalyan, Ha Trong Nguyen, and Chris Ryan. "School Completion: What We Learn from Different Measures of Family Background." *Longitudinal Surveys of Australian Youth,* Research Report 59, July 5, 2012.

Huntsinger, Carol, and Paul Jose. "Parental Involvement in Children's Schooling: Different Meanings in Different Cultures." *Early Childhood Research Quarterly* 24, no. 4 (2009): 398-410.

Huntsinger, Carol, Paul Jose, Shari Larson, Dana Balsink Krieg, and Chitra Shaligram. "Mathematics, Vocabulary, and Reading Development in Chinese American and European American Children over the Primary School Years." *Journal of Educational Psychology* 92, no. 4, (2000): 745-760.

Ingram, Dale. "Family Plot." *Tulsa World,* October 18, 2009.

Jae-yun, Shim. "Shadow of Higher Education." *The Korea Times,* Nov. 30, 2011.

Jauhiainen, A., J. Kivirauma, and R. Rinne. "Status and Prestige through Faith in Education: The Successful Struggle of Finnish Primary School Teachers for Universal University Training." *Journal of Education for Teaching: International Research and Pedagogy* 24, no. 3 (November 1998): 269.

Johnson, Jean, Jon Rochkind, and Amber Ott. "Are We Beginning to See the Light?" *Public Agenda,* June 2010.

Johnson, Sandy Scaffetta. *Oklahoma Teacher Education Programs Under the Microscope: A Study of Oklahoma Elementary Education Mathematics Content Preparation.* Oklahoma City: Oklahoma Business and Education Coalition, 2005.

Joerres, Jeff. "CEO Working Summit Synopsis." Panel at the *Atlantic's* New Work Era Summit, July 19, 2011, Washington, DC.

Jordan, Jennifer. "A Higher Standard." *The Providence Journal*, October 11, 2009.

Kaczorowska, Teresa. "The New Need to Improve." *Gazeta Wyborcza*, September 2, 1999. Translation by Sarah Zarrow.

Kalbarczyk, Adam. "Against Gymnasium." *Gazeta Wyborcza*, October 1, 1998. Translation by Sarah Zarrow.

Kamm, Henry. "The Past Submerged: Wroclaw, Once German Breslau, Is Now a Vigorously Polish City." *The New York Times*, February 19, 1966.

Kanervio, Pekka. "Challenges in Educational Leadership in Finnish Municipalities." Paper presented at the 6th International Symposium on Educational Research, Kempton Park, South Africa, July 19-23, 2010.

Kang, Shin-who. "67 Percent of Private Cram Schools Overcharge Parents." *The Korea Times*, April 14, 2009.

Khan, Salman. *The One World Schoolhouse: Education Reimagined.* New York: Hachette Book Group, 2012.

Killackey, Jim, and Mick Hinton. "Outlook Uncertain for Literacy Passport." *Daily Oklahoman*, March 26, 1995.

Killackey, Jim. "State Education Secretary Urges High School Graduation Test." *Daily Oklahoman*, July 30, 1997.

Kim. *Kim's AFS Journey* (blog). http://kimsafsjourney.blogspot.com/.

Kim, Hee-jin. "BAI Finds Several Big Loopholes in Admission System." *Korea JoongAng Daily*, January 25, 2012.

Kim, Mi-ju, and Park Su-ryon. "Students Rely on Hagwon More Than Public Schools." *Korea JoongAng Daily*, February 19, 2010.

Kim, Young-hwa. "Consequences of Higher Educational Expansion in Korea: Trends in Family Background and Regional Effects on Higher Educational Attainment, 1967-1984." *Korean Social Science Journal* 18 (1992): 139-153.

Kivirauma, Joel, and Kari Ruoho. "Excellence Through Special Education? Lessons from the Finnish School Reform." *International Review of Education/Internationale Zeitschrift Fur Erziehungswissenschaft* 53, no. 3 (2007): 283-302.

Koedel, Cory. "Grading Standards in Education Departments at Universities." *Education Policy Analysis Archives*, 19 (2011): 1-23.

The Korea Times. "Education Warning." Nov. 25, 2011.

Korean Culture and Information Service. *Facts about Korea.* Seoul: Ministry of Culture, Sports, and Tourism, 2009.

Kruczkowska, Maria. "Reform Without Miracles." *Gazeta Wyborcza,* May 27, 1998. Translation by Sarah Zarrow.

Kupiainen, Sirkku, Jarkko Hautamäki, and Tommi Karjalainen. *The Finnish Education System and PISA.* Helsinki: Ministry of Education Publications, 2009.

Kwon, Hyunsoo. "Inclusion in South Korea: The Current Situation and Future Directions." *International Journal of Disability, Development & Education,* 52.1 (2005): 62.

Landers, Jim. "Finland's Education System a Model for Dallas." *The Dallas Morning News,* February 8, 2009.

Langworth, Richard, ed. *Churchill by Himself: The Definitive Collection of Quotations.* New York: PublicAffairs, 2011.

Lee, Hyo-sik. "Private Education Costs Fall for Second Year." *The Korea Times,* February 17, 2012.

Lee, Ki-Bong. "The Best of Intentions: Meritocratic Selection to Higher Education and Development of Shadow Education in Korea." Ph.D. diss., Pennsylvania State University, 2003.

Lee, Robert. "18-year-old Murders Mom, Hides Body in Apartment." *The Korea Herald,* November 24, 2011.

Leinwand, Steven, and Alan Ginsburg. *Measuring Up: How The Highest Performing State (Massachusetts) Compares to the Highest Performing Country (Hong Kong) in Grade 3 Mathematics.* Washington, DC: U.S. Department of Education and The Urban Institute, 2009.

Lemov, Doug. *Teach Like a Champion.* San Francisco: Jossey-Bass, 2010.

Lerner, Lawrence, Ursula Goodenough, John Lynch, Martha Schwartz, and Richard Schwartz. *The State of State Science Standards: Oklahoma.* Washington, DC: Thomas B. Fordham Institute, 2012.

Loveless, Tom. *How Well Are American Students Learning? With Special Sections on High School Culture and Urban School Achievement.* Washington, DC: Brookings Institute, 2001.

Loveless, Tom. *How Well Are American Students Learning? With Sections on Arithmetic, High School Culture, and Charter Schools.* Washington, DC: Brookings Institute, 2002.

Luxembourg Income Study (LIS) Inequality and Poverty Key Figures, http://www.lisdatacenter.org, Luxembourg: LIS. Accessed 2012.

Lyytinen, Jaakko. "Helsinki Parents at Pains to Avoid Schools with High Proportion of Immigrants." *Helsingin Sanomat,* January 1, 2011.

Magnuson, Katherine, and Jane Waldfogel, eds. *Steady Gains and Stalled Progress: Inequality and the Black-White Test Score Gap.* New York: Russell Sage Foundation, 2008.

Mandara, Jelani. "An Empirically Derived Parenting Typology." Paper presented at the Achievement Gap Initiative Conference, Harvard University, Cambridge, June 29, 2011.

Manyika, James, Susan Lund, Byron Auguste, Lenny Mendonca, Tim Welsh, and Sreenivas Ramaswamy. *An Economy That Works: Job Creation and America's Future.* McKinsey & Company, June 2011.

Marshall, Paula A. *Sweet as Pie, Tough as Nails.* Tulsa: Expert Message Group, 2011.

May, Henry, Angela Duckworth, and Erling Boe. *Knowledge vs. Motivation: What Do International Comparisons of Achievement Test Scores Really Tell Us?* Unpublished manuscript, 2012.

McKinsey & Company. *The Economic Impact of the Achievement Gap in America's Schools.* April 2009.

MetLife, Inc. *The MetLife Survey of the American Teacher: Teachers, Parents and the Economy.* New York: MetLife, 2012.

Miliband, Ed. "On Social Mobility." Speech at the Sutton Trust-Carnegie Corporation Social Mobility Summit, London, UK, May 22, 2012.

Moskowitz, Eva, and Arin Lavinia. *Mission Possible: How the Secrets of the Success Academies Can Work in Any School.* San Francisco: Jossey-Bass, 2012.

Mourshed, Mona, Chinezi Chijioke, and Michael Barber. *How the World's Most Improved School Systems Keep Getting Better.* London: McKinsey & Company, 2010.

Michigan State University News. "MSU Scholars Help Minnesota Become Global Leader in Math." December 9, 2008.

Na, Jeong-ju. "Bounty Hunters Targeting 'Hagwon.'" *The Korea Times,* September 18, 2012.

Na, Jeong-ju. "Cram Schools Turning to NEAT to Boost Revenue." *The Korea Times,* February 8, 2012.

National Council on Teacher Quality. *It's Easier to Get into an Education School than to Become a College Football Player.* Washington, DC: National Council on Teacher Quality, 2011.

National Council on Teacher Quality. *Teacher Quality Roadmap: Improving Policies and Practices in LAUSD.* Washington, DC: National Council on Teacher Quality, 2011.

National Governors Association. *Benchmarking for Success: Ensuring U.S. Students Receive a World-Class Education.* Washington, DC: National Governors Association, the Council of Chief State School Officers, and Achieve, Inc., 2008.

National Science Board. *Science and Engineering Indicators 2010.* Arlington, VA: National Science Foundation, 2010, Chapter 4.

Nixon, Ron. "Congress Blocks New Rules on School Lunch." *New York Times,* November 15, 2010.

Northeastern State University. *Fact Book: Academic Year 2010-2011.*

Obama, Barack. "State of Union address." January 25, 2011.

Obama, Barack. "Remarks by the President on the 'Education To Innovate' Campaign." Washington, D.C., November 23, 2009.

Office of State Finance, State of Oklahoma. *FY 2011 Executive Budget.* Accessed 2012.

Official Statistics of Finland. *Special Education.* Helsinki: Statistics Finland, 2012.

OECD. *Building a High-Quality Teaching Profession: Lessons from Around the World.* Paris: OECD Publishing, 2011.

_____. "Child Well-being Module—CO4.1: Teenage suicide (15-19 years old)," Social Policy Division, Directorate of Employment, Labour and Social Affairs. Updated October 2011.

_____. "Country Statistical Profile: Poland." *Country Statistical Profiles: Key Tables from the OECD.* 2011.

_____. "Country Statistical Profile: United States." *Country Statistical Profiles: Key Tables from the OECD.* 2011.

_____. *Education at a Glance 2011: OECD Indicators.* Paris: OECD Publishing, 2011.

_____. *Education at a Glance 2012: OECD Indicators.* Paris: OECD Publishing, 2012.

_____. *Education at a Glance 2013: OECD Indicators.* Paris: OECD Publishing, 2013.

_____. *The High Cost of Low Educational Performance: The Long-Run Economic Impact of Improving PISA Outcomes.* Paris: OECD Publishing, 2010.

_____. "The Impact of the 1999 Education Reform in Poland." OECD Education Working Papers No. 49. OECD Publishing, Paris, 2011.

_____. *Improving Lower Secondary Schools in Norway 2011.* Paris: OECD Publishing, 2011.

_____. *International Migration Outlook 2012.* Paris: OECD Publishing, 2012.

_____. *Knowledge and Skills for Life: First Results from the OECD Program for International Student Assessment (PISA) 2000.* Paris: OECD Publishing, 2001.

_____. *Learning for Tomorrow's World: First Results from PISA 2003*. Paris: OECD Publishing, 2004.

_____. *Let's Read Them a Story! The Parent Factor in Education*. Paris: OECD Publishing, 2012.

_____. *Mathematics Teaching and Learning Strategies in PISA*. Paris: OECD Publishing, 2010.

_____. *Measuring Student Knowledge and Skills: A New Framework for Assessment*. Paris: OECD Publishing, 2000.

_____. *Messages from PISA 2000*. Paris: OECD Publishing, 2004.

_____. *Pathways to Success: How Knowledge and Skills at Age 15 Shape Future Lives in Canada*. Paris: OECD Publishing, 2010.

_____. *PISA In Focus No. 6: When Students Repeat Grades or Are Transferred Out of School: What Does It Mean for Education Systems?* Paris: OECD Publishing, 2011.

_____. *PISA in Focus No. 10: What Can Parents Do to Help Their Children Succeed in School?* Paris: OECD Publishing, 2011.

_____. *PISA Released Items: Mathematics*. Paris: OECD Publishing, 2006.

_____. *PISA 2009 Results: What Students Know and Can Do (Vol. I)*. Paris: OCED Publishing, 2010.

_____. *PISA 2009 Results: Overcoming Social Background (Vol. II)*. Paris: OECD Publishing, 2010.

_____. *PISA 2009 Results: What Makes a School Successful? Resources, Policies and Practices (Vol. IV)*. Paris: OECD Publishing, 2010.

_____. *PISA 2012 Results: Excellence Through Equity (Vol. II)*. Paris: OECD Publishing, 2013.

_____. *PISA 2012 Results: What Students Know and Can Do (Vol. I)*. Paris: OECD Publishing, 2013.

_____. *Quality Time for Students: Learning In and Out of School*. Paris: OECD Publishing, 2011.

_____. *Strong Performers and Successful Reformers in Education: Lessons from PISA for the United States*. Paris: OECD Publishing, 2011.

_____. *Student Learning: Attitudes, Engagement, and Strategies*. Paris: OECD Publishing, 2004.

_____. *Students with Disabilities, Learning Difficulties, and Disadvantages: Policies, Statistics, and Indicators*. Paris: OECD Publishing, 2007.

_____. "Suicides." *Health: Key Tables from OECD*, No. 17, October 30, 2012.

_____. *Take the Test: Sample Questions from OECD's PISA Assessments*. Paris: OECD Publishing, 2009.

Oklahoma High School Indicators Project. *Remediation Report, Fall 2010.* Oklahoma City: Oklahoma State Regents for Higher Education, 2010.

Oklahoma State Department of Education. *Sallisaw Public School No Child Left Behind Act Annual Report Card 2008-2009.* Oklahoma City, 2009.

Oklahoma State Department of Education. *Sallisaw Public School No Child Left Behind Act Annual Report Card 2009-2010.* Oklahoma City, 2010.

Oklahoma State Department of Education. *Sallisaw Public School No Child Left Behind Act Annual Report Card 2010-2011.* Oklahoma City, 2011.

Oklahoma State Department of Education. *Superintendent's Salary Listing.* Oklahoma City, 2011.

Oklahoma Commission for Teacher Preparation, *Teacher Preparation Inventory 2012.* Oklahoma City: OCTP, 2012.

Orfield, Gary, and Chungmei Lee. *Historic Reversals, Accelerating Resegregation, and the Need for New Integration Strategies.* Los Angeles: The Civil Rights Project/*Proyecto Derechos Civiles,* 2007.

Paige, Rod. "U.S. Students Average Among International Peers." U.S. Department of Education press release. Washington, DC, December 4, 2001.

Parmar, Parminder, Sara Harkness, and Charles M. Super. "Teacher or Playmate? Asian Immigrant and Euro-American Parents' Participation in Their Young Children's Daily Activities." *Social Behavior and Personality: An International Journal,* 36 (2008): 163-174.

Pennsylvania Department of Education. "SAT and ACT Scores." http://www. portal.state.pa.us/portal/server.pt/community/data_and_statistics/7202/ sat_and_act_scores/674663. Accessed 2012.

Peterson, Paul E., and Carlos Xabel Lastra-Anadón. "State Standards Rise in Reading, Fall in Math." *Education Next* 58, no. 4 (2010): 12-16.

Peterson, Paul E., Ludger Woessmann, Eric A. Hanushek, Carlos X. Lastra-Anadón. *Globally Challenged: Are U.S. Students Ready to Compete? The Latest on Each State's International Standing in Math and Reading.* PEPG Report No: 11-03, August 2011.

Poehlman, Lindsay. *2011-2012 International Youth Exchange Statistics.* Alexandria, VA: The Council on Standards for International Educational Travel, 2012.

Price, Marie, and Barbara Hoberock. "Legislative Roundup: Education Committee Backs 'High-Stakes' Student Testing.'" *Tulsa World,* March 8, 2005.

Rahn, Kim. "Student Kills Mother, Keeps Body at Home for 8 Months." *The Korea Times,* Nov. 24, 2011.

Ravitch, Diane. "What Can We Learn from Finland?" *Bridging Differences* (blog), *Education Week*. October 11, 2011.

Ravitch, Diane. Speech at "Save Our Schools" rally on the National Mall. Washington, DC, July 30, 2011.

Rich, Vera. "Minister Who Got His Sums Wrong Is Forced to Quit." *THE*, August 4, 2000.

Richtel, Matt. "In Classroom of Future, Stagnant Scores." *New York Times*, September 3, 2011.

Ripley, Amanda. "Ban School Bake Sales." *Slate*, September 5, 2013.

_____. "Brilliance in a Box: What Do the Best Classrooms in the World Look Like?" *Slate*, October 20, 2010.

_____. "The Case Against High-School Sports." *The Atlantic*, October 2013.

_____. "The New Smart Set." *Time*, September 30, 2013.

_____. "Rhee Tackles Classroom Challenge." *Time*, November 26, 2008.

_____. "Teacher, Leave Those Kids Alone." *Time*, October 3, 2011.

_____. "What Makes a Great Teacher?" *The Atlantic*, January/Febuary 2010.

_____. "The World's Schoolmaster." *The Atlantic*, July/August 2011.

Robelen, Erik W. "Study Links Rise in Test Scores to Nations' Output." *Education Week*, January 25, 2010.

Rolland, Megan. "National Group's Plan to be Used: Kern Decries School Standard." *The Oklahoman*, October 7, 2011.

Rolland, Megan, and Tricia Pemberton. "Raising Bar for Final Tests Leaves Some Feeling Worry." *The Oklahoman*, April 3, 2011.

Rotherham, Andrew J. "When It Comes to Class Size, Smaller Isn't Always Better." *Time*, March 3, 2011.

Rothwell, Jonathan. *Housing Costs, Zoning, and Access to High Scoring Schools.* Washington, DC: Brookings Institute, 2012.

Sachs, Jeffrey. Interviewed on *Commanding Heights*. Public Broadcasting System, June 15, 2000.

Sahlberg, Pasi. *Finnish Lessons: What Can the World Learn from Educational Change in Finland?* New York: Teachers College Press, 2011.

Schmidt, William, and Curtis McKnight. *Inequality for All: The Challenge of Unequal Opportunity in American Schools.* New York: Teachers College Press, 2012.

Schmidt, William, Maria Teresa Tatto, Kiril Bankov, Sigrid Blömeke, Tenoch Cedillo, Leland Cogan, Shin Il Han, Richard Houang, Feng Jui Hsieh, Lynn Paine, Marcella Santillan, and John Schwille. *The Preparation Gap: Teacher Education for Middle School Mathematics in Six Countries (MT21 Report).* East Lansing: Michigan State University, 2007.

Schneider, Mark. "The International PISA Test." *Education Next* 9, no. 4 (Fall 2009).

Scholastic and the Bill & Melinda Gates Foundation. *Primary Sources: 2012 – America's Teachers on the Teaching Profession.* Scholastic U.S.A., 2012.

SciMathMN. *Minnesota TIMSS: The Rest of the Story: A Summary of Results as of October 2009.* SciMathMN, 2009.

Scott, Joan. "Testimony by Professor Joan Wallach Scott Before the Pennsylvania General Assembly's House Select Committee on Student Academic Freedom." November 9, 2005.

Seligman, Martin E.P., Karen Reivich, Lisa Jaycox, and Jane Gillham. *The Optimistic Child: A Proven Program to Safeguard Children Against Depression and Build Lifelong Resilience.* New York: Houghton Mifflin, 2007.

Seth, Michael J. *Education Fever: Society, Politics, and the Pursuit of Schooling in South Korea.* Honolulu: University of Hawaii Press, 2002.

Shin-who, Kang. "Private Education Spending to Be Halved." *The Korea Times*, January 27, 2010.

Shockley, Martin Staples. "The Reception of *The Grapes of Wrath* in Oklahoma." *American Literature* 15, no. 4 (1944): 351-361.

Simola, Hannu, and Risto Rinne. "PISA Under Examination: Changing Knowledge, Changing Tests, and Changing Schools." *Comparative and International Education,* 11, Section V (2011): 225-244.

Song-ah, Kim. "Living in Harmony with Disabled." *The Korea Times,* November 25, 2009.

Sorensen, Clark W. "Success and Education in South Korea." *Comparative Education Review,* 38, no. 1 (1994).

Suh-young, Yun, and Na Jeong-ju. "Nation Holds Breath for Most Crucial Test." *The Korea Times,* November 10, 2011.

Suh-young, Y. "My Dream Is to Reshape Korea's Education." *The Korea Times*, September 21, 2011.

Statistics Korea. *The 2010 Survey of Private Education Expenditure.* 2011.

Steinbeck, John. *The Grapes of Wrath.* New York, NY: Penguin Group, 1939.

Tauber, Robert T. *Classroom Management: Sound Theory and Effective Practice.* Westport: Praeger Publishers, 2007.

Taylor, Leonore. "Finns Win, but Australian Students Are a Class Act." *Australian Financial Review,* December 5, 2001.

Time. "Northern Theatre: Sisu," January 8, 1940.

_____. "Time Poll Results: Americans' Views on Teacher Tenure, Merit Pay, and Other Education Reforms," September 9, 2010.

Toffler, Alvin. *Future Shock.* New York: Random House, 1970.

Tucker, Marc S., ed. *Surpassing Shanghai: An Agenda for American Education Built on the World's Leading Systems.* Cambridge: Harvard University Press, 2011.

UNICEF. *Child Poverty in Perspective: An Overview of Child Well-Being in Rich Countries.* Florence: UNICEF Innocenti Research Centre, 2007.

U.S. Department of Education. Education Dashboard. http://dashboard.ed.gov. Accessed 2012.

U.S. Department of Education, National Center for Education Statistics. *Table B.1.70: Average combined mathematics literacy scores of 15-year-old students, by national quartiles of the PISA index of economic, social and cultural status (ESCS) and jurisdiction: 2003.* International Data Table Library, 2012. http://nces.ed.gov/surveys/international/tables/B_1_70.asp. Accessed 2012.

U.S. Department of Education, National Center for Education Statistics. *Table M8: Average scores of 15-year-old students on PISA mathematics literacy scale, by national quarters of the PISA index of economic, social and cultural status (ESCS) and education system: 2012.* PISA Data Explorer, 2013. http://nces.ed.gov /surveys/pisa/pisa2012/pisa2012highlights_3d.asp. Accessed 2013.

U.S. Department of Education, National Center for Education Statistics. *Digest of Education Statistics, 2010: Table 3: Enrollment in educational institutions, by level and control of institution: Selected years, 1869-70 through fall 2019.*

U.S. Department of Education, National Center for Education Statistics. *Digest of Education Statistics, 2010: Table 45: Children 3 to 21 years old served under Individuals with Disabilities Education Act, Part B, by type of disability: Selected years, 1976-77 through 2008-09.*

U.S. Department of Education, National Center for Education Statistics. *National Assessment of Educational Progress (NAEP).* Various years, 1990–2011, Mathematics Assessments.

U.S. Department of Education, National Center for Education Statistics. *Table 8: Average number of public school teachers and average number of public school teachers who were dismissed in the previous year or did not have their contracts renewed based on poor performance, by tenure status of teachers and state: 2007–08.* Schools and Staffing Survey (SASS), Public School District Data File, 2007–08.

U.S. Department of Education, Institute of Education Sciences, National Center for Education Statistics. *Table 194: Current expenditure per pupil in average daily attendance in public elementary and secondary schools, by state or jurisdiction.* Various years, 1959-60 through 2007-8.

U.S. Department of Education, Institute of Education Sciences, National Center for Education Statistics. *Table 135: American College Testing (ACT) Score Averages, by Sex: 1970-1997.*

U.S. *News and World Report.* "College Ranking Lists: Top 100 Lowest Acceptance Rates, Fall 2011." Accessed December 2012.

Walsh, Kate, and Christopher O. Tracy. *Increasing the Odds: How Good Policies Can Yield Better Teachers.* Washington, DC: National Council on Teacher Quality, 2004.

Walsh, Kate, Deborah Glaser, and Danielle Dunne Wilcox. *What Education Schools Aren't Teaching about Reading and What Elementary Teachers Aren't Learning.* Washington, DC: National Council on Teacher Quality, 2006.

Wang, Aubrey, Ashaki Coleman, Richard Coley, and Richard Phelps. *Preparing Teachers Around the World.* Princeton: Educational Testing Service, 2003.

Whelan, Fenton. *Lessons Learned: How Good Policies Produce Better Schools.* London: Fenton Whelan, 2009, p. 7.

Window & Door. "Therma-Tru to Close Oklahoma Manufacturing Facility." January 26, 2009.

Winerip, Michael. "Despite Focus on Data, Standards for Diploma May Still Lack Rigor." *New York Times*, February 5, 2012.

Won, Seoung Joun, and Seunghee Han. "Out-of-School Activities and Achievement Among Middle School Students in the U.S. and South Korea." *Journal of Advanced Academics* 21 no. 4 (August 2010): 628-661.

World Economic Forum. *The Global Competitiveness Report 2012-2013: Full Data Edition.* Geneva: World Economic Forum, 2012.

Yoon, Ja-young. "Foreign Investors Eye Education Market." *The Korea Times*, September 12, 2008.

Yun, Suh-young. "'My Dream Is to Reshape Korea's Education.'" *The Korea Times*, September 21, 2011.

notes

prologue: the mystery

1   *Crap:* Ripley, "Rhee Tackles Classroom Challenge."

2   *Kimball Elementary School:* Ripley, "What Makes a Great Teacher?" Unemployment rate for Ward 7 comes from the D.C. Strategic Workforce Investment Plan.

3   *Dance of the Nations:* The graphic, updated in July 2012 for this book, was also scheduled to appear in Hanushek and Woessmann's forthcoming book, *The Knowledge Capital of Nations.*

4   *American kids were better off:* OECD, *PISA 2012 Results (Vol. II)*, Table II.2.13a, 212.

4   *Twenty-seven other nations:* The PISA test, the most sophisticated international test of teenagers' critical thinking skills, is administered by the OECD. For this book, I relied primarily, though not exclusively, on PISA data. (For more on why, see notes for page 15, "*Other international tests*," p. 258.) In an effort to be fair and consistent, I did not include non-countries (i.e., Hong Kong, Shanghai, or Macao-China) when I derived rankings from PISA data.

Also, I considered countries with exactly the same average PISA score to occupy the same ranking. (In other words, since the most affluent kids in Australia and Germany had the same mean math score, I considered both countries to rank about tenth in the world, not tenth and eleventh.)

The PISA test does not collect data on parental income per se, partly because students do not generally know how much money their parents earn. The test does however measure socioeconomic status by asking students about their parents' education levels, occupations, and the number of books and computers in their home, and so on. Their answers make up something that the OECD calls the index of students' economic, social, and cultural status (ESCS). Students' answers to these kinds of questions tend to be surprisingly accurate—and the results can better predict educational success than income alone.

The index reveals that American kids who ranked in the top quartile on the ESCS index in 2012 scored below their top-quartile peers in twenty-seven other countries in math (see U.S. Department of Education, *Table M8*).

Outside a handful of researchers at the OECD and the U.S. Department of Education, few people seem to have noticed this index, possibly because it is so hard to find. Instead, various education bloggers and commentators have seized on another, more readily available breakdown of scores. That data shows how different *schools'* students did on PISA within the United States, broken down by the percentage of students receiving free or reduced-price lunch at those schools. Nothing wrong with that. And, indeed, that data, included in a U.S. Department of Education publication, shows that U.S. schools with very few low-income kids performed very well on PISA compared to U.S. schools with high numbers of low-income kids. It is a useful way to compare schools *within* the United States.

However, these same bloggers concluded that kids in affluent American schools performed better than *all kids* in Finland or other top-performing countries. Education pundit and New York University research scientist Diane Ravitch has repeatedly made this claim—on television and in print. "If you look at the latest international test scores, our schools that are low-poverty schools are number one in the world," Ravitch said at the 2011 *Save our Schools* rally on the National Mall. "They're ahead of Finland! They're ahead of Korea. Number one. The schools that are less than 10 percent poor and the schools that are 25 percent poverty are equal to the schools of Finland and Korea, the world leaders. Our problem is poverty, not our schools."

That is nonsense. Other countries do not have data on which students would qualify for free or reduced-price lunch under U.S. regulations; that is an American policy with American definitions. This breakdown of PISA scores came from a survey of principals conducted in the United States *only*. The OECD does not collect comparable data from principals in any other country. So we cannot use the free-lunch data to compare different countries' results.

For example, Finland has less than 5 percent child poverty using one standard definition of poverty (i.e., the percentage of people earning less than 50 percent of the median income for *Finland*). That definition of poverty is totally different and unrelated to the criteria used to qualify kids for free or reduced-price lunch in the United States (i.e., parents earning less than 185 percent of the *U.S.* poverty level).

The bottom line: The only existing way to compare how kids at different income levels do on PISA is to use PISA's own index of socioeconomic status. That is the data I have cited here and throughout the book. That data does not show that low-poverty U.S. schools rank number one in much, unfortunately, except perhaps spending per student.

4   *Beverly Hills:* Greene and McGee, "When the Best Is Mediocre."

5   *Research and development:* National Science Board, *Science and Engineering Indicators.* The United States still invests more money in absolute dollars than any other nation in research and development. It's worth nothing, however, that the U.S. rate as a portion of GDP now falls below several other education superpowers, including Finland and Korea.

5   *The world had changed:* Author interviews with Craig Barrett, former Chair and CEO of Intel, March 27, 2012; Sir James Dyson, founder of the Dyson Company, June 1, 2011; Bill Gates, chairman of Microsoft, August 18, 2010; Sir John Rose, former CEO of Rolls-Royce, December 5, 2011; executives at Adecco, a global staffing and recruiting agency, December 14, 2011; as well as economists, public officials, and other business leaders around the world.

5   *Apple pies:* Author interviews with Paula Marshall, CEO of the Bama Companies, on November 9, 2011, and Shelly Holden, vice president of people systems at the Bama Companies, on December 16, 2011.

5   *Manpower:* Joerres, *Atlantic* panel. "The bar has risen," Joerres said. "Salespeople are the hardest to find—not because people don't want to do it. Companies have changed the entire definition of what it means to sell."

5   *Twenty countries:* High-school graduation rates for 2011 come from OECD, *Education at a Glance 2013,* Table A2.1a.

6   *Norway:* Child poverty rates come from the Luxembourg Income Study (LIS) analysis of poverty around the world. Children are considered poor if they live in a household earning less than 50 percent the median household income in their country of residence. Scientific literacy scores come from OECD, *PISA 2009 Results (Vol. I).* Norway's average scale score was 500 compared to the US score of 502.

7   *President Barack Obama:* In his 2011 State of the Union address, President
     Obama applauded South Korean teachers' reputation as "nation builders."
     He spoke admiringly of Korean parents in 2009 remarks for the "Educa-
     tion to Innovate" campaign.

8   *Survey:* This survey, conducted in collaboration with AFS in the spring
     of 2012, included 202 former exchange students from fifteen countries.
     Marie Lawrence from the New America Foundation helped design and
     administer the survey and analyze the results. A detailed summary of the
     methodology and results can be found in the appendix.

chapter 1: the treasure map

13   *Andreas Schleicher:* Details about the history of PISA come from many in-
     terviews with Andreas Schleicher, in-person, on the phone, and via email
     and Skype, between 2010 and 2012; interviews with Thomas Alexander;
     and archived newspaper clips from around the world. More details about
     Schleicher can be found in Ripley, "The World's Schoolmaster."

14   *A third of a million teenagers:* OECD, *Messages from PISA 2000.* The coin
     question comes from the OECD's *PISA Released Items.*

15   *Other international tests:* There are other tests besides PISA, each of which
     provides valuable data in its own right; for the purposes of this book, I was
     most interested in which countries prepared students to think, learn, and
     thrive in the modern economy. PISA was designed with this purpose in
     mind. The OECD's 1999 report, *Measuring Student Knowledge and Skills,*
     describes the difference between PISA and other international tests this
     way:
          "The knowledge and skills tested . . . are defined not primarily in terms
     of . . . national school curricula but in terms of what skills are deemed to be
     essential for future life. This is the most fundamental and ambitious novel
     feature of OECD/PISA. . . . PISA examines the degree of preparedness
     of young people for adult life and, to some extent, the effectiveness of
     education systems. Its ambition is to assess achievement in relation to
     the underlying objectives (as defined by society) of education systems,
     not in relation to the teaching and learning of a body of knowledge. Such
     authentic outcome measures are needed if schools and education systems
     are to be encouraged to focus on modern challenges."
          That said, no test is perfect, so it's important to consider multiple met-

rics and keep an open mind. To decide which countries to feature in this book, I used many different data points, including high school graduation rates, college attainment rates, spending per pupil, rankings of national competitiveness, and other economic indicators, as well as data from a variety of tests (including TIMSS, PIRLS, and NAEP).

As it turns out, international test results tend to be rather consistent. (The correlation between TIMSS 2007 and PISA 2006 was 0.93.) There are some differences worth mentioning, though. For example, American kids usually do somewhat better on TIMSS than on PISA, especially in reading. But TIMSS is given to fourth and eight graders, and PISA is taken by fifteen-year-olds (most of whom are in tenth grade).

Since we know that American students' abilities seem to degrade the longer they go to school (relative to other countries), PISA was more useful for my purposes. It not only measured students' abilities to apply knowledge to solve real-world problems (whereas TIMSS is a test of school curriculum); PISA also captured students' abilities closer to the end of their compulsory schooling, measuring the cumulative effects of education systems rather than the midpoint.

15   *"We were looking for the ability to think creatively:"* Taylor, "Finns Win, but Australian Students Are a Class Act."

16   *The education minister strode into the room:* Author interview with Jouni Välijärvi, professor at the Finnish Institute for Educational Research, University of Jyväskylä, on May 13, 2011. Välijärvi attended the Helsinki press conference and was interviewed on television afterward.

16   *"A tragedy for German education:"* "Bildungsstudie - Durchweg schlechte Noten," *FOCUS,* and Bracey, "Another Nation at Risk."

16   *Others blamed video games:* Heckmann, "Schlechte Schüler wegen schlecht gebildeter Lehrer?"

17   *A gulf of more than ninety points:* The data on the performance of affluent and less-affluent teenagers in the United States and around the world on the 2000 PISA is from Figure 6.1 on page 141 of the OECD report, "Knowledge and Skills for Life."

17   *"Average is not good enough:"* Paige, "U.S. Students Average among International Peers."

17   *Immigrants could not be blamed:* OECD, *Strong Performers and Successful Reformers in Education,* 29.

17   *Private school:* Compared to many other countries, the United States does not have a large proportion of students in private school. However, the

PISA sample for the United States does include private-school students. OECD, *Strong Performers and Successful Reformers in Education*, 47.

17   *Early childhood program:* OECD, *PISA 2012 Results (Vol. II)*, 95.

18   *Money did not lead to more learning:* OECD, *Strong Performers*, 28.

18   *"And he tells me the truth:"* Author interview of U.S. Secretary of Education Arne Duncan, March 21, 2011.

18   *"The most important man in English education:"* Gove, "The Benchmark for Excellence."

18   *PISA attracted critics:* For one critique of PISA, see Schneider, *Education Next*. My own conclusion is that these critics raised important points, particularly regarding the challenges of extrapolating causation from PISA data. Schleicher and his colleagues at the OECD have imperfect information, and their own biases, of course. Still, on balance, the data from PISA represents an important portal into a large, complex problem. It seems better to attempt to understand what differentiates education systems (with caution) than to abstain from the conversation altogether.

21   *"A TV reporter showed this graph:"* OECD, *Take the Test*.

21   *Flu-shot notice:* OECD, *Take the Test*.

22   *Vitamin C:* OECD, *PISA Released Items*.

23   *"Good job!":* The PISA folks declined to translate my performance into a precise numerical score since a country's mean score is normally derived from the aggregate score of all the kids who took the test. There are different versions of the test booklet given to different students to come up with a balanced sample. So, I can't say with precision how I did compared to all kids in Finland or Korea. However, it seems safe to assume that we inhabit the same league, since I got all but one question right. I am of course, much older than PISA test-takers, so this does not mean much. But, anecdotally speaking, I can tell you that there was nothing on the test that I wouldn't want my own child to know and be able to do by the age of fifteen. PISA is many things, but it is not rocket science.

23   *"The hallmark of American education:"* Scott, "Testimony by Professor Joan Wallach Scott."

24   *U.S. teenagers ranked twenty-sixth:* OECD, *PISA 2009 Results (Vol. I)*. Note that students from Shanghai, which is part of China, earned, on average, the highest score in the world on PISA in 2009. I did not include Shanghai in my rankings for this book because Shanghai is not a country and not representative of China as a whole. (Millions of children in China still lack access to a basic education, despite exaggerated media

accounts of China's educational dominance.) If I had included Shanghai (and Hong Kong), the United States would rank lower in every subject.

Data from PISA can be most easily accessed using the PISA International Data Explorer, located at http://nces.ed.gov/surveys/pisa/idepisa/.

24 *Second in the world:* OECD, *PISA 2009 Results (Vol. IV)*, Table IV.3.21b. There are many ways to compare spending on education, all of them flawed. After looking at the options, it seemed most useful and fair to rely on OECD data for cumulative expenditures by educational institutions per student aged six to fifteen. The figures are in equivalent U.S. dollars, converted using purchasing power parity.

One downside of this figure is that it does not include all of high school (or prekindergarten). Since the PISA test score data is based on fifteen-year-olds, these figures do correspond to the most relevant years for our purposes.

A bigger downside is that these numbers do not include families' private spending on tutoring and other educational supplements (although the figures do include private *school* expenditures in most countries, including the United States). As discussed in more detail in the portions of the book focused on Korea, that spending can be very high in Asian countries in particular. But, in all cases, most education spending flows through the school systems, which is where these numbers come from.

24 *One-to-one match:* Robelen, "Study Links Rise in Test Scores to Nations' Output," and OECD, *The High Cost of Low Educational Performance.*

24 *One to two trillion dollars:* McKinsey & Company, *Economic Impact.*

24 *A better predictor:* The predictive power of PISA was analyzed in a longitudinal study of thirty thousand Canadian teenagers who took the test in 2000. OECD, *Pathways to Success.*

chapter 2: leaving

27 *Pretty Boy Floyd:* Ingram, "Family Plot."

27 *Officially classified as poor:* Poverty rates for Sallisaw School District from the Bureau of the Census, American Community Survey, 2005-9 Summary Tables, generated using American FactFinder.

27 *On the state test:* In 2009, when Kim was finishing eighth grade, six out of ten of her Sallisaw classmates scored proficient or better on Oklahoma's standardized test. Oklahoma State Department of Education, "Sallisaw Public School No Child Left Behind Act Annual Report Card 2008-2009."

27   *But that test was notoriously easy:* Peterson and Lastra-Anadón, "State
      Standards Rise in Reading, Fall in Math."

27   *On a more serious test:* I'm talking here about the National Assessment of
      Educational Progress (NAEP), which is the largest nationally representative
      test continually administered in the United States. In Oklahoma and other
      states, the sample does not include enough students to offer district-level
      results. But since Sallisaw's scores did not differ dramatically from statewide
      averages on other tests, it is fairly safe to assume that Sallisaw's NAEP re-
      sults would be comparable to the statewide results (if such data existed).

      To put Kim's experience in context, I referred here to the 2009 NAEP
      results. That year, 23 percent of Oklahoma eighth graders achieved pro-
      ficient or advanced scores in math. In 2011, the number rose slightly to
      27 percent, which was still below the national average of 34 percent. U.S.
      Department of Education, *National Assessment of Educational Progress.*

27   *If states were countries:* Oklahoma's world ranking comes from the 2011 re-
      port, *Globally Challenged* (Peterson et al.), which creates a statistical crosswalk
      between PISA and NAEP data in order to rank states' performance relative
      to countries. The figure on pages 8-9 of the report shows that Oklahoma
      ranks eighty-first in the list of countries and states (not including territories).

31   *SAT scores:* In critical reading, Kim did better than 40 percent of Oklaho-
      ma's college-bound seniors. But she performed better than a whopping 69
      percent of seniors nationwide. Why such a big difference? It turns out that
      only about 6 percent of Oklahoma graduates took the SAT (compared to
      48 percent nationally). So, Oklahoma's average SAT scores were higher than
      they were for the nation. Most Oklahoma students took the ACT instead.

      Meanwhile, Kim did much worse in math, as she'd expected. In math, she
      scored better than just 5 percent of Oklahoma SAT-takers and 15 percent
      of students nationwide. In writing, she did slightly better, scoring higher
      than 14 percent of the Oklahoma seniors and 34 percent of all U.S. seniors.

      At a high level, Kim's strengths and weaknesses were not all that differ-
      ent from that of American students nationwide. She excelled in reading
      and tanked in math.

33   *More than doubled:* The increase in Oklahoma education spending is in
      constant dollars and comes from U.S. Department of Education statistics
      on per pupil expenditures.

33   *Teachers' aides:* During the 1986 to 1987 school year (earliest available
      data), Oklahoma had 3,825 instructional aides; by the 2010 to 2011 school
      year, the state employed 8,362 aides. To be fair, the student population rose

11 percent during the same time period. But the ratio of students-to-aides still went from 155:1 to 79:1. Meanwhile, Oklahoma's student-to-teacher ratio went from 17:1 to 16:1 over the same time period. Figures compiled through Common Core of Data "Build a Table" site, National Center for Education Statistics (http://nces.ed.gov/ccd/bat/).

33   *Lowered the student-to-teacher ratio:* Working with the Oklahoma State Department of Education, the earliest data I could find was student-to-teacher ratios going back to the 1976-1977 school year. Since then, the ratio had gone from 20.21 students per teacher to a low of 15.01 in the 2000-2001 school year. Since then, the ratio had crept up slightly to 16.11 for the 2011-2012 school year.

33   *Over half the state budget:* In Oklahoma's FY11 budget, education rang in at $3.6 billion—out of a total $6.7 billion in spending.

33   *End-of-school test:* Across the developed world, students in school systems that require standards-based external exams perform over sixteen points higher on average on the PISA test than those in schools that do not require such tests. These kinds of tests exist in Finland, Korea, and Poland, among other countries. They also exist in some U.S. states, but are not generally very rigorous.

For the tortured history of this test in Oklahoma, see Hinton, "Legislature Junks High School Grad Test Requirement"; Killackey and Hinton, "Outlook Uncertain for Literacy Passport"; Hinton, "Governor to Require 'Literacy Passports'"; and Price and Hoberock, "Legislative Roundup."

For more on how end-of-school tests impact performance around the world, see OECD, *Strong Performers and Successful Reformers in Education*, pgs. 49-50 and 243. For me, the most memorable part of that section was this:

"In the United States, high school students may be led to believe that the outcome is the same whether they take easy courses and get Ds in them or take tough courses and get As. Either way, they might think, they can get into the local community college and get on with their lives. Contrast this with a student of the same age in Toyota City, Japan, who wants to work on the line at a Toyota plant. That student knows that she must get good grades in tough subjects and earn the recommendation of her principal, so she takes those tough courses and works hard in school. . . . One of the most striking features of the American education system, in contrast with the education systems of the most successful countries, is its failure to provide strong incentives to the average student to work hard in school."

34   *"Kids have a really good detector":* Killackey, "State Education Secretary Urges High School Graduation Test."

34   *"Lost generation":* Archer, "Bill Would Lift Required Graduation Testing."

34   *530 superintendents:* By comparison, Finland has 399 superintendents for the entire country—a far larger land area with over 1 million more residents than Oklahoma. See Kanervio, "Challenges in Educational Leadership in Finnish Municipalities."

35   *One of the top earners:* Sallisaw's median household income between 2006 and 2010 was $30,229, according to the Bureau of the Census. Superintendent salaries come from the Oklahoma State Department of Education.

35   *Hardly unusual:* Usually, no one pays attention to the return on education spending—despite it being one of the largest items in any state budget. In a dramatic break with precedent, Ulrich Boser did a study in 2011 on the productivity of American school districts. This analysis showed huge variation from place to place, with the highest-spending districts being among the least efficient.

     Seen through this lens, Sallisaw's education results, while unimpressive in absolute terms, were a relative bargain, given the small amount of money spent per student. For more, check out the interactive map that accompanied that report, available at http://www.americanprogress.org/.

35   *More involved parents:* Americans' views on parental involvement (and all things) vary depending on how you ask the question. But it seems fair to say that parental involvement is a widespread concern. A 2010 *Time* magazine poll of one thousand U.S. adults included the following question (percentage agreeing in parentheses):

"What do you think would improve student achievement the most?"
More involved parents (52 percent)
More effective teachers (24 percent)
Student rewards (6 percent)
A longer school day (6 percent)
More time on test prep (6 percent)
No answer/don't know (6 percent)

35   *They were in fact showing up:* MetLife, *The MetLife Survey of the American Teacher.*

35   *Nine out of ten parents:* Herrold and O'Donnell, *Parent and Family Involvement in Education, 2006–07 School Year.*

36   *Nearly one in four:* Oklahoma State Department of Education, *Sallisaw Public School No Child Left Behind Act Annual Report Card 2010-2011.*

37   *Remedial classes:* Oklahoma High School Indicators Project, *Remediation Report, Fall 2010.*

For Sallisaw's Class of 2010 alumni entering college as freshmen, the remediation rate was 55 percent. The statewide remediation rate for Oklahoma high school graduates attending state colleges and universities that fall was 38 percent.

Nationwide data for the 2010 class was not yet available, and comparisons from one locality to the entire country are always complicated. But as one point of reference, about 36 percent of first-year undergraduates nationwide reported having taken a remedial course in 2007 to 2008. At public two-year institutions, about 42 percent said they had taken a remedial course. See Aud et al., *The Condition of Education 2011,* Indicator 22: Remedial Coursetaking.

37   *One out of two Oklahoma university students:* Denhart and Matgouranis, *Oklahoma Higher Education.*

38   *One or two thousand American high school students:* Poehlman, *2011–2012 International Youth Exchange Statistics.*

39   *Teenagers in Finland did less homework:* OECD, *Mathematics Teaching and Learning Strategies in PISA.*

40   *Not even tiny New Hampshire:* The Class of 2011 in New Hampshire performed at about the same level of students in Hungary and France. New Hampshire's teenagers were outperformed by their cohorts in eighteen other places including Canada, Japan, New Zealand, and Finland. See Peterson et al. *Globally Challenged.*

40   *Among the least challenging in the nation:* Lerner et al., *The State of State Science Standards: Oklahoma.* The state's science standards received an F in this report. The document to which this report refers (the one that does not mention evolution) is the *Priority Academic Student Skills (PASS)* standards for science, which were updated in 2011

43   *Door and window factory: Window & Door,* "Therma-Tru to Close Oklahoma Manufacturing Facility."

43   *Blue Ribbon Downs:* Adcock, "Sallisaw: A Blue Town."

chapter 3: the pressure cooker

46   *Busan:* Busan used to be known as Pusan. They are the same place. The spelling was officially changed in 2000.

53   *"Love stick"*: The Korean government had outlawed corporal punishment shortly before Eric arrived. It was a controversial decision, one with
which Eric's principal and the local superintendent did not entirely agree.
Teachers complained, worried they would have even less control of their
sleepy students if they couldn't hit them.

But certain kinds of physical punishments were still allowed—like taps
with the so-called love sticks or even forcing kids to stay in a push-up
position for twenty minutes or to run laps around a field. Occasionally,
more Draconian habits resurfaced.

One afternoon, an older man that Eric hadn't seen before came into
his classroom and called up three boys who had been disruptive earlier in
the day. He lined them up at the front of the classroom and told them
to present their hands, palms down. Then he rapped their knuckles with
a ruler, one boy at a time, said Eric, who saw the boys flinch. Then they
slouched back to their seats.

Worldwide, corporal punishment in schools is outlawed in about one
hundred nations, including Afghanistan, China, Finland, Germany, Sweden, the United Kingdom, and Poland, according to the Global Initiative
to End All Corporal Punishment of Children. So far, the United States
is not one of those countries, although thirty-three states do have bans
in place.

More information on international comparisons can be found here, including interviews with children themselves about the humiliation caused
by physical punishment at school: http://www.endcorporalpunishment.org/.

55   *Only 2 percent of seniors:* Korean Education Ministry officials. This figure
refers to the portion of all two- and four-year college students admitted
in 2012 to Korea's so-called SKY Universities: Seoul National University,
Korea University, and Yonsei University.

57   *American tests were not high stakes for students:* In a 2011 survey of 10,000
public-school teachers by Scholastic and the Gates Foundation, only
45 percent of teachers said their students took standardized tests seriously. See Scholastic and the Bill & Melinda Gates Foundation, *Primary
Sources: 2012 – America's Teachers on the Teaching Profession.*

57   *A small fraction of teachers:* The stakes were higher for teachers in some
places but, as of 2012, the vast majority of U.S. teachers were not evaluated based on test scores, despite widespread anxiety over such practices.
In some places—like Washington, D.C., and Memphis—a minority of
teachers had started to be reviewed based in part on the growth in their

students' test scores over time (compared to other students who had started the year at a similar level of performance). The rest of their evaluations were based on other things, including classroom observations. In 2011, about 6 percent of teachers in D.C. and fewer than 2 percent of teachers in Memphis lost their jobs after receiving exceptionally poor evaluations, according to my interviews with education officials in both places in 2012.

58   *"You Americans see a bright side":* Author interview with Korean Minister Lee Ju-ho on June 9, 2011, in Seoul.

59   *In tenth-century Korea:* Lee, "The Best of Intentions," 23.

59   *New words had to be coined:* Sorensen, "Success and Education in South Korea."

59   *Student-teacher ratio of 59:1:* Cavanagh, "Out-of-School Classes Provide Edge." Korea's current ratio is closer to 28:1.

59   *Only a third of Korean kids:* Seth, *Education Fever.*

59   *Nobody got accepted because he was good at sports:* Lee, "The Best of Intentions."

60   *About 40,000 percent:* GDP figures from Korean Culture and Information Service, *Facts about Korea,* 87.

60   *Education acted like an antipoverty vaccine in Korea:* Kim, "Consequences of Higher Educational Expansion in Korea."

61   *Dropout rates:* The dropout rate for Minnetonka High School comes from the Minnesota Department of Education online Data Center, accessed in November 2012. The dropout rate for Namsan, Eric's Korean high school, comes from my interview with the principal in June 2011.

To be fair, Namsan only admits 70 percent of the students who apply, while Minnetonka must take all students in the zoned jurisdiction. However, even with its selectivity, Namsan has a more impoverished student body, with about 17 percent qualifying for a full tuition subsidy due to their parents' low-income levels. (This formula is complex, but in general, qualifying families must earn less than $20,000 or so.) By contrast, at Minnetonka, only 8 percent of students qualify for free or reduced price lunch under the federal guidelines (which comes out to about $29,000 or less for a family of four). While these are two totally different measures, they give us some rough indication of the relative affluence of the Minnetonka student body.

61   *High salaries:* Teachers in Minnetonka, earned $61,000 on average according to Minnesota Department of Education statistics. According to the principal of Namsan, Eric's school in Korea, teachers earned about

$45,000 on average. When adjusted for purchasing power parity, the Korean salary is worth about $61,000, or the same as the Minnetonka salary.

There are, of course, many ways to compare teachers' earnings. However, suffice it to say that teachers in both of Eric's schools could afford a similar standard of living (although the Korean teachers earned less per hour, given Namsan's longer school day and year).

61   *Stabbed his mother:* Rahn, "Student Kills Mother, Keeps Body at Home for 8 Months"; Lee, "18-year-old Murders Mom, Hides Body in Apartment."

62   *Some went so far as to accuse the mother:* Jae-yun, "Shadow of Higher Education." The quote about "pushy" mothers comes from a 2011 unsigned editorial in the *Korea Times*.

62   *"One of the pushy 'tiger' mothers":* Korea Times, "Education Warning."

62   *Hundreds of students were accused of lying:* Kim, "BAI Finds Several Big Loopholes in Admission System."

62   *Highly educated elementary school teachers:* Minister Lee himself confirmed this rather bluntly in an interview by Kang Shin-who in the *Korea Times*: "Our teachers are better than those in the U.S."

62   *The top 5 percent:* Barber and Mourshed, *How the World's Best-Performing School Systems Come Out on Top*, 19. Interestingly, Korean elementary teachers were not always so carefully chosen. For many years, the teachers in training attended less prestigious two-year colleges. But, in the early 1980s, those education colleges became four-year universities offering more rigorous training and boosting the status of the profession. This history is almost identical to the story of Finland, which also consolidated its middling training programs into the more elite university system (albeit a decade or so earlier). Coolahan, *Attracting, Developing and Retaining Effective Teachers*.

This proven approach—elevating the selectivity and rigor of the teaching profession at the very beginning of teachers' careers—has never been attempted on a large scale in the United States, despite its obvious logic.

62   *Top of the world:* Schmidt et al., *The Preparation Gap.*

63   *Fateful mistake:* Ibid. *The Economist*, "How to be the Top."

63   *"Quality of an education system":* Barber and Mourshed, *How the World's Best-Performing School Systems Come Out on Top*, 16.

63   *Less than 1 percent:* In 2011, about 750 underperforming Korean teachers were sent for two months of training; another fifty were told to get six months of training. In all, 800 out of about four hundred thousand teachers received the training, which comes out to a mere .2 percent. Stephen

Kim, a *Time* magazine freelancer and a professional translator in Seoul, got these numbers from Korean education officials in September 2011.

63 *Some simply refused to go:* Author interviews with Korean educators in Seoul who asked not to be named for fear of retribution.

64 *Down just 3.5 percent:* Author interview with Minister Lee.

64 *Tricked-out classrooms:* There is remarkably little comparative data on technology investments around the world. It remains possible that technology holds great potential for schools, especially since it can personalize learning. So far, however, despite extravagant financial investments in technology, U.S. schools have not realized major benefits in productivity or effectiveness. And the American teenagers I followed for this book uniformly reported that they did not miss the high-tech devices they had in their U.S. classrooms.

For more detail on what other exchange students said about technology, see the results of the survey in the appendix and Ripley, "Brilliance in a Box."

65 *Only 15 percent of teenagers took afterschool lessons:* OECD, *PISA 2009 Results (Vol. IV),* Table IV.3.17b.

65 *Lee thought Finland was a far better national model:* Yun, "'My Dream is to Reshape Korea's Education.'"

65 *Just one in ten kids took afterschool lessons:* OECD, *PISA 2009 Results (Vol. IV),* Table IV.3.17b.

chapter 4: a math problem

70 *Math eluded American teenagers:* OECD, *PISA 2009 Results (Vol. I).*

70 *Math had a way of predicting kids' futures:* ACT, *Crisis at the Core,* and Hanushek et al., "Teaching Math to the Talented."

70 *Eighteenth in math:* U.S. Department of Education, *Table B.1.71.*

71 *American third graders:* Leinwand, *Measuring Up.* This study found that, even in Massachusetts, the highest performing state in the country, third graders were being asked less demanding math questions than kids their age in Hong Kong.

71 *Less than half were prepared for freshman-year college math:* ACT, *The Condition of College & Career Readiness 2011.* Only 45 percent of high-school graduates who took the ACT test in 2011 met the college readiness benchmark in math. The benchmark was based on the minimum score

needed to have a 50 percent chance of earning a B or higher in a fresh-man-year college math class. (Keep in mind that only half of high-school graduates took the ACT to begin with, so ability levels for the entire population would presumably be significantly lower.)

72   *"Success is going from failure to failure":* Langworth, *Churchill by Himself,* 579.

72   *Minnesota:* Peterson, *Globally Challenged,* 8-9 and SciMathMN, *Minnesota TIMSS.*

74   *American textbooks:* Schmidt and McKnight, *Inequality for All.*

75   *Sixty minutes per day:* MSU News, "MSU Scholars Help Minnesota Become Global Leader in Math."

75   *The Common Core:* For more on the potential value of the Common Core, along with the controversy, see Ripley, "The New Smart Set."To read the actual Common Core Standards, go to www.corestandards.org.

76   *A larger universe of math:* In his book *The One World Schoolhouse,* Salman Khan, founder of Khan Academy, writes persuasively about the problem of stove-piping in U.S. schools:

   "Genetics is taught in biology while probability is taught in math, even though one is really an application of the other. Physics is a separate class from algebra and calculus despite its being a direct application of them . . . In our misplaced zeal for tidy categories and teaching modules that fit neatly into a given length of class time, we deny students the ben-efit—the physiological benefit—of recognizing connections."

77   *Fourth graders said their math work was too easy:* Boser and Rosenthal, *Do Schools Challenge our Students?*

77   *Schools that did not even offer algebra courses:* Schmidt and McKnight, *Inequality for All.*

77   *In 2009, most American parents surveyed:* Johnson, Rochkind, and Ott, "Are We Beginning to See the Light?"

chapter 5: an american in utopia

84   *It made everyone more serious about learning:* When I visited Kim in Fin-land, I wondered if her impressions of her fellow students were skewed by the fact that she was at an academic high school in Pietarsaari—not a vocational one, where the less-driven students might have ended up. Kim disagreed, pointing out that she was comparing the drive of students in her

AP and honors classes in the United States to the students in her Finnish academic school—and still noticing the same disparity in engagement.

In any case, the dropout rate of Finland's vocational schools (about 8 percent) was still much lower than the dropout rate of the vast majority of U.S. high schools. Partly due to an infusion of resources from the government, Finland's vocational schools were generally more popular than U.S. vocational schools. So, it is likely that the student level buy-in was high at the vast majority of schools in Finland, not just Kim's school.

84 *Teachers rarely got fired anywhere:* OECD, *Strong Performers and Successful Reformers in Education,* 238. Many U.S. education reformers insist that unions are the reason for the country's mediocre education outcomes. After all, U.S. teachers' unions have a history of adversarial relations with government, and over the years, specific union leaders have obstructed basic, common sense changes at the expense of millions of students.

That said, the top performing countries in the world have unions, too. These countries offer irrefutable evidence that it is possible (and preferable) to radically improve entire systems *with* teachers' unions, rather than against them. That cooperation is much more likely to work if teaching has already evolved into a knowledge-worker profession, with high standards of entry and rigorous training (a development that has not yet happened in the United States and most countries worldwide). Consider this excerpt from the OECD report, *Strong Performers:*

"[M]any of the countries with the strongest student performance also have the strongest teachers' unions, beginning with Japan and Finland. There seems to be no relationship between the presence of unions, including and especially teachers' unions, and student performance. But there may be a relationship between the degree to which the work of teaching has been professionalised and student performance."

84 *She knew the odds were still against her:* Author interviews with Tiina Stara, in-person and over email and Skype, in 2011 and 2012.

85 *Only 20 percent of applicants were accepted:* The acceptance rate for the University of Jyväskylä in the mid-1980s comes from Ossi Päärnilä, who works in the Finnish literature department and kindly researched the historical acceptance rates at my request. Acceptance rates today vary depending on which department and university students select; but most Finnish teacher-training programs take between 5 and 20 percent of applicants.

85 *About as selective as Georgetown or the University of California, Berkeley:* U.S. News and World Report, "College Ranking Lists."

85   *Just one out of every twenty education schools:* Walsh, Glaser, and Wilcox.
      *What Education Schools Aren't Teaching about Reading and What Elemen-
      tary Teachers Aren't Learning.*

85   *"A Finnish teacher has received the highest level of education in the world":*
      Jauhiainen, Kivirauma, and Rinne, "Status and Prestige through Faith in
      Education," 269.

85   *Norway is not choosy about who gets to become a teacher:* OECD, *Improving
      Lower Secondary Schools in Norway 2011.*

86   *Norwegians have fretted:* Afdal, "Constructing Knowledge for the Teach-
      ing Profession."

86   *Even the most privileged among them:* U.S. Department of Education, *Table
      B.1.70.* Norway's most advantaged teenagers rank twentieth in math
      compared to other countries' top quartile students.

87   *He'd decided to become a teacher mostly so he could become a football coach:*
      Author interviews with Scott Bethel via phone and email in 2012.

87   *Nearly two dozen teacher-training programs:* Oklahoma Commission for
      Teacher Preparation, *Teacher Preparation Inventory 2012.*

87   *They were rewarded with high grades:* Koedel, "Grading Standards in Edu-
      cation Departments at Universities."

88   *It also has a 75 percent acceptance rate:* Northeastern State University, *Fact
      Book: Academic Year 2010-2011.* The university did not respond to requests
      for historical acceptance rates dating back to the time of Bethel's admis-
      sion.

88   *The university's typical ACT score is lower:* Northeastern State University,
      Fact Book: Academic Year 2010-2011 and ACT, *2010 ACT National and
      State Scores.* In 2010, incoming freshmen at NSU had an average ACT
      score of 20.1, compared to 21 for the U.S. overall. (The average for Okla-
      homa in 2010 was 20.7.)

88   *A master's degree did not make American teachers better at their jobs:* For a
      summary of this research and other insights into what does (and does not)
      seem to make teachers stronger, see Walsh and Tracy, *Increasing the Odds.*

88   *Two and a half times the numbers of teachers it needed:* Greenberg, Pomer-
      ance, and Walsh. *Student Teaching in the United States.* About 186,000
      new teachers graduate in the U.S. each year. About 77,000 actually take a
      teaching job.

88   *Finland, it turns out, had its own No Child Left Behind moment:* Simola and
      Rinne, "PISA Under Examination," and Landers, "Finland's Educational
      System a Model for Dallas."

88 *Central authorities approved textbooks:* Aho, Pitkänen, and Sahlberg, *Policy Development and Reform Principles of Basic and Secondary Education in Finland Since 1968.*

89 *Opponents argued that the new system was elitist:* Jauhiainen, Kivirauma, and Rinne, "Status and Prestige through Faith in Education," 266-267.

89 *Some university leaders objected, too:* OECD, *Stronger Performers and Successful Reformers in Education,* 117-135:

"University leaders initially resisted the idea that teaching was anything more than a semiprofession and feared that advocates for other semiprofessions like nursing and social work would now clamor to give their training programs university status. Their real worry was that the admission of teacher education candidates would lead to a dilution of academic standards and a consequent loss of status. Over time, however, as the new university-based teacher education programs were designed and built, these fears were not borne out."

90 *This liberation worked only because of all the changes that had come before:* To be fair, other writers, some of them Finnish, have disparaged the country's top-down, centralization phase as a total mistake. Instead, they cite the later phase—in which schools and teachers received more autonomy—as the key cause of Finland's success. And they recommend that other countries jump to that phase immediately.

However, veteran teachers and reformers in Finland told me that Finland needed to go through both phases, in that order. The centralizing, top-down phase, which included the creation of more rigorous teacher-training programs, made the subsequent period of decentralization possible in the 1980s and 1990s. Without raising all levels to a respectable baseline, there could never be trust.

Irmeli Halinen, a former teacher and reformer, and a member of the Finnish Education Evaluation Council, put it this way in our 2011 interview: "It's so difficult to speculate, but I think it would have been very difficult to be more collaborative in the first phase. People have to learn to work together. The national authorities have to learn to trust teachers, and the teachers have to learn to trust the national authorities. And that's a slow process—to learn to trust. I don't think we were ready for that in the beginning of the 1970s."

92 *"It will disenfranchise too many students":* Jordan, "A Higher Standard."

92 *"I have the utmost confidence":* Ibid.

92 *The percentage of minority students studying to be teachers:* In 2012, with the higher standards in place, minorities represented 9.24 percent of students admitted to Rhode Island College's education school—a rate slightly higher

than the previous four-year average of 8.8 percent. That rate could change, of course, but it was an early, hopeful sign that raising standards did not necessarily lead to a whiter teaching corps. Figures for 2008 to 2012 provided in December 2012 via email by Alexander Sidorkin, Dean of Rhode Island College's Feinstein School of Education and Human Development.

93   *Only two out of ten American teachers:* August, Kihn, and Miller, *Closing the Talent Gap.* In the class of 1999, about 23 percent of new U.S. teachers had SAT or ACT scores that were in the top third of the distribution for all college graduates. Only 14 percent of teachers in high-poverty schools had top-third scores.

93   *Higher academic standards to play football:* National Council on Teacher Quality, "It's Easier to Get into an Education School Than to Become a College Football Player."

93   *A grade-point average of just 2.5 or higher:* Details about Northeastern State University's current and past requirements come from a review of current policies, a list of the admissions requirements for the Teacher Education program from 1990 as well as email correspondence with former education dean Kay Grant, who joined the NSU faculty in 1985.

93   *The national average for the ACT back then was 20.6:* U.S. Department of Education, *Table 135.*

93   *Less than half of American high-school math teachers majored in math:* Schmidt and McKnight, *Inequality for All.*

94   *"A large majority of elementary education majors are afraid of math":* Johnson, *Oklahoma Teacher Education Programs Under the Microscope.*

94   *Most of the material was at a tenth or eleventh grade level:* Education Trust, "Not Good Enough."

94   *Knew about as much math as their peers in Thailand and Oman:* Center for Research in Mathematics and Science Education, *Breaking the Cycle.* One line from the executive summary bears repeating: "U.S. future teachers are getting weak training mathematically, and are just not prepared to teach the demanding mathematics curriculum we need, especially for middle schools, if we hope to compete internationally."

94   *An average of twelve to fifteen weeks of student teaching:* Wang et al., *Preparing Teachers Around the World,* 21-23. For a more thorough account of student teaching within the United States, see Greenberg, Pomerance, and Walsh, *Student Teaching in the United States.*

95   *The world's highest paid teachers lived in Spain:* Relative to other workers with college degrees, teachers in Spain earned more in 2010 than teach-

ers in all other developed countries surveyed, including Germany, Finland, France, Korea, Poland, and the United States. OECD. *Building a High-Quality Teaching Profession*, 13.

99   *About four hundred Finnish kids travel to the United States:* Poehlman, *2011–2012 International Youth Exchange Statistics.*

99   *Elina came to America:* I first read about Elina in a newspaper story (see Gamerman, "What Makes Finnish Kids So Smart?"). To learn more, I tracked Elina down and interviewed her in 2010, and again in 2012.

101   *Over half of American high schoolers echoed Elina's impression:* Boser and Rosenthal, *Do Schools Challenge Our Students?*

101   *In my own survey of 202 foreign-exchange students:* Details from this survey are contained in the appendix. Some of the results were mirrored in surveys conducted by the Brown Center on Education Policy a decade earlier. That study included a larger sample size, so the results may be more robust. In all, Loveless surveyed 368 foreign-exchange students and 328 Americans studying abroad. A majority of both groups agreed that their U.S. classes were easier. See Loveless, *How Well Are American Students Learning? With Special Sections on High School Culture and Urban School Achievement*, and Loveless, *How Well Are American Students Learning? With Sections on Arithmetic, High School Culture, and Charter Schools.*

chapter 6: drive

107   *Thirteen countries and regions:* Borgonovi and Montt, "Parental Involvement in Selected PISA Countries and Economies." The thirteen countries and regions that participated in the parents' survey were Croatia, Denmark, Germany, Hong Kong, Hungary, Italy, Korea, Lithuania, Macao (China), New Zealand, Panama, Portugal and Qatar. Since the United States and other countries chose not to participate in this survey, we don't know for sure if the dynamics would be comparable in those places. But it was interesting to see that clear patterns emerged even among these very different, far-flung thirteen locales.

For a less academic, more reader-friendly report on the same survey, see OECD, *Let's Read Them a Story!*

107   *Parents who volunteered in their kids' extracurricular activities had children who performed worse:* Borgonovi and Montt, "Parental Involvement in Selected PISA Countries and Economies," Table 3.1b. Specifically, parents

were asked if they had volunteered in extracurricular activities, such as a book club, school play, sports, or field trip over the last academic year.

109   *Fifteen-year-olds whose parents talked about complicated social issues:* Ibid., 18.

109   *Research from within the United States echoed these findings:* Henderson and Mapp, *A New Wave of Evidence,* and Dervarics and O'Brien, *Back to School.*

109   *Parent Teacher Association parenting:* To learn more about the different forms parental involvement takes in different countries, see Ripley, "Ban School Bake Sales." For more about the dangers of praise and the self-esteem parenting movement (and specific ideas about what parents can do differently), see Bronson and Merryman, *Nurture Shock,* and Seligman et al., *The Optimistic Child.*

   For more on the differences between Asian and Caucasian parenting in the United States, see Chao, "Chinese and European American Mothers' Beliefs about the Role of Parenting in Children's School Success."

   See also Parmar, "Teacher or Playmate," a 2008 study of highly educated Asian and European-American parents with children enrolled in the same preschools. The study revealed that while Asian and European parents spent about the same amount of time with their children—and allowed their children to watch about the same amount of television—the parents did different things with their kids. The Asian parents spent over three hours a week engaged in preacademic activities with their young children—learning letters and numbers, playing alphabet and number games, and visiting the library. The European parents spent just twenty minutes per week engaging in these activities.

110   *Parents who participated in a PTA had teenagers who performed worse:* Borgonovi and Montt, "Parental Involvement in Selected PISA Countries and Economies," Table 3.1b. Parents in thirteen countries and regions were asked if they had participated over the past academic year in local school government, such as a parent council or school management committee. Less than one-third of parents said they had done so in every case. Parents who had participated tended to have children who scored significantly lower in reading than parents who had not.

110   *Coach parents:* For an intriguing analysis of the parent as trainer, see Chao, "Beyond Parental Control and Authoritarian Parenting Style."

110   *Actually enjoy reading and school more than their Caucasian peers:* Carol Huntsinger and her colleagues have conducted fascinating research on the parenting styles and learning outcomes of Chinese-American kids. See Huntsinger and Jose, "Parental Involvement in Children's Schooling."

110 *Nor did a coach parent have to be Asian:* One obvious question is whether Finnish parents more closely resemble Korean or American parents. It is hard to get comparative data on this, and many Finns anecdotally report that play is the primary goal of elementary education in their country. *Play* can mean many things, however; some forms of play seem to lead to enormous learning and growth, and other forms do not. There is some evidence that totally unstructured free play is not as central to early childhood education in Finland as it is in the United States (Hakkarainen, "Learning and Development in Play").

My sense is that Finns are not as regimented nor as competitive as Korean parents, generally speaking, and that they have a more holistic approach to education at home and at school. That said, both cultures value self-reliance, humility, and direct communication in ways that might make many American parents uncomfortable. I suspect that the subtle cues that Korean and Finnish parents send to children about their capabilities, and how they can do better, may be similar and worth studying in more detail.

110 *European-American parents who acted more like coaches tended to raise smarter kids, too:* Huntsinger et al., "Mathematics, Vocabulary, and Reading Development in Chinese American and European American Children over the Primary School Years," 758.

111 *Scored twenty-five points higher on PISA:* OECD, *PISA in Focus No. 10.*

111 *If parents simply read for pleasure:* OECD, *Let's Read Them a Story!,* Chapter 5.

111 *85 percent of American parents surveyed:* Dweck, "Caution—Praise Can Be Dangerous."

112 *Same effect on PISA scores as hours of private tutoring:* Andreas Schleicher made this assertion in Friedman, "How about Better Parents?"

113 *"Warmth and strictness":* Lemov, *Teach like a Champion.*

113 *Researcher Jelani Mandara:* Mandara, "An Empirically Derived Parenting Typology."

113 *"In high school, Asian immigrant parents really have a more hands-off approach":* Author interview with Ruth Chao on September 7, 2011.

116 *Everything was more demanding, through and through:* This difference comes through in the data but also in person. When I visited Finland and Korea, it was obvious that both places had their problems. But going there was like watching a professional soccer game when you'd been playing junior varsity all your life. It was the same game, but everything seemed more fluid, less random. Pervasive rigor had raised these systems to another level.

117 *The education superpowers believed in rigor:* The OECD report, *Strong Performers and Successful Reformers in Education,* describes this difference on page 231:

"Many nations declare that they are committed to children and that education is important. The test comes when these commitments are weighed against others . . . .When it comes down to it, which matters more, a community's standing in the sports leagues or its standing in the student academic achievement league tables? Are parents more likely to encourage their children to study longer and harder or to want them to spend more time with their friends or playing sports?"

118 *Sports were central to American students' lives and school cultures:* The centrality of sports in U.S. schools is a fascinating oddity that bears further research. We know from the 2009 PISA dataset that 98 percent of U.S. high schools offered sports as an extracurricular activity, compared to 71 percent in Finland, for example. We don't, however, understand all the many ways this difference affects the lives of kids.

A survey of exchange students conducted a decade before this one found a similar consensus about sports: Eight out of ten exchange students said that it was more important to their American friends to do well in sports compared to students in other countries. (See Loveless, *How Well Are American Students Learning? With Special Sections on High School Culture and Urban School Achievement,* and Loveless, *How Well Are American Students Learning? With Sections on Arithmetic, High School Culture, and Charter Schools.*)

Those reports also pointed out that schools and students can excel at both sports and academics. They are not mutually exclusive, and athletes can, of course, be scholars. Still, it is hard to measure how the glorification of sports undermines academics in the minds of all the other American students (most of whom, it should be noted, are not serious athletes and never will be).

For more about the (rarely acknowledged) trade-offs between sports and academics, see Ripley, "The Case Against High-School Sports."

118 *American students spent double the amount of time playing sports:* Won and Han, "Out-of-School Activities and Achievement Among Middle School Students in the United States and South Korea."

119 *About 10 percent of Kim's classmates played sports in Finland:* Author email correspondence with teacher Tiina Stara on May 27, 2012.

120 *More and more studies:* The study of how personality impacted earnings started with Marxist sociologists and economists like Samuel Bowles and Herbert Gintis, who wrote a book called *Schooling in Capitalist America.* The research into all kinds of noncognitive skills accelerated in the 1980s, 1990s, and 2000s, led by scholars like James Heckman at the University of

Chicago and Angela Lee Duckworth at the University of Pennsylvania, among others.

120 *Best predictor of academic performance was not the children's IQ scores:* Duckworth and Seligman, "Self-Discipline Outdoes IQ in Predicting Academic Performance of Adolescents."

120 *Motivation, empathy, self-control, and persistence:* Almlund et al., "Personality Psychology and Economics."

121 *Researchers at the University of Pennsylvania had an idea:* Boe, May, and Boruch, *Student Task Persistence in the Third International Mathematics and Science Study.*

122 *When May repeated the analysis with the 2009 PISA data:* May, Duckworth, and Boe. *Knowledge vs. Motivation.*

123 *It even predicted how long people lived:* Almlund et al., "Personality Psychology and Economics."

chapter 7: the metamorphosis

124 *The children of Breslau:* For a richly detailed, gripping account of the siege of Breslau—and the history of the city before and after—see Davies and Moorhouse, *Microcosm.*

125 *Sometimes before they'd been abandoned by their owners:* Ibid, 432.

126 *They renamed Adolf Hitler Street:* Kamm, "The Past Submerged."

126 *Hyperinflation took hold:* Sachs, interviewed on the PBS program, *Commanding Heights.*

127 *Nearly one in every six Polish children lived in poverty:* Measuring child poverty is a complicated business. There are different ways to do it, none of them very good. In this case, I've chosen to use the Luxembourg Income Study analysis of poverty around the world. By this metric, children were considered poor if they lived in a household earning less than 50 percent the median household income in their country.

The latest data for Poland was from 2004, which meant that it did not reflect the effects of the global recession that began in late 2007. Still, the LIS data set was the only one I found that allowed comparisons of child poverty in Finland, the United States, South Korea, *and* Poland. In 2004, about 16 percent of Poland's children were living in poverty, under this definition. Nearly 21 percent were living in poverty in the United States that same year.

It's worth noting that the OECD's analysis of the socioeconomic status of students around the world (known as the Economic, Social and Cultural Index) found something different than the measures of poverty based on income. By this more holistic metric, which takes into account parents' education levels, occupations, and the number of books and computers in the home, among other factors, 21 percent of Poland's fifteen-year-olds were living in the least advantaged category in 2009 compared to 10 percent of teenagers in the United States See OECD, *PISA 2009 Results (Vol. I),* Table 1.2.20.

127   *Poland ranked dead last:* UNICEF, *Child Poverty in Perspective,* 2-4.

127   *The average reading score of Polish fifteen-year-olds shot up twenty-nine points:* PISA International Data Explorer, accessed December 2012.

127   *Almost three-quarters of a school year of learning:* OECD, *The High Cost of Low Educational Performance,* 3.

129   *"We demand a playground!":* Czajkowska, "Kids Revolt."

131   *"We have to move the entire system":* Author interview with Mirosław Handke on April 16, 2012. Translation by Justine Jablonska.

131   *"Give students a chance":* Mourshed, Chijioke, and Barber, *How the World's Most Improved School Systems Keep Getting Better.*

132   *School systems that used regular standardized tests tended to be fairer places:* OECD, *PISA 2009 Results: (Vol. IV).*

132   *Delaying tracking meant creating four thousand new junior high schools:* Mourshed, Chijioke, and Barber, *How the World's Most Improved School Systems Keep Getting Better.*

133   *That autonomy was the fourth reform:* Author interview with Handke.

133   *"This is our ticket to Europe and the modern world":* Kruczkowska, *"Reform Without Miracles."*

134   *"We can look forward to a deterioration in the standard of education":* Kalbarczyk, "Against Gymnasium."

134   *There were a lot of distractions:* Author interview with Jerzy Wiśniewski on May 18, 2011.

134   *On September 1, 1999:* Author interview with Handke and *Catholic Information Agency,* "Gniezno."

134   *"Not hammering redundant information into the head":* Kaczorowska, "The New Need to Improve."

134   *60 percent of Poles:* Rich, "Minister who got his sums wrong is forced to quit."

135   *"The only other developed country still opposed is Turkey":* Author interview with Wiśniewski.

135   *Over two-thirds scored in the rock-bottom lowest literacy level:* OECD, *Strong Performers and Successful Reformers in Education,* 225.

135 *Thirteenth in reading and eighteenth in math:* OECD, *Learning for Tomorrow's World*, 81, 281.

136 *Despite spending less than half as much money:* OECD, *PISA 2009 Results (Vol. IV), Table IV.3.21b.* As of 2007, Poland was spending about $39,964 to educate a single student from age six to fifteen, the age at which students took the PISA test; meanwhile, the United States was spending about $105,752 to do the same thing. Figures are in equivalent U.S. dollars, converted using purchasing power parity.

136 *Poland's poorest kids outscored the poorest kids in the United States:* For reading results, see OECD, *PISA 2009 Results (Vol II)*, 152; for math results, see U.S. Department of Education, *Table B.1.70.*

136 *84 percent of Polish students graduated from high school in 2011, compared to 77 percent in the U.S.:* OECD, *Education at a Glance 2013*, Table A2.1a.

136 *PISA scores for U.S. kids remained largely unchanged:* U.S. students' performance in math and reading remained about the same between 2000 and 2009; science scores did go up a bit in 2009 compared to 2006, ringing in at about average for the developed world. OECD, *Strong Performers and Successful Reformers in Education*, 26.

136 *The variation in scores from one Polish school to the next had dropped:* OECD, *Strong Performers and Successful Reformers in Education.*

136 *Over one-third of Polish teens scored in the top two levels of literacy:* OECD, "The Impact of the 1999 Education Reform in Poland."

136 *The delay in tracking:* Ibid.

137 *The reforms had postponed the gap, not eliminated it:* Ibid.

137 *Tracking tended to diminish learning and boost inequality:* Hanushek and Woessmann, *Does Educational Tracking Affect Performance and Inequality?*

138 *The applied track:* Author interview with Principal Mark Blanchard and teachers at Gettysburg High School.

139 *A uniquely American policy:* Schmidt and McKnight, *Inequality for All.* "Teachers, principals, school superintendents, and school board members may see their policies with respect to tracking in practical, harmless terms . . . .[In fact] what we are experiencing is the hidden destruction of the hopes of millions of children."

139 *About a third of kids got special help:* Hancock, "Why Are Finland's Schools So Successful?"

140 *Only 2 percent repeated a grade in Finnish primary school: PISA In Focus No. 6* and PISA 2009 dataset.

140   *The poorest school districts spent 20 percent less:* U.S. Department of Education, Education Dashboard.

140   *One of the most obvious differences between the United States and other countries:* Tucker, *Surpassing Shanghai.*

140   *In almost every other developed country:* OECD, *Strong Performers and Successful Reformers in Education,* 32. Student-teacher ratios did not necessarily reflect quality, but the ratio did reflect spending power and the values of the larger society.

141   *He figured he could fix Gettysburg:* Author interviews with Blanchard in person and via email in the spring and summer of 2012.

141   *The school spent almost twice as much per student:* Boser, *Return on Educational Investment.*

142   *No one dropped out because "bonehead English" went away:* Author interviews with Blanchard.

143   *All jobs had gotten more complex, including blue-collar jobs:* For a vivid case study of how blue-collar jobs have changed, see Davidson, "Making it in America."

143   *The state's own test, which wasn't very hard:* The lack of rigor in the Pennsylvania state test (the PSSA) is evidenced by the fact that 78 percent of eighth graders tested proficient in math on the PSSA—but only 39 percent tested proficient on the NAEP.

143   *When Tom's classmates took the SAT:* Pennsylvania Department of Education, "SAT and ACT Scores."

146   *Spałka and other principals had about $4,681 to spend:* OECD, "Country Statistical Profile: Poland," Education Expenditure Per Student: Non-tertiary.

146   *Compared to $11,000 per student in Gettysburg:* OECD, "Country Statistical Profile: United States," Education Expenditure Per Student: Non-tertiary. Separately, Principal Blanchard estimated that Gettysburg spent about $11,000 per student as of 2012.

146   *"We're not too excited about the reforms":* Author interview with Urszula Spałka on May 20, 2011. Translation by Mateusz Kornacki.

147   *It hadn't changed enough:* For an excellent, in-depth analysis of the phases of reforms that countries go through to get from poor to fair, fair to good, good to great, and, finally, great to excellent, see Mourshed, Chijioke, and Barber, *How the World's Most Improved School Systems Keep Getting Better.* The report includes a detailed assessment of the trajectory of Poland and 19 other countries, illustrating the importance of systems-based reforms that occur in sequence.

chapter 8: difference

152 *She felt like two people:* The description of Kim's depression is based in part on her blog post: "I swear one side of my head was metaphorically curled up with ice cream and watching a romantic comedy and cuddling a box of Kleenex, the other side was lacing up her combat boots, swiping that black grease under her eyes and finding the latest edition of, *I swear I'm mentally stable. Let me rationally convince you of this.*"

153 *"A compound of bravado and bravery":* Time, "Northern Theatre: Sisu."

155 *The big matriculation exam:* Details on Finland's graduation test come from Sahlberg, *Finnish Lessons,* and author interviews with Finnish educators.

156 *Performed over sixteen points higher on PISA:* OECD, *Strong Performers and Successful Reformers in Education,* 256.

156 *Finnish kids cited the high number of tests as one reason that they didn't like school:* Kupiainen, Hautamäki, and Karjalainen, *The Finnish Education System and PISA,* 22.

156 *Many states had some kind of graduation test:* Center on Education Policy, *State High School Exit Exams.* As of 2012, twenty-five states had exit exams, a policy affecting seven out of ten U.S. public-school students.

156 *But kids didn't need much* sisu *to pass them:* Ibid. In most states that had exit exams, the tests were not designed to measure students' readiness for careers or college, and colleges did not consider the results in admissions decisions. Students who failed the exam could retake it four to six times in their final year of high school in most states. Twenty-two states allowed students to circumvent the test by taking another kind of exam altogether, doing a project, creating a portfolio of their work, or requesting a waiver.

Opposition to the exams was fierce in many states. Critics often included teachers' unions and advocates for students with special needs.

156 *New York State Regents exam:* Winerip, "Despite Focus on Data, Standards for Diploma May Still Lack Rigor."

157 *One-third the time of Finland's test:* To graduate, New York students had to take five Regents exams, each of which lasted three hours, for a total of fifteen hours of testing (compared to fifty hours total in Finland).

157 *Only 20 percent of Finnish teenagers said they looked forward to math lessons:* OECD, *Learning for Tomorrow's World,* Figure 3.2.

157 *About half of Finnish kids said they got good grades in math:* Ibid, Figure 3.6.

158 *Only 3 percent of Finland's students had immigrant parents:* OECD, *Education at a Glance 2011,* Table A5.2.

158 *Eighty-four points below white students:* Fleischman et al., *Highlights From PISA 2009,* 14.

158 *As if the white kids had been going to school two extra years:* OECD, *Let's Read Them a Story!,* 31. In general, thirty-nine score points in PISA is considered the equivalent of one year of formal schooling.

159 *The other half was more complicated:* Magnuson and Waldfogel, eds. *Steady Gains and Stalled Progress.*

159 *Teenagers' aspirations at age fifteen could predict their futures:* Homel et al., "School Completion."

159 *White American teens performed worse than all students in a dozen other countries:* Peterson et al., *Globally Challenged.*

159 *New York State had fewer white kids:* Hanushek, Peterson, and Woessmann, *U.S. Math Performance in Global Perspective,* 17.

160 *Asian-Americans did better than everyone:* Fleischman et al., *Highlights From PISA 2009,* 14.

160 *Gap between PISA reading scores for native and immigrant students:* OECD, *Education at a Glance 2011,* Table A5.2.

160 *Poor American students had become more concentrated:* Rothwell, *Housing Costs, Zoning, and Access to High Scoring Schools.*

160 *Most white kids had majority white classmates:* Aud, Fox, and KewalRamani, *Status and Trends in the Education of Racial and Ethnic Groups.*

160 *More likely to attend majority black or Hispanic schools:* Orfield and Lee, *Historic Reversals, Accelerating Resegregation, and the Need for New Integration Strategies.*

160 *In Singapore, the opposite happened:* OECD, *Strong Performers and Successful Reformers in Education,* 159-176.

161 *The number of foreigners had increased over 600 percent:* OECD, *International Migration Outlook 2012,* Table A.1.

163 *Teachers changed their behaviors in a hundred small ways:* Tauber, *Classroom Management.*

164 *Special education:* The research on special education around the world leaves much to be desired. Different places define special needs in different ways—sometimes within the same country. It is therefore extremely difficult to make meaningful comparisons.

Special ed students do participate in PISA in most developed countries—but in 2003 they represented only 1.4 percent of the total sample worldwide. And here again, different definitions made comparisons almost impossible. (For more on PISA data and special education, see OECD, *Students with Disabilities.*)

We do know that most countries seem to be moving away from seg-regating special needs kids in separate schools and toward the Finland model, which is to say, including special needs students in traditional classrooms and training teachers to differentiate instruction accordingly.

In fact, while Finland probably leads the world in this area, it's fair to say that the United States is ahead of many top-performing countries in Asia. Of all special ed students in the United States, about 95 percent receive ser-vices in regular schools, according to Department of Education statistics.

In the pressure cooker of South Korea, on the other hand, special needs children and their families are often ignored or denigrated. They have little chance of winning the Iron Child competition, so they reside in the margins. "People often view students with disabilities as stubborn, irresponsible, unsocialised and incapable," according to Hyunsoo Kwon, in a 2005 article from the *International Journal of Disability, Development & Education*. Kim Song-ah, a high school student writing in the *Korea Times*, noted that although special ed students attended regular classes for part of the day, "[N]obody, classmates and teachers alike, cares about their presence . . . Frankly, we are rather indifferent to them." According to the Ministry of Education, Science and Technology, fewer than 1 percent of Korean students received special education services in 2007. Over a third of them attended separate schools.

Ironically, the more children a country categorizes as special needs, pro-portionally speaking, the more equitable the system seems to be. But once so labeled, kids must still remain in mixed classrooms for as long as possible with highly trained teachers who can meet their needs. This pattern sup-ports a theme that recurs throughout the international research: Keeping children of different abilities and backgrounds *together* in the same class-room tends to lift the performance of everyone, everywhere in the world.

164   *Finland had one of the highest proportions of special education kids in the world:* Kivirauma and Ruoho, "Excellence Through Special Education?"

164   *One in four Finnish kids:* Official Statistics of Finland, *Special Education.*

164   *One in eight American students received special education:* U.S. Department of Education, *Digest of Education Statistics, 2010: Table 45.*

164   *"Our parents on this side don't have the know-how":* Ripley, "What Makes a Great Teacher?"

167   *"Undoubtedly we all want to live in a multicultural and tolerant atmosphere":* Lyytinen, "Helsinki Parents at Pains to Avoid Schools with High Pro-portion of Immigrants."

168   *11 percent of children in the United States were enrolled in private schools:* U.S.
Department of Education, *Digest of Education Statistics, 2010: Table 3.*

168   *Less than average for the developed countries:* OECD, *Education at a Glance
2011,* Table C1.4.

168   *Private schools did not add much value:* OECD, *Strong Performers and Successful Reformers in Education,* 47.

168   *Three-quarters of kids attended high schools that competed for students:* Ibid,
45-46.

chapter 9: the $4 million teacher

169   *Andrew Kim earned $4 million in 2010:* Author interview with Andrew
Kim in Seoul on June 7, 2011. I was unable to independently confirm
Kim's salary, but the amount was within the range of what Korea's most
successful hagwon instructors are known to earn.

170   *Three of every four Korean kids participated in the private market:* Statistics
Korea, *The 2010 Survey of Private Education Expenditure.*

170   *In 2011, their parents spent over $18 billion:* Lee, "Private Education Costs
Fall for 2nd Year."

170   *Investments from places like Goldman Sachs:* Yoon, "Foreign Investors Eye
Education Market."

172   *Something U.S. teachers were rarely asked to do before being hired:* National
Council on Teacher Quality, *Teacher Quality Roadmap,* 12. In this survey
of Los Angeles teachers, only 13 percent of recent hires had been asked to
teach a sample lesson as part of their interviews.

172   *U.S. schools dismissed about 2 percent of teachers annually:* U.S. Department
of Education, *Table 8.*

173   *Most Korean teenagers preferred their hagwon instructors:* Kim and Su-ryon,
"Students Rely on Hagwon More Than Public Schools."

173   *Private tutoring did seem to lead to higher test scores:* Choi, Calero, and Escardíbul, *Hell to Touch the Sky.*

173   *PISA data for the entire world suggested that the quality of afterschool lessons mattered more:* OECD, *Quality Time for Students,* 14. Students from
high-performing countries spent less time, on average, taking afterschool
lessons and studying on their own.

174   *Eight out of ten Korean parents said they felt financial pressure:* Kang, "67
Percent of Private Cram Schools Overcharge Parents."

174 *Convinced that the more they paid, the more their children learned:* Na, "Cram Schools Turning to NEAT to Boost Revenue."

175 *Some 900 Korean students had their SAT scores canceled:* Arenson, "South Korea."

175 *Charging double and sometimes quintuple the allowable rates:* Kang, "67 Percent of Private Cram Schools Overcharge Parents."

175 *Nine out of ten Supreme Court and high court justices:* Chae, Hong, and Lee, "Anatomy of the Rank Structure of Korean Universities."

175 *Korea's suicide rate for fifteen- to nineteen-year-olds:* OECD, "Child well-being Module—CO4.1."

175 *Korea's overall suicide rate was one of the highest in the world:* OECD, "Suicides," 2010.

176 *On patrol with the study police:* Author interview with Cha Byoung-chul on June 8, 2011, and Ripley, "Teacher, Leave Those Kids Alone."

176 *Ratting out various hagwons:* Na, "Bounty Hunters."

chapter 10: coming home

181 *Six million more Americans without high-school diplomas:* Manyika et al., *An Economy that Works*, 2.

181 *Marshall ran the Bama Companies, an Oklahoma institution:* I cannot do justice to Paula Marshall's fascinating story in this book. To learn more about how she went from being a teen mother to the CEO of Bama, check out her book, *Sweet as Pie, Tough as Nails.*

185 *Online education had grown 400 percent:* Eger, "www.school.com."

185 *Jerry McPeak introduced a bill to repeal the mandate:* Oklahoma House Bill 2755, titled the "Freedom to Succeed Act."

185 *"We're going to brutalize and bully those children":* Greene, "Graduation Testing Bill Advances."

186 *"If we keep rolling these limits back, students are not going to take this seriously":* Rolland and Pemberton, "Raising Bar for Final Tests Leaves Some Feeling Worry."

186 *Fewer than 5 percent of Oklahoma's 39,000 high school seniors:* Estimate per Oklahoma State Department of Education officials as of September 2012.

186 *6 percent of seniors who did not pass Finland's far more rigorous graduation exam:* In English, more information about Finland's matriculation exam can be found at http://www.ylioppilastutkinto.fi/en/index.html. The

Finnish version of the site included the failure rate for 2010, the most recent data available as of August 2012. Translation by Tiina Stara.

186   *"There are some kids that just can't test well":* Archer, "Owasso Board Joins High-Stakes Testing Protest."

186   *The United States was ranked number seven:* World Economic Forum, *The Global Competitiveness Report 2012-2013.*

193   *Finland ranked second in the 2012 World Happiness Report:* Helliwell, Layard, and Sachs, eds, *World Happiness Report.*

193   *"If you want the American Dream":* Miliband, "On Social Mobility."

194   *"The Common Core State Standards are federalization of education":* Rolland, "National Group's Plan to Be Used."

195   *William Taylor taught math:* Ripley, "What Makes a Great Teacher?" and author interviews between 2009 and 2012.

197   *At BASIS public charter schools:* Author interview with Olga and Michael Block, cofounders of the BASIS charter schools, in Washington, D.C., on April 9, 2013.

197   *A special new version of the PISA test:* America Achieves, *Middle Class or Middle of the Pack?*

appendix I: how to spot a world-class education

208   *Average class size:* Rotherham, "When It Comes to Class Size, Smaller isn't Always Better."

210   *An epic Gates Foundation research study:* Bill & Melinda Gates Foundation. *Learning About Teaching.*

215   *"Great vision without great people is irrelevant":* Collins, *Good to Great.*

217   *"Joyful rigor":* Moskowitz and Lavinia, *Mission Possible.*

appendix II: AFS student experience survey

220   *1,376 Americans went abroad:* Poehlman, *2011-2012 International Youth Exchange Statistics.*

220   *The Measures of Effective Teaching Project:* Bill & Melinda Gates Foundation. *Learning about Teaching.*

221   *The Brookings Institute surveys:* Loveless, *How Well Are American Students Learning? With Special Sections on High School Culture and Urban School*

Achievement, and Loveless, *How Well Are American Students Learning? With Sections on Arithmetic, High School Culture, and Charter Schools.*

221 *Math skills tend to better predict future earnings:* Hanushek, Peterson, and Woessmann, "Teaching Math to the Talented," 12.

226 *The findings from the 2001 and 2002 Brookings Institute surveys:* Loveless, *How Well Are American Students Learning? With Special Sections on High School Culture and Urban School Achievement,* and Loveless, *How Well Are American Students Learning? With Sections on Arithmetic, High School Culture, and Charter Schools.*

227 *United States children lead highly structured lives:* Hofferth, "Changes in American Children's Time, 1997-2003."

231 *Excessive, vague, or empty praise has corrosive effects:* Henderlong and Lepper, "The Effects of Praise on Children's Intrinsic Motivation."

231 *Tendency of math class to "stay busy and not waste time":* This question was inspired in part by a question used in the Tripod survey—an instrument designed by Harvard University's Ronald Ferguson and analyzed by the Gates Foundation in the aforementioned MET study (see Bill & Melinda Gates Foundation. *Learning about Teaching*). We were not attempting to replicate that survey, of course. Still, that particular question seemed like a good way to help respondents assess the relative rigor of their math classes.

232 *Tendency of math teachers to "accept nothing less than our full effort":* Ibid.

index

Page numbers in *italics* refer to illustrations

about the author

Amanda Ripley is an investigative journalist for *Time*, *The Atlantic*, and other magazines. She is the author of *The Unthinkable: Who Survives When Disaster Strikes—and Why*. Her work has helped *Time* win two National Magazine Awards. She is currently an Emerson Senior Fellow at the Emerson Collective. She lives in Washington, D.C., with her husband and son.